Growth in Grace and Knowledge: Lectures and Speeches on Practical Theology 1949-1992

Growth in Grace and Knowledge: Lectures and Speeches on Practical Theology 1949-1992

C. Ellis Nelson

Nortex Press
Austin, Texas

Book design by Jeanne French

Published by Nortex Press
P. O. Box 90159
Austin, Texas 78709-0159

Library of Congress Cataloging-in-Publication Data

Nelson, Carl Ellis, 1916-
Growth in grace and knowledge: lectures and speeches on practical theology: 1949-1992/ C. Ellis Nelson.
p. 290 cm.
Includes bibliographical references.
ISBN 0-89015-874-6 (alk. paper)
1. Christian education. 2. Theology, Practical. I. Title.
BV1471.2.N39 1992
268--dc20 92-19747
CIP

Contents

Contents

Preface

Several times in the past few years I have been asked by doctoral students in the field of religious education to supply the text of some unpublished essay or speech I wrote years ago. In response to those requests I have become aware of the importance of documents for historical research. This collection of essays, lectures and speeches is published to provide data about the second half of the twentieth century for students of protestant education and for historians. This book, printed in a limited edition, will be distributed to the libraries of higher educational institutions where professors are engaged in research and teaching in the field of practical theology.

I was ordained in May, 1940 and taught one course in Christian education the next fall at Austin Presbyterian Theological Seminary, the seminary from which I had graduated. From that time until now I have been involved in a variety of educational aspects of practical theology. Most of this time has been spent in teaching and research, but there have been periods when I worked directly with churches and lay people. Those periods include some years as minister to students at The University of Texas, as the national Director of Youth Work for the Presbyterian Church, U.S., as president of Louisville Presbyterian Theological Seminary, and as a teacher in the churches my family attended. During this period, 1940-1992, I wrote a variety of essays, speeches, and books, which are listed in chronological order in the bibliography. Most of the published items can be retrieved through libraries or through the Presbyterian Historical Center, Montreat, North Carolina 28757. Many of the unpublished items are collected in this volume.

The items in this collection are arranged chronologically in order to display the development of ideas. On the first page of each article is a footnote giving the occasion for which the manuscript was prepared. This should help the reader understand the reason for the topic and for the style of writing. A few extemporaneous speeches that were recorded and then transcribed are also included.

The use of inclusive language for God and generic terms for humankind did not become an issue until the early 1970s. When I became aware of the importance of this matter I changed my writing style. The articles from the 1970s on reflect that change. The problem was what to do with essays written in the earlier period. Since they are historical documents the modern reader should be able to interpret them as readers must do with all documents written in that era. However, in order to be consistent, my student assistant, Rose Gander, worked through the earlier lectures and substituted inclusive language for God and generic terms for humankind if the change did not alter the meaning of the passage.

I find writing difficult and time-consuming. I prefer the classroom situation where I can lay out a line of thought and then respond to questions, corrections, or other points of view. However, I learned early in my teaching career that students did not always hear what was said, or they were so absorbed in taking notes that they were not able to reflect on the meaning of the lecture. The same is true of speeches given to groups of religious leaders or to adults in the congregation. So I formed the habit of writing speeches or of supplying the audience with a rather full outline, including quotations and references. This procedure produced most of the manuscripts in this collection.

Growth in Grace and Knowledge

The title deserves an explanation. When I went to Union Theological Seminary, New York, in 1957, as professor of Religious Education and Psychology I found a teaching situation new to me. The tradition at Union which President Van Dusen delighted to explain was for the senior professor in each field to teach the required course in the B. D. curriculum. In 1957 this meant James Muilenburg taught the Introductory course in Old Testament, John Knox the New Testament, Cyril Richardson and Wilhelm Pauck Church History, Reinhold Niebuhr Ethics and John Bennett and D. D. Williams Theology. Having been called as the tenured professor in religious education, I was assigned the required course for B. D. students.

The quota for the entering class of B. D. students was ninety, but in the late 1950s and early 1960s the pressure on enrollment was so great that Union would over-enroll on the assumption that some would drop out. Until the curriculum was changed in the mid-1960s, I had a class of ninety to one hundred in the required course. Three class meetings per week were the standard for required courses, but the professors usually lectured for only two of these. The other hour was spent in discussion groups of about fifteen students led by tutors selected by the professor from among the doctoral students in that field.

The required introductory courses were surveys of the whole field. The professors compared and contrasted their approach to other approaches so that at the end of the course the student would have a general knowledge of the field as well as an overview of how others resolved the underlying issues. It was assumed the students with this working knowledge of the field would then select courses suited to their academic background and vocational interest.

Under these circumstances I prepared a syllabus on the theological, biblical, and social science foundations for the field of religious education with discussion of the different agencies of religious education, such as the Sunday school and home, and characteristics of age groups in the church. All of the lectures were accompanied by full outlines so there could be some discussion in class and a ready reference for use in the discussion groups. However, at that time there was considerable concern for a proper theological and biblical base for subjects in the practical field, so I wrote a rather full text for the lectures in that part of the course so we could use most of the available time for discussion rather than presenting the material orally. I duplicated those lectures for classroom use under the title *Growth in Grace and Knowledge* (1961). The reference is to 2 Peter 3:18. Sections of that work were expanded and used for the Sprunt Lectures (1965) and published as *Where Faith Begins* (1967).

As I look back on my work I realize that the preparation of the syllabus for the introductory course in religious education at Union brought together my first twenty years of reading, research and practical experience and set the foundation for my lectures and writing since that time. It seems appropriate to use the title of those essays for this collection of papers.

Appreciation

Putting these papers together and making them available in book form was made possible by the cooperation of many friends and the help of several institutions. A grant from the Lilly Endowment, Inc., and contributions from individuals paid for the cost of publication. Jack Stotts, president of Austin Presbyterian Theological Seminary, supported this project by making the staff and the facilities of the seminary available for my use. Dorothy Andrews typed the first draft of the manuscript. Jeanne French transferred the manuscript to a word processor, composed the pages for the printer, and corrected errors as she worked. Prescott Williams undertook the difficult task of working through the papers in order to provide some consistency in style without changing the content of the essays. I deeply appreciate the help of these institutions and people in preparing this manuscript for publication. I hope the essays and speeches will assist future generations of protestants to understand the issues which engaged our attention during the last half of the twentieth century.

Austin, Texas C.E.N.
April, 1992

1

The Importance of Christian Education for Adults

Dr. Robert Hutchins, Chancellor of the University of Chicago, has been preaching what he considers the good news of damnation. His sermonic approach to the complex problems caused by our use of the atomic bomb indicates his pleasure in a crisis severe enough to force adults to think. In his excitement he has said that it is already too late to train a new generation of youth. We must redirect the interest of adults or America will cause the downfall of Western Civilization.

Without sharing Hutchins' pessimism we may be instructed by his emphasis on education. The day must end when we can believe that education, and particularly Christian education, is designed exclusively for children and youth.

The educational situation in our churches demonstrates our preoccupation with children and youth. One can stand by almost any Presbyterian Church on a Sunday morning and see the cars drive up and discharge their loads of children. With a quick eye one can see the driver in housecoat or pajamas as he/she drives on. To indicate further the exclusiveness of the Sunday School as a child's experience of religion, we hear the children conclude their session with, "Sunday School is over and we are going home." The continual use of this song illustrates our Church's tolerant attitude toward educational heresy. A theological mistake of the same magnitude would result in excommunication.

Statistically, the facts are overwhelming. Whereas children under 15 make up only 17% of the population of the Presbyterian Church, they make up over 50% of the Sunday School enrollment.

There is, of course, good reason for this regrettable lack of adult education. Historically, the modern religious education movement

---

Installation address as professor of Christian Education, Austin Presbyterian Theological Seminary, Austin, Texas, September 15, 1949.

evolved from an interest in children. When Robert Raikes started his Sunday School in 1780, he was motivated by Colonel Townly's complaint that children in the pin factory district of Gloucester were devoid of education and manners. This concern for illiterate and underprivileged children was the characteristic mark of the Sunday School movement for five decades. When the movement spread across America, its evangelistic impulse was directed toward children on the ever receding Western Frontier.

Organized youth work was begun in 1882 with the founding of Christian Endeavor as an activity program for youth but also as a revolt against the child-centered emphasis of the Sunday School. Begun outside denominational influence, the youth organizations were later incorporated into the program of the churches.

However, in America there is also a cultural situation that glorifies youth. One cultural anthropologist said that America is the only country on earth where children know more than their parents. Again, there is good reason for America's unusual interest in youth. During the early decades of this century we received wave after wave of immigrants. Their children, not incubated in the Old World Culture, were soon more at home in America than their parents. In that same period of time, America became a technical culture where the distinguished role in human affairs was played by the scientists and the technicians. With such a premium placed on knowledge, young persons came into their glory. Today if a physicist at the age of 25 unravels another atomic secret he/she is a military, political and intellectual hero as well as a professional success. If any of you have had a 17 year old son or daughter repair your radio or start a stalled motor in your car, you are forced by circumstances to admit that he/she knows more about some subjects than you.

Our technical culture plus our material wealth has not only produced a leisure class in America but it has made possible a long adolescent period. Nowhere else in the world do we find the period from puberty to responsible adulthood so far extended as we do in America. The adolescent of leisure is strictly an American innovation who has appeared only since the turn of the century. Our culture not only has produced these unusual circumstances but it likewise demands a prolonged period of preparation in order that the machines of a scientific age be manned with skilled technicians.

Thus, the historical development of religious education plus the unique configuration of our emerging technical society focuses attention on children and youth. Promoters in our church and in our community do not fail in their efforts if somehow they can link their project with the welfare of children and youth.

Having gone this far in an analysis of the reasons behind our emphasis on religious education for children and youth, allow me to put these comments in proper perspective. I do not underestimate the value of Christian Education for children, for to do so would be to become a traitor to my family. I do not regret one erg of energy or one dime of money I have invested in the youth movements with which I have been associated in the past. Rather, from these experiences I now know that before we can go much farther with Christianizing our children and youth we must devote more than a tithe of our efforts to adult education.

Why?

In the first place we must recognize that adults set the cultural pattern. The cultural atmosphere in which children live shapes their affective behavior as truly as food, exercise and living conditions effect their physical growth. For example, most of us have referred to the generation of youth after the first World War as "Flaming Youth." Often we rest the blame with youth itself or more frequently assign the cause of this jazz age to the breakup of moral standards occasioned by the war. A more understandable and sounder reason is advanced by Goodwin Watson in *Youth After Conflict* when he demonstrates that the jazz age was the logical outcome of the modernism which took root soon after the turn of the century. He traces this modernism in religion, art, movies, music, literature and other cultural areas. The first World War simply speeded up a cultural process which had been at work for two decades. It was the cultural situation that incubated a generation of youth we have dubbed "Flaming Youth."[1]

Adults *continue* to set the cultural pattern. Today, American culture has taken on some of the characteristics of a religion. Millions pay their respects to the great American values: pleasure, money, success. If we seriously desire to make Christian values come alive in American culture, we will have to plan our strategy in terms of adults.

A second reason is that adults are in positions of authority. Adults set the pace, they form the laws of the land, make up the responsible leadership of the community. This fact is so obvious it is strange we have so long neglected this group through which results could so quickly be felt in our community life.

A third factor that enhances the importance of this age group is the gradual shift in age distribution in the U. S. population. Up until recent years the age distribution chart looked like the profile of a Christmas tree: it was broad at the bottom and tapered gently to a point at the top. The broad portion at the bottom represented the larger proportion of children in relation to the number of adults. However, that figure is now changed and is continuing to change. The age distribution chart will soon look like the profile of an ornamental shrub, pruned to look like a shaft with a rounded top. To be specific, in 1900 only 55.7% of the population was over 20 years of age, whereas in 1960 70.7% of the population will be over 20 years of age. Students of population trends say that our population will become stabilized after 1960 and the new permanent fact to be understood is that adults, and particularly older adults, will be present in large numbers.

In the light of these circumstances, what factors should characterize the church's efforts in adult education? Obviously, preaching is adult education, and many other activities of the church train adults in specific tasks. But since our concern this evening is primarily the educational program, the suggestions are aimed in that direction.

What must be the approach of an educational program designed to meet the needs previously mentioned?

First, it must be based on a type of Bible study that will help adults understand God's will for their lives and free them from cultural standards.

Much of our uncertainty today arises from our incomplete understanding of God's will for our lives. The Bible is not only an unread book, it is unintelligible to large numbers. Rather than try to fix blame on the laziness or indifference of adults themselves, let us try a different hypothesis. Could it be that we ministers and other leaders have been too intrigued with a critical study of the Bible? Our seminary training is oriented in that direction, and rightly so. It is also natural that when we graduate we use the same methods of Bible study on adults that we learned in seminary.

In Oslo, Norway two summers ago during the Youth Conference sponsored by the World Council of Churches, I got a glimpse of what a personal devotional study of the Bible could mean. In a small French-speaking group the Bible was studied according to a pattern very strange personal devotional study of the Bible could mean. In a small French-speaking group the Bible was studied according to a pattern very strange to Americans. First, the Bible passage was read, verse by verse, and questions of interpretation settled. Then the leader went from person to person asking each this question: "What does this passage mean to you?" The two Americans were keen in their understanding of what the passage meant to Paul and the early church. They also offered a fine analysis of its application to the church today. But the French leader insisted with his question "What does it mean to you?" The Americans saw for the first time what it meant to wrestle with God's Word for a revelation of God's will for an individual life.

This call is a call to go beyond content and criticism. It is a plea that we not rest with an "application" of the Bible to present conditions. The new adult education must cause adults to seek God's will for their lives in God's Word.

You may say, this is too difficult. Such a study is what we expect of our ministers. Indeed we should look to our clergy for guidance, but nothing will take the place of laypersons seeking God's will for their lives in God's word. Such a process would restore the creative and wholesome elements of the old testimonial but in the framework of God's revelation rather than in the emotionalism of the community group.

Searching for the will of God in and through the story of God's self-disclosure characterizes a group of prophets who lived in the eighth and seventh centuries B.C. These prophets, some laypersons and some with official status, had an uncanny ability to see social and political situations through the eyes of God. We might designate them "thoughtful" prophets in order to distinguish them from ordinary prophets who emerged soon after the Israelites entered Canaan.

Ordinary prophets had a well-defined role in Israel. They may be designated "ecstatic" prophets for they sought the will of God by non-rational methods. Saul was caught up in a spirit of prophecy and later, in Elisha's time, prophets formed small communities. Their prestige was great. Kings listened to their advice (I Kings 20:13-15) and the common people visited them for guidance in personal affairs (1 Kings 4:18-25). They sought to discern God's will by visions (I Sam. 19:18-24), divination, sorcery and necromancy (Deut. 18:9-14; Lev. 19:26, 31; 20:6; I Sam. 28:7, 9).

In contrast the thoughtful prophets refused to be identified with the ecstatic prophets. Amos said:

> I am no prophet, nor a prophet's son; but I am a herdsman, and a dresser of sycamore trees. . . . (Amos 7:14)

Jeremiah divorced himself from the clairvoyant people with these words:

> So do not listen to your prophets, your diviners, your dreamers, your soothsayers, or your sorcerers . . . for it is a lie which they are prophesying to you. . . . (Jer. 27:9-10)

The thoughtful prophets taught on the basis of observable data, using their rational faculties rather than the non-rational feelings of the ecstatic prophet. When Isaiah let go his blast at the ecstatic prophets they lost caste in Israel and never again were an important factor in the religious life of the Israelites. Isaiah said the ecstatic prophets were liars (Isa. 9:15-16). And he later said they erred in vision, stumbled in judgment, were full of vomit and could not teach knowledge (Isa. 28:7-9). So magic was cleared out of Israel and God's will became known by God's Word and was based on observable conditions in the marketplace.

These thoughtful prophets were committed to finding God's will for their lives through a study of God's self-disclosure in their history. This type of Bible study assumes that God has a will for the world that is different from the will of political leaders and that God desires a style of life different from that approved by culture.

This kind of Bible study will free us from our cultural standards. There is no free country in the world today where people are more slaves to culture than America. Not only in dress but also in thought patterns we follow the pied piper of fad and fashion. For example, the pollster can dip into various classes, sample opinion, and be confident that what a few think, that all in that class or occupational group will think. The sociologist, likewise, sees class distinctions in which certain attitudes and values are clearly visible. Examples of how class values function in society will be found in the "Yankee City Series" of sociological studies edited by W. Lloyd Warner. A more recent study of a family life in a social setting is August B. Hollingshead's *Elmtown's Youth*. In this volume. Hollingshead gives the results of his study of 535 families in a Midwestern town. Concerning religion, this sociologist said,

> The impression gradually grew that religion to these adolescents is comparable in a way to wearing clothes or taking a bath. It is something one has to have or to do to be acceptable in society.[2]

Remember, it is Hollingshead's thesis in this study that the social class to which the family belongs determines the personal attitudes and beliefs of the children. This social structure was shown to be a more determining factor in one's beliefs than the church. How far have we departed from Paul's instruction:

> Do not be conformed to this world but be transformed by the renewal of your mind, that you may prove what is the will of God, what is good and acceptable and perfect (Rom. 12:2).

Religion, no, let us be more specific, Protestantism, in this Midwestern town was so conformed to the social pattern it had lost its distinctiveness. How can the church ever hope to produce an evangelical Christianity in that community until the adults who structure the social situation experience the dynamic qualities of the Christian faith that will free them from cultural standards?

In this regard, Jacques Maritain is correct in saying that the aim of modern education must be rooted in the individual. Its fruits will not be an individualistic personality but an individualism which has a living center of conviction from which personal conscience, idealism and courage will flow.[3]

We must start our adult education with Bible study dependent on a study of God's Word in terms of our own need to know God's will, thus giving us power to become free from cultural standards.

The other pole around which our adult education must revolve is that of the parent as an educator.

How did we forget in religious educational circles that the parent is not only the first but also the most important educator? One suspects that the lack of interest in parents may have been a byproduct of the liberalism of the early decades of this century that permeated educational as well as theological circles. The liberal religious educator was determined to build "the happy democracy of God," and parents, of course, would just get in the way. Fortunately, this attitude was shared by only a few responsible religious education leaders and today we find a movement back to the fundamental thesis that the parents are the first and most important teachers of religion.

Our adult education will therefore see parents and families not only as the objects of Christian education efforts but also as the agents by which Christian education becomes operative in the lives of children.

Such was the position of education in the Old Testament. The parents were held responsible for their children's conduct and beliefs. If a son became unmanageable, the parents brought him to the elders of the city for punishment (Deut. 21:18-21). Delinquency was always adult, *not* juvenile; for responsibility rested on the man as head of the home. We recall that most of the festivities of the Israelites were family festivals used to inculcate the meaning of God's revelation. Even the great national events were interpreted to children by the parents. When Joshua set up a second monument, he did not forget the educational significance.

> . . . that this may be a sign among you, when your children ask in time to come, 'What do those stones mean to you?' Then you shall tell them that the waters of the Jordan were cut off before the ark of the covenant of the Lord. . . . (Jos. 4:6-7)

The New Testament carries over the Hebrew conception of the parents' responsibility to educate their children in the faith. Paul has in mind spiritual as well as material things when he writes,

> If any one does not provide for his relatives, and especially for his own family, he has disowned the faith and is worse than an unbeliever (1 Tim. 5:8).

If we honestly consider parents as teachers of Christianity, then we must consider training them for this great responsibility.

Biologically speaking, becoming a parent is not unusual. Spiritually speaking, becoming a parent of a Christian child is most difficult.

We are faced at once with the difference between intellectual concepts of faith and faith's emotional expression. Too often we assume that if a child has the proper intellectual concepts, i.e., knows the correct verbal formulations, then he/she is a child of faith. Much mischief has been done by that notion. A child is not a child of faith until he/she also has learned the emotional expression. Emotional expressions are learned just as are intellectual concepts, but in a different way. The child must not only know that God is the Creator, but he/she must also possess the corollary emotional expression of reverence.

With such a principle in mind, we see more clearly the role of the parent as teacher. Emotional expressions are learned in the context of participation. Only to a limited degree can the Sunday School teacher teach a child basic Christian attitudes, for the teacher sees the child only one hour per week, and then in an artificial social environment. The parent, however, has limitless opportunities in countless specific social situations to teach the child both the content of faith and its appropriate emotional expressions.

Many churches and groups within the religious education movement have, within recent years, been changing their terminology to Christian education. This outward shift in nomenclature is symptomatic of a deeper shift of emphasis. The emerging Christian education movement is characterized by a new concern for theology, a new respect for the history of the church, and above all, a new effort at enlisting the home as a teaching institution to complement the teaching efforts of the church. This shift of emphasis may appear simple, but actually it involves new curriculum procedures, different leadership techniques, and a radical change in methods. However, any change is justified if we bring Christian education back into the family where the child learns the appropriate emotional expression as well as the content of our faith.

Our plea for adult education is in conflict with neither our concern for the Christian nurture of children nor our interest in youth activities. Rather, our hope is in an adult education which will cause spiritual values to become more operative in the lives of all church members and which will reinforce the Christian nurture of our children and youth.

Notes

1 Goodwin Watson, *Youth After Conflict* (New York: Association Press, 1947) 48-194.

2 August B. Hollingshead, *Elmtown's Youth* (New York: John Wiley, 1949) 244.

3 Jacques Maritain, *Education at the Crossroads* (New Haven: Yale UP, 19 43) 9-10.

2

The God of the Bible

The Bible is basic to and inseparable from the Christian Faith. If some great social catastrophe should jar our American scene, disrupt our Christian institutions, destroy our churches and programs of Christian education, we would instinctively protect and preserve our copies of the Bible. For the scriptures together with our personal experience and fellowship with other believers would be our inspiration and guide for rehabilitating the Christian Faith.

Furthermore, the Bible itself is so closely related to the teaching function, that one can hardly think of the Bible without considering it in relation to one's own personal edification, as the background for the message proclaimed by the preacher, or as the content of our teaching program. "Torah" is to the Jewish mind a comprehensive name for divine revelation, covering not only the "law" of Moses, the teaching of the prophets and wise ones, but also many oral traditions and interpretations of God's revelation. Gunnar Östborn in his brilliant and comprehensive treatment of this word has come to the conclusion that the very word "torah" does not mean "to cast" or "to throw" (stemming from the priestly tradition of casting lots for divine guidance). Specifically, he finds that the word is a directive to instruct in the law.[1] Thus "torah," the comprehensive word the Jews use for the Old Testament, is not only an identification of the content, that is, the "law," but also a command that it shall be taught.

E. F. Scott has indicated in his book, *The Purpose of the Gospels*, that they were written because Christianity was working towards self-consciousness.[2] The Gospels were written when the first phase of the

---

Lecture given to the Children's Work Section, Division of Christian Education, National Council of Churches, Columbus, Ohio, February 10-12, 1952.

struggle with the Roman world was over, as a documentation of the life of Jesus to be used in a further expansion of the Christian Church. Matthew's account ends on a note of confident assurance: the risen Lord says to the faithful, "Go forth, therefore, and teach all nations. . . ." The letters from Paul to the various churches he established were written to teach "the more excellent way," to correct abuses, and to answer questions--thereby demonstrating the highest role a teacher can perform, that of making clear the will of God.

Our problems begin when we seek to describe the God of the Bible and to trace out God's will. Prior to the Reformation the Bible was often used as proof text for the doctrines formulated by the theologians and approved by the church. Christians were not expected to use the Bible nor understand its message; for them religious life was taken care of by their participation in the sacraments, particularly the mass, and their individual problems were handled by the priest.

It is often said that the reformers substituted the authority of the Bible for the authority of the church. This in a sense is true, for they opened the Bible to the average church member, and insisted that it be taught in the schools in the vernacular translation. They also set an example of biblical preaching that has probably never been equalled. However, their concept of the Bible was not that rigid "cover-to-cover" authoritarianism which we often observe today.

Holding to a high concept of inspiration, the reformers appealed to the Bible as their only guide for faith and practice. Yet their attitude toward books of the Bible and toward certain passages indicated they were not searching for proof texts but were seeking the great underlying purposes of God. They rejected the Apocrypha. Luther was outspoken in his preference for the letters of Paul and considered the Gospels of Matthew, Mark, and Luke a rather good introduction to Christianity, especially for children![3] His attitude toward the Epistle of James reads:

> Many sweat to reconcile St. Paul and St. James, as does Melanchthon in his Apology, but in vain. "Faith justifies" and "faith does not justify" contradict each other flatly. If anyone can harmonize them I will give him my doctor's hood and let him call me a fool. Let us banish this epistle . . . for it is worthless. It has no syllable about Christ. . . . The ancients saw all this and did not consider the epistle canonical.[4]

Although Calvin was much more careful in his language and precise in his judgments concerning the canonicity of various books, he pointed out many errors in the Bible record in his commentaries. He did not believe Samuel wrote the book by that name, and he surmised that the priest Eleazar wrote the outline of the book of Joshua and that its composition was worked out by someone else.

The creative age of the Reformation was followed by the period of Protestant scholasticism; formulations of faith were adopted by various groups, but only one, the Swiss Helvetica (1675), included the idea of the verbal inerrancy of Scripture.

But new knowledge and new discoveries pressed in on people's minds. At the beginning of the 19th century William Smith had proven that rock is stratified and that the chronological order of the strata can be determined by the fossils contained in them. The latter part of the 19th century saw the publication of Charles Lyell's *Antiquity of Man* (1863) and Charles Darwin's *Descent of Man* (1871). With the publication of these books, the whole cosmology changed. The idea of evolution struck with such force and logic that even the person on the street could follow the concept that higher forms: humans, institutions and ethics developed from lower and cruder life. After all, the Victorian age was a "good" age, complete with fair economic prosperity, development of industrial power, relative peace in the world, and the discovery of many basic laws in physics. Incidentally, the conflict of this newer scientific approach to life and the old view is well illustrated in Simpson's experience with the discovery of the anesthetic qualities of chloroform. People said this was not of God and they would not use artificial means to kill pain. Simpson is reported to have replied that the Bible says, before God performed the operation on Adam of removing his rib to make Eve, God put Adam in a deep sleep!

The mood of the age was against anything being credited to faith that could be explained by natural law. After all, people were learning the most important facts about life from a systematic investigation of natural law; the evidence was too handy and the results were too profitable to abandon even in the field of religion. It was in that atmosphere that historical or higher criticism of the Bible developed.

> It proceeded on the primary assumption that the literature of the Bible is to be studied in the first instance as one would study any other literature. Its central concern therefore, was with the questions

of date, authorship, composition, literary structure, and history. While such questions had always been a concern of biblical scholars, their answers were now sought with extraordinary diligence in the new freedom which Protestantism and the spirit of inquiry made possible. The chief interest soon centered in the unraveling of the various literary strata in the Pentateuch and the Gospels. In the course of time the startled Christian would begin to hear not only of J, E, D, P, Mk, and Q, but also of J1, J2, E1, E2, R, H, M, L, and so forth.[5]

Looking back on that age we are amazed at its productivity in Biblical studies. Archaeological societies were formed by the great universities. Definitive issues of Hebrew-English Lexicons and dictionaries of the Bible were published. Comprehensive critical commentaries were issued, such as the *International Critical Commentary* and the *Cambridge Bible for Schools and Colleges*. When we add to that list the monumental list of individual works by scholars and the founding of scholarly Journals, we begin to grasp the magnitude of biblical work that was done when people turned their minds to the critical study of the Bible.

Christendom was torn by heresy trials both in America and Scotland, for the God of the higher critic's Bible was quite different from the traditional concept.[6] The reorientation of the church to the new critical views of the Bible was as revolutionary as Copernicus' announcement that the world was round.

We cannot trace the whole reaction to the new views, for we are primarily interested in setting the stage for the newer developments of the study of the Bible. However, let us pause long enough for station identification and get clearly in mind the God of the higher critics' Bible.

It is generally thought that Harry Emerson Fosdick's two books on the Bible, *The Modern Use of the Bible*, (1927), and *A Guide to Understanding the Bible*, (1938), present the clearest and most comprehensive summary of the higher critical views. Commenting on the great work the higher critics had done, Fosdick indicates its value by saying:

> It means that we can trace the great ideas of Scripture in their development from their simple and elementary forms, when they first appear in the earliest writings, until they come to their full maturity

> in the latest books. Indeed, the general soundness of the critical results is tested by this fact that as one moves up from the earlier writings toward the later he can observe the development of any idea he chooses to select, such as God, man, duty, sin, worship. Plainly we are dealing with ideas that enlarge their scope, deepen their meaning, are played upon by changing circumstance and maturing thought, so that from its lowliest beginning in the earliest writings of the Hebrews any religious or ethical idea of the Bible can now be traced, traveling an often uneven but ascending roadway to its climax in the teaching of Jesus.[7]

Such an approach to the Bible naturally produced a different type God and Fosdick eagerly describes this God: "As the early writings of the Old Testament clearly reveal, Jehovah, at first one among many gods, dwelt with his own special people and exercised no jurisdiction beyond their boundaries."[8]

Perhaps the idea of a person developing a concept of God is nowhere more winsomely stated than in these words:

> Start now with this tribal morality and the roadway leading up to the New Testament, where all boundaries are down and God is calling all humanity into his kingdom, is alike one of the most significant that man ever traveled and one of the most rewarding that man can study now. To see in the Bible new world-contacts breaking down the old walls of isolation, to watch prophets enlarging their thought of God and thereby widening their sense of moral obligation, to feel the significance of great hours of vision, as when Isaiah hears God say, "Blessed be Egypt my people, and Assyria the work of my hands, and Israel mine inheritance," to rejoice in the widening internationalism of books of propaganda, like Jonah, until at last, under the influence of Jesus, religion is universalized, human personality regardless of national or racial lines is made the supreme treasure, men of every tribe, tongue, people, and nation are welcomed into one brotherhood, and a kingdom for God on earth is promised to which men shall come from east, west, north, and south--so to see the Bible is to enter creatively into what God was really doing in that amazing spiritual development whose record the Bible is.[9]

This view frankly states that many things ascribed to God in the Old Testament are "intellectually ruinous" and cannot be harmonized with the God of the New Testament.[10] Furthermore, this approach will appeal to the scientifically trained modern generation, for it will remove most of the miracles as adornments added to the simple gospel by editors who wanted to make the story better than it really was.[11]

Four ways are given whereby a person can know the Bible: first, be acquainted with the beauty spots; second, study individual books; third, study characters; and, fourth, understand the progressive revelation. The main positive use of the Bible, according to Fosdick, is that it teaches which abiding experiences are to be applied to the changing categories we face.[12]

Nowhere was the progressive revelation theory more quickly adopted or more widely used than in the field of religious education. Nothing could be more natural. As Fosdick had pointed out, this concept of God eliminated most of the problems of the Bible in one way or another; it fitted into the mood of a generation that was filled with idealism and trained in the scientific method. It emphasized experience and, therefore, meshed nicely with the child-centered curriculum which was being developed by secular educators. The underlying idea of progressive revelation was so patent on the surface and so harmonious with evolution of everything else we know about the world that the case was won by simply stating the theory.

W. C. Bower might be taken as a typical illustration, for he faced this problem in his book *The Living Bible* published in 1936. Seven years later while still professor of religious education at the Divinity School of the University of Chicago, he restated his position in *Christ and Christian Education*. In this later book, for example, he holds the Bible up as the "most precious part of our Christian heritage." However, he does not advocate that it be taught, at least not in the usual sense of that word. His language is as follows:

> Now, at least in the progressive areas of general education, we are coming to feel that it is not the business of education to "teach" themselves; but rather to provide conditions in which the growing members of society may have the experience of communication, of the quantitative aspects of living, of science as a method of thought, of the values expressed in literature, and of the arts as creative expressions of beauty, through the *use* of language, mathematics,

science, literature, and the arts as resources provided by a growing culture for meeting the issues of contemporary living. So in Christian education the Bible as the most precious record of our religious past is coming to be thought of as a resource to be *used* in the interpretation, enrichment, and guidance of genuinely vital and authentic experience of the living God in contemporary life.[13]

Specifically, Bower cites five ways the Bible can be brought into functional relation to our own experience:

1. We must begin with people where they are in their interaction with their real and present world rather than with the canonized Bible, which is a deposit of past religious living.

2. In order to avail ourselves of the resources of the Bible, it is necessary to rearrange the assembled parts of its literature according to the genetic origin by distributing its several portions along the time span of more than a thousand years.

3. When, however, we have reconstructed the historical situations out of which the various parts of the literature of the Bible grew, we come upon the third consideration--the selective use of the Bible. There is much in the Bible that is not relevant to our life in the modern world.

4. We need to see the literature of the Bible and the experience which it records in their historical perspective. . . . One must think of *stages* in the *growth* of Hebrew religious thought, practices, and institutions. . . .

5. To bring the Bible into functional relation to our present experience it is necessary, therefore, to extract the enduring values of the Bible from their concrete historical contexts, so that they may be released for use in the enrichment and guidance of our own experience under the changed historical conditions in which we live.[14]

Most of us who have planned curricula materials will recognize our use of these principles. We will also recall the many hours we have dedicated to the task of distilling spiritual truths from the Bible which would apply to specific life experiences of a particular age group in a specific church.

It is possible for one to get so absorbed in this functional approach that even the God of the liberal critical Bible becomes just another god, a time prisoner of an ancient people. This seems to be the view of E. J. Chave in his 1947 book, *A Functional Approach to Religious Education*. Out of the 161 pages in the book, hardly more than five are given to a discussion of the place of the Bible. The longest section is only two paragraphs long and the first paragraph reads as follows:

> So with the use of the Bible, one may have simple, naive beliefs regarding its supernatural character, or critical-historical understanding of its nature, values, and relative significance in the story of religion. There is no inevitable religious experience in Bible study; for, as is well known, the Bible has been used to justify all kinds of evil, and many people have only a smattering of cultural knowledge without any appreciation of its inspiring teachings. There are various reasons for the widespread attachment to the Bible, but undoubtedly one of the main reasons is the traditional belief in a supernatural God, who was supposed to have given this book as a revelation of his will and purpose for man. The only justifiable use for the Bible from a religious standpoint is one in which its historical and developmental character is fully appreciated and understood and in which its insights and patterns of behavior are critically evaluated. One is not necessarily religious when he employs the gangster tactics of Samson, the fanatical attitudes of Jeremiah, the dogmatic spirit of Paul, or the violence of Jesus in expediting reforms. The Bible is an interesting book, portraying the developing religious ideas of a small group of people in ancient times. There are innumerable other books in the literature of the ages, and more to be written, which may serve the purpose of helping young and old to think and to live religiously. To treat the Bible as a unique and isolated revelation of truth is to deny the essential quality of growth in the cosmic process and to ignore the experiences of the vast majority of people as inconsequential. The Bible must take its place in the vast array of religious literature and, without presumption as to uniqueness, prove its worth by the insights which it gives to intelligent and receptive minds.[15]

Thus Chave sees the Bible as one of many interesting books that can be used for the development of the religious life. Elsewhere in his book, he indicates that belief in God may or may not be assumed, and, if assumed, it matters not if God be personal or impersonal.[16] One can ask, "Isn't this the ultimate stopping point for the liberal view of the Bible?" The answer is no. One final step can be taken. One can set up a program for the inculcation of spiritual values without reference to the Bible or to God: this has now been done by the Educational Policies Commission of the National Education Association in their 1951 book, *Moral and Spiritual Values in the Public Schools*. The word Bible does not appear in that book and the word God is mentioned but twice: once to state that our country was founded by God-fearing people, and again when the Bill of Rights is quoted as guaranteeing freedom to worship God according to the mandate of one's own religious convictions.[17]

To summarize, what was the concept of God that emanated from the critical study of the Bible? *First*, God was progressively revealed in the Bible, especially in the Old Testament. Religion in its various stages of growth started as primitive animism and polydemonism. It then developed from polytheism and henotheism into ethical monotheism. Such a concept tended to subordinate theology to history and literature; for one could not study the theological content of a Biblical passage or book without knowing its complete historical setting, and all the critical studies concerned the actual text. As a result, Biblical theology became almost non-existent.

Second, God revealed Godself and God's will in historical situations in the Bible; but the account is so overlaid with editorial emendations, redactors' comments, and omissions, that it is not trustworthy as a guide except perhaps for the period in which it was finally written. The principal illustration is the Pentateuch. These books do not tell us much about Moses and the religion of the people because the material was edited by men in the 8th century who had developed an advanced ethical monotheism. This theory tended to make the biblical account untrustworthy and to set up science and reason as the proper guides for understanding the Bible.

Third, the God of the Bible, particularly of the New Testament, dealt with persons on a personal basis inspiring them through religious experiences to build the kingdom of God. The church as such was discounted and passages referring to it were considered inferior in teaching value to the "high" ethical teachings of Jesus. This view tended to shift major interest to our problems and social conditions, since all we could transpose from the Bible was the subjective religious experience that would provide the motivation for us to solve our present social problems.

Each of these three major concepts of the higher critics' God is being challenged. New findings in the field of archaeology have practically removed the old concept that monotheism evolved from polytheism; form criticism has struck a serious and perhaps fatal blow at the idea that the Old Testament biblical account cannot be considered trustworthy beyond the period when the passage was assembled; and the rise of "realistic theology" and biblical theology has raised serious doubts about the adequacy of a faith apart from the Word of God. Let us take each of these newer developments in turn.

Archaeology and Monotheism

In 1872, George Smith, while reading through some clay tablets discovered at Nineveh, found some stories that paralleled the flood story of the Bible. His discovery so excited the *Daily Telegraph* of London that he was offered 1000 guineas to go to Nineveh and search for more tablets. He was very successful, finding not only more tablets with stories concerning the flood but also many creation stories which seemed to parallel the Biblical accounts. Thus the archaeologists started the gathering of factual data concerning the folklore, religion and social customs of the near eastern people in whose lands the Israelites lived. As the excavations yielded more and more knowledge of the ancient people, the evidence seemed to prove beyond a reasonable doubt that the religion of the Hebrews was syncretistic: that is, made up like a modern bride out of "something old, something new, something borrowed." But in the last two decades many archaeologists have unearthed new data; they have begun to be impressed not with the areas in which the Hebrew faith is like that of other Semitic people, but the marked dissimilarities which cannot be accounted for by any other known religion of the period and which go counter to all empirical evidence.

W. F. Albright of Johns Hopkins University is primarily responsible for this new turn of events through the publication of his book, *From the Stone Age to Christianity* in 1940. The sub-title "Monotheism and the Historical Process" shows his interest; but the entire book is written from the historical, archaeological and critical point of view. In the three page epilogue Albright clearly separates himself from the older view of progressive revelation. His words are as follows:

> Nothing could be farther from the truth than the facile belief that God only manifests Himself in progress, in the improvement of standards of living, in the spread of medicine and the reform of abuses, in the diffusion of organized Christianity.[18]

The case which Albright builds for Hebraic monotheism has been adopted by many younger scholars, particularly G. Ernest Wright, who presents it along with his own original research in a brief booklet entitled, *The Old Testament Against Its Environment.* In this book the case is stated in three questions.[19]

First, is the concept of growth adequate to explain the Bible? The concept of growth is not abandoned, for obviously the theology of Paul is not that of the Book of Kings. However, "The idea of development lays emphasis inevitably upon the process of human discovery rather than on revelation, on gradual evolution rather than on mutation," according to Wright. Both development and revelation must be kept in mind. The history of Israel contains many primitive survivals, but can a system of theology be reconstructed from them? It is not possible to do so with the polytheisms of Egypt, Babylon; or of any other nation of the ancient world. Why, therefore, can we assume that we can reconstruct the theology of Israel by fragments of data about early Hebraic practices?

Secondly, some biblical writers show little interest in the development of ideas. How did Israel become a nation apart from the God actually depicted in the early account? The prophets did not invent this concept. Social conditions occasioned by the shift from a nomadic to an agricultural life would not effect the idea of their being God's chosen people. A glance at environment only proves that the Canaanite religion was the most disintegrative factor Israel had to face.

The third question that starts us on this new path is, "What is the Israelite mutation which made the particular and peculiar evolution of biblical faith a possibility?" Even though Israel borrowed from many sources, the uniqueness of her faith is still there. Now what caused her to improve on her sources, or why did she alter all that she took from others, and why always in the direction of the basic monotheistic faith which runs through the Bible?

These three questions asked of the older critical view anticipate the answer by more precise archaeological data. Animism, which was thought to be the beginning of Israel's faith in primitive form, is now known to have left the states of all near eastern people before the history of Israel began; by the third millennium B.C. all the people of that region had a highly developed polytheism. These gods were not known through rational analysis but through the experiences of life. The polytheist's problem was the power of nature over which he had no control yet on which he was dependent. Humanity was caught in the interplay of gigantic forces to which one must adjust. Gods were created to represent the various forms of nature, sometimes numbering into the thousands.

But the Old Testament, written as it was in the midst of a polytheistic world, is entirely different. Professor Frankfort, an authority on ancient polytheism, says that the differences between the faith of Israel and polytheism are as great and significant as the differences between the Greek philosophers and the old superstitions. What were the differences?

First, God was not the product of abstract thought but was known because God had chosen God's people, delivered them from slavery, given them a law and a land. God was defined in terms of what God did: God brought Israel out of the land of Egypt, out of the house of bondage (Ex. 20:2). God was a God of historical event. In polytheism the religious metaphors are all drawn from nature. In Israel's faith the metaphors of nature, borrowed from Canaanite religion, were not basic, for their God could transcend nature as well as history and the historical experience was first.

Second, Israel's theology was never expressed in categories of duality of sex. Male and female were part of the created world of polytheism but never a part of Israel's theology--indeed, Biblical Hebrew has no word for goddess.

Third, Israel's God was surrounded by a type of holiness and prohibition of images not known by other religions. No image of deity is ever mentioned, not even in the temple of Solomon, although many Israelites had small figures of Canaanite goddesses as even the Old Testament indicates. It is interesting to note that these are always female deities--no male deity has ever been found in an Israelite home.

Fourth, the gods of the polytheists were connected with the world through almost every animal and bird. The God of Israel was related to humanity and history as no other creature of the world, and it is from these categories that the language of the Bible describes God. More could be said to indicate the data available but the direction of the proof is clear. The God of Israel is not a god who slowly evolved from polytheism: the two faiths rest on different foundations. The faith of Israel breaks suddenly into a history which predisposes and predetermines the course of biblical history. Furthermore, this faith shows a state of tension between God and the world. Although God created the world, the Hebrew, because of sin, saw a disharmony between the will of God and the existing order. Although the Israelites desired peace, they lived under this tension; social revolution was expected and discussed. Contrariwise, the polytheist lived in a tolerant world in which the goal was integration of the gods with and within the social order of humanity, so that the status quo was the desired end of humanity's relation to the gods.

Form Criticism and the Biblical Record

The second major turn in the academic world can be treated briefly. Just fifty years ago (1901) the German scholar Hermann Gunkel published a commentary on Genesis utilizing what we now know as form criticism.[20] His work is not well known in the English speaking world since his books have not been translated, but his influence has been felt in the past few decades by American scholars. The old critical view held that the material in a given document or book must be used for reconstructing the social and religious life of the period in which it was composed or edited. This was the principle that underlay the whole Mosaic era and assumed that the prophets were not reformers but rather the authors of the Hebrew faith. Form criticism accepts the basic outline of the older literary criticism, but it assumes that the documents are not innovations but rather the final written crystalization of the history of Israel. Wright states the matter in these words:

> In these last stages we have to do with the work of individual compilers whose greatness lay not so much in their invention of material, not in their ascription of current practices back into Mosaic or other antiquity, but rather in the way they gathered, organized and unified old traditions by various means, chiefly by an overall theme which was the product of intensive theological reflection. At the heart of the Yahwist's work, for example, is the unifying thread of a confessional recital of God's saving acts (a Heilsgeschichte), derived ultimately from old forms of confession used at the Tabernacle (so Gerhard von Rad). Such a point of view involves a closer attention to

the nature and peculiarity of written material as a whole, and particularly to the long history of the tradition which lies behind the final literary form. It thus means that the age of a document does not determine the date of the material employed by it. Each item of tradition has its own history which must be examined on its own merits. Consequently, the history of Israel cannot be reconstructed simply by dating final literary compositions; and the ground is cut from under the older Wellhausenian assumptions.[21]

Form criticism has brought theology back into the picture, for the Bible now presents itself as a collection of narratives written by people who were concerned with propagating the faith. Let us then turn to the final consideration of this paper, the formulation of modern Biblical theology.

Biblical Theology

The swing from the older liberal views has been so general that American scholars have been producing first-rate books on Biblical theology at the rate of almost one a year for the past decade. Look at this list:

1943 - Floyd V. Filson, *One Lord, One Faith*
1944 - G. Ernest Wright, *The Challenge of Israel's Faith*
1946 - N. H. Snaith, *The Distinctive Ideas of the Old Testament*
1946 - Millar Burrows, *An Outline of Biblical Theology*
1946 - Paul S. Minear, *Eyes of Faith*
1949 - Otto J. Baab, *The Theology of the Old Testament*
1950 - F. C. Grant, *An Introduction to New Testament Thought*
1950 - Paul S. Minear, *The Kingdom and the Power: An Exposition of the New Testament Gospel*
1951 - G. Ernest Wright, *The God Who Acts: Biblical Theology as Recital*

It is impossible and unfair to attempt a quick review of these books, and obviously the authors do not agree. However, it is possible to point out the direction that Biblical Theology is taking and particularly to indicate its content. Four general comments can be made.[22]

First, there is a fresh recognition of the authority of the biblical revelation. Professor H. H. Rowley puts it this way:

> The newer attitude still recognizes the clear marks of progress in the Biblical revelation, yet it does not reduce revelation to discovery. It does not cease to be interested in the development of religion, but its center of interest is not in man but in God. It does not find the story of man's growth in the understanding of God of such absorbing interest that it becomes an end in itself, but rather seeks to perceive in every stage of the progress that which is enduringly true of God.[23]

O. J. Baab describes the process by saying that a Biblical theology must unhesitatingly use all the scientific techniques available including history, archaeology, criticism, etc.; yet with all this we cannot leave out the one thing that makes the Bible possible, that is, the religious consciousness of the writers. Baab explains:

> The Old Testament's "Thus saith the Lord" or "The Word of the Lord is like a burning fire in my bones" and scores of similar statements demonstrate conclusively the orientation of its prophets and saints toward the God who spoke to and through them. The critic may declare that these men were mistaken, and confused a personal ethical urge with divine revelation, but he must acknowledge the existence of these passages and offer an explanation of their prominence.
>
> Apart from this fact of the Old Testament's religious consciousness, any real understanding of this literature is impossible. The expert may exercise his skill in extricating from the records of the life of biblical man information respecting social customs and economic and political institutions. Yet the dead past which the historian thus reconstructs remains dead, because the quickening power of religious faith which once animated it eludes him.[24]

Baab points out that two criteria must be established in order to create a positive Biblical theology: first, a logical consistency concerning the character of God; and second, a proof of the character of this God by God's relation to people in history. Regarding the first point of consistency on the part of God, he says:

> Here the difficulty of our task is apparently insurmountable. How can logical consistency be found when the reader is confronted by many

gods and by contradictory traits of the one God? In the Old Testament, God appears to be a strange being, wrathful and vindictive, merciful and benevolent, righteous and vengeful, creative and destructive, a fierce fighter, a loving father, concerned for but one people, ruling over all men. . . . How can the student of biblical theology find God among these gods? Is there a unitary Being which the Old Testament writings present with convincing unanimity? Examination reveals that there is, even though various characteristics of the divine nature may be over-emphasized to the point of distortion in certain books or sources.

The Hebrew Scriptures are in fundamental agreement as to the power, holiness, righteousness, and redemptive love of God, notwithstanding that his rule is nationalistic in some writings and universal in others, or creative and constructive in some and righteously destructive in others. Even such books as Leviticus show how the good and holy God of Israel may be approached. He is central in the elaborate Temple ritual. The Book of Judges, containing considerable evidence of crude religious feeling and practice, as a book is a remarkable documentation of the moral majesty of a God who rules the history of men or, in particular, the men of Israel.

It is true that this consistency is by no means perfect, for the Hebrew writers were more interested in the drama of life than in the nature and relationship of ideas. They reported those personal and national experiences which seemed to them significant in revealing the nature and purposes of God. Further, Old Testament books, particularly Genesis, contain legendary source material, the contradictory portions of which were frequently left undisturbed by compilers. When an entire biblical book is surveyed, however, the undeveloped religious ideas which it contains may possibly be viewed as archaisms or unexpurgated survivals from a primitive cultural period.

It is significant that no Old Testament author or editor is conscious of being an innovator in his presentation of truth. All assume the continuity with the past of the message which they record. Israel's greatest creative thinkers--the prophets--constantly assume and maintain that their messages carry the weight of historical experience. They exhort and condemn in the light of past revelation, going back even to the days of the Exodus to support their contentions.[25]

The second principle is the test of the character of God in the experience of people. Here we follow Baab again:

> The God of the Hebrews is a living God, revealing his righteousness and mercy in the continuing historical process. Political events and social conflicts are always viewed by the biblical writers in terms of the nature and will of God. History is never regarded as the result of natural forces operating automatically; instead, it is the account of man's obedience to or defiance of, the divine will. The character of God is demonstrated by the events of history, never by pure reason alone. It is a striking fact that Israel's monotheism came to its full glory and maturity after the nation had fallen and the righteousness of God had been tragically verified. In national defeat was seen convincing proof of the reality of the God of history.
>
> The national tragedy, which such prophets as the Second Isaiah turned into spiritual triumph, rested upon the fact of man's rebellious will. His collective sin lay in flaunting the will of God and in worshipping the gods which he had made with his own hands but which actually were the projections of his own unregenerate desires. . . . Man through his creation has a spiritual nature, a capacity for worship and moral commitment, and the power to deny his divine sonship in sinfulness and self-centered living. . . . Man is made for God and goodness. When he willfully sets his face against God, he brings ruin upon himself and upon his fellows. . . . The candid portrayal found there is supported by the events of Hebrew history. What the Old Testament teaches us about man it makes convincing by showing us man in action.[26]

Second, a part of this fresh discovery of the authority of the Bible is an emphasis on its essential unity. The older liberal critical view of the Bible ascribed a certain kind of unity to the two testaments, but the emphasis was on the development of religious ideas, on the various levels of spiritual attainment, on the contrasts between the prophets and the writers of the J documents, or the dissimilarity between the theology of Paul, Peter and John. The biblical scholar during the past ten years has rediscovered the essential unity of God's word. Witness A. M. Hunter's book, *The Unity of the New Testament* or Professor R. V. G. Tasker's *The Old Testament in the New Testament*. A summary of Tasker's view runs like this:

> . . . the main theme of the Bible is the covenant-relationship between God and man, a relationship which was initiated by God for the reconciliation of sinful man to Himself. First He entered into a covenant-relationship with the Israelites, whom He called out of Egypt for the special purpose of revealing through them His purposes for mankind; and later in the person of His incarnate Son He inaugurated a new covenant with the new Israel. The membership of this new Israel consisted of all who accepted Jesus both as the Christ, who fulfilled the prophecies made to the Old Israel, and as the Saviour, who by His death and resurrection had won salvation for all mankind.[27]

F. C. Grant in his 1950 book, *An Introduction to New Testament Thought* states the matter thus:

> . . . the New Testament is essentially a continuation and further development of the thought of the Old Testament, with a new orientation and emphasis which were completely to distinguish it from the contemporary but divergent development of rabbinic Judaism. For a rounded view it is necessary to take into account the Old Testament thought on every point. The Old Testament is even more important than the apocalyptic literature, important as that is. . . . So true is this relation between the two Testaments that one might almost take a book on Old Testament theology and merely substitute New Testament references and illustrations for those which it cites. . . . One thing is certain--the New Testament writers presuppose the Old Testament pattern of thought, phraseology, and conceptions a dozen times for every reference or allusion to apocalyptic. Even the apocalypse of John is far more dependent on the Old Testament than upon the 'apocalyptic literature' of the period.
>
> In brief, what we call New Testament theology is chiefly derived from the Old Testament as read and interpreted by the early Christians. The other factors, drawn from their own religious experience and their reflections upon it, affected the interpretations, not the data.[28]

This emphasis on the unity of the Bible is occasioned by four developments. First, the neo-orthodox theology seeks for the Word of God in the Scripture which is applicable to our condition at this time;

such a search naturally sees a unity in the Bible. Second, the older concern for deference to the Hellenistic background of the New Testament is giving way to a rediscovery of the Old Testament. Hoskyns and Davey (1931) showed that the meaning of the important words in the New Testament was to be found in the Septuagint, and Manson said that same year that the New Testament was to be understood in the light of the Old Testament conception of the "saving remnant."[29] Third, there is the newer understanding of the Bible as not just the history but the holy history of God's people, to be read and understood from within the orbit of the religious community which it describes. Fourth, recent work by scholars shows the unity of each of the testaments. For example, Baab says this about the Old Testament:

> There is a great difference between the God of the J writer and the God of Second Isaiah, but there is also a deep likeness. For both men God was the righteous, redemptive, self-revealing Creator of humankind and the Lord of history. . . . Thus the very fact that the Hebrews consisted of one highly self-conscious, continuing, historical community lends plausibility to the supposition that there was and is only one Old Testament theology.[30]

Third, the general emphasis of the new understanding of the Bible is the recovery of the theological significance of the Scripture. Biblical criticism, which did so much to clear up the nature of the books of the Bible as to date and composition and historical setting, should have led scholars into a profound evaluation of the theology involved. Instead, it became an end in itself. One of the reasons we are getting so many books in the field of Biblical theology is that the critical work has been done so well and the actual meaning of the passages has been so clearly defined, that scholars are putting the muscle of meaning back on the skeleton of fact. Manson in his brilliant essay on "The Failure of Liberalism to Interpret the Bible as the Word of God" says this:

> Where, then, is the point at which Liberalism took the wrong theological turning? All the evidence before us points in one direction: the mischief was begun when the working hypotheses of natural science were allowed to become the dogmas of theology. At that moment God's revelation of himself gives way to man's thought about God. God's mighty acts give place to man's evolving

civilization. In order to come to terms with nineteenth-century science, Liberalism had to fall out with historical Christianity. The Gospel had to be reduced to a message about God; and the essence of the message had to be found in a few simple beliefs, held with great tenacity and promulgated with great force by Jesus, who becomes the author of a strong reforming movement in Judaism rather than the saviour of the world.

We realize today that, in its every essence, the religion of the Bible is concerned with the life of mankind in relation to the will of a living and active God. The things that men will and do, and the eternal purpose of God and his control over history, are intimately bound together. That God created the world and man; that he did so for some good purpose of his own; that he is constantly watching over the course of history; that he actively governs its development; that in Christ he has made the decisive intervention--these convictions are so fundamental to the Christian religion that to give them up is not to reform Christianity but to abandon it.

But the Christian religion is concerned with a God who reveals himself above all in history. This fact has consequences of vital importance. It means that history takes on a new significance, that the outstanding events in which the voice of God has been heard, or his hand discerned, must be studied with the same passion for accuracy that the scientist gives to a chemical analysis. If God has in fact spoken through prophetic oracles or the words of Jesus and his disciples, then it becomes a matter of vital importance to establish the true text and to ascertain the exact meaning of the Biblical records.

We have to begin by using all our powers and all our resources for the simple end of establishing what the Bible says and what it means when the words are taken in their plain sense.[31]

Fourth, the revival of biblical theology is bringing about an awareness of the interrelation of the Bible and the Church. The Bible is the product of the believing community. The church existed years before the scriptures of the New Testament were circulated and several hundred years before the canon was set. This Book, then, is the record of the saving acts of God in history. It is a holy history. So we are reminded that there are two great facts to our Christian experience. We can sing

Jesus loves me, this I know
For the Bible tells me so.

We can also sing

Jesus loves me, this I know
For my parents told me so.

Notes

1 Gunnar Östborn, *Torah in the Old Testament* (Lund: Hakan Ohlssons Boktryckebi, 1945) 170.
2 E. F. Scott, *The Purpose of the Gospels* (New York: Charles Scribner's Sons, 1949) 19-25.
3 This section is indebted to G. Ernest Wright's article "The Christian Interpreter as Biblical Critic," *Interpretation*, 2 (1947): 131-152.
4 Wright 135.
5 Wright 139.
6 G. Ernest Wright, "The Study of the Old Testament," *Protestant Thought in the Twentieth Century*, ed. Arnold Nash (New York: Macmillan, 1951) 18.
7 H. E. Fosdick, *The Modern Use of the Bible* (New York: Macmillan, 1924) 7-8.
8 Fosdick 13.
9 Fosdick 14.
10 Fosdick 27.
11 Fosdick 131-167.
12 Fosdick 97-129.
13 W. C. Bower, *Christ and Christian Education* (New York: Abingdon-Cokesbury, 1943) 80-81.
14 Bower 89-97.
15 E. J. Chave, *A Functional Approach to Religious Education* (Chicago: UP, 1947) 112-113.
16 Chave 25.
17 *Moral and Spiritual Values in the Public School* (Educational Policies Commission, National Educational Association of the United States, Washington, D. C., 1951).
18 W. F. Albright, *From the Stone Age to Christianity* (Baltimore: John Hopkins Press, 1940) 310.
19 G. Ernest Wright, *The Old Testament Against Its Environment* (Chicago: Henry Regnery Company, Chicago, 1950) 9-29.
20 J. L. Mihelic, "The Influence of Form Criticism on the Study of the Old Testament," *The Journal of Bible and Religion* 19 (1951) 120.
21 G. Ernest Wright, "The Study of the Old Testament," 27.
22 The material in this section follows the outline given by Raymond Abba in his article "Recent Trends in Biblical Studies," *Scottish Journal of Theology*, 4 (1951) 235-240.
23 Quoted in the article by Abba cited above, page 235.
24 O. J. Baab, "Old Testament Theology: Its Possibility and Methodology," *The Study of the Bible Today and Tomorrow*, ed. R. Willoughby, (Chicago: UP, 1947) 413-414.

25 Baab 415-416.
26 Baab 417.
27 Quoted in the article by Abba cited above, page 237.
28 F. C. Grant, *An Introduction to New Testament Thought* (New York: Abingdon-Cokesbury, 1950) 16-17.
29 Abba, 238.
30 O. J. Baab, *The Theology of the Old Testament* (New York: Abingdon-Cokesbury, 1949) 252.
31 T. W. Manson, "The Failure of Liberalism to Interpret the Bible as the Word of God," *The Interpretation of the Bible*, ed. C. W. Dugmore (London: Society for Promoting Christian Knowledge, 1944) 101-105.

3

The Glory, Jest and Riddle of the World: Man

Alexander Pope sets the perennial problem in these words from Epistle 11.I of his *Essay on Man.*

Know then thyself, presume not God to scan;
The proper study of mankind is man.
Placed in this isthmus of a middle state,
A being darkly wise, and rudely great:
With too much weakness for the stoic's pride,
He hangs between; in doubt to act, or rest;
In doubt to deem himself a god, or beast;
In doubt his mind or body to prefer;
Born but to die, and reasoning but to err;
Alike in ignorance, his reason such,
Whether he thinks too little, or too much:
Chaos of thought and passion, all confused;
Still by himself abused, or disabused;
Created half to rise, and half to fall;
Great lord of all things, yet a prey to all;
Sole judge of truth, in endless error hurled;
The glory, jest, and riddle of the world!

Humans, the riddle of the world, cannot answer their own questions. Perhaps the greatest triumph of humans has been the conquest of the physical universe during the past two centuries; yet this success creates a bigger problem. The scientific skills that produced penicillin also manufacture the materials for bacteriological warfare.

Prepared for Children's Work Section, Division of Christian Education, National Council of Churches, meeting in Columbus, Ohio, February 10-12, 1952.

Still, the human mind seeks to solve the riddle; and our concern in this paper is the recent attempt to shape a Christian answer in harmony with the facts of modern history.

Liberal American theology, under which all of us grew up and in which many of us were schooled, was based on the goodness and perfectibility of human nature and society. John Bennett, who at one time was a devotee of liberal theology, has said that all that was characteristic of liberalism could be accounted for in its basic doctrine of faith in humankind. His words in 1933 were as follows:

> . . . The premise of liberalism is faith in man and his highest values as the clue to the nature of God. This faith in man makes possible confidence in human reason and insight as the basis of authority in religion. It makes possible the emphasis upon the immanence of God. It makes possible the identification of the divinity of Christ with his ideal humanity. It makes possible the optimistic faith in progress which is now under such a cloud. It makes possible the attitude toward other religions which we find in the early chapters of the Laymen's report. I think that the best short-cut to an understanding of the present theological situation is to realize that liberalism diverges from orthodoxy and neo-orthodoxy in its various forms in its doctrine of man, and that other differences follow from that.[1]

Liberal theology was optimistic about humans, believing that they could improve their social situation, control their irrational outbursts of hate, and perfect their life in history. These desirable goals were rooted in the concept of a human ability to control nature and society. Humans, it was thought, did not fall from goodness as in the Adam-Eve story but rather rose by evolutionary process to the high estate they now enjoy.

One of the finest treatments of the idea of humans as sinners is the book titled *Man as Sinner*, written by Mary Francis Thelen in 1946. In tracing the reaction to the liberal concept of humans, Thelen shows that liberal theologians were not too interested in sin, for they were busy perfecting the arguments for God in the light of the biological theory of evolution and the idea of progress.[2]

F. R. Tennant of Trinity College, Cambridge, became the spokesman for the liberal concept by formulating a philosophical system in which sin was rationally explained. Tennant strikes at the traditional concept of a human's plight by denying original sin. He gives three reasons for his denial. *First*, there was no literal, historical "fall." Original human nature was without conscience. Communal living in primitive society was governed by group mores. Later, when conditions changed and humans reflected on applying the old mores to new social conditions, conscience emerged. The clash between conscience and group ethical practices is the condition that produces sin. *Second*, there is no bias toward sin. There is actual sin everywhere; but this can be explained simply by showing how impossible is a sinless life, rather than by saying that man inherits a tendency toward evil. *Third*, sin is really a problem of the will and is not inherited. Humans admit that sin is universal; but affirm that the problem of sin can be solved by forgetting that human inheritance has anything to do with it. We inherit a free will, not sin, and the will can overcome sin.

Tennant's definition of sin is ". . . disobedience to the moral law which the sinner understands, . . . and to which he is therefore morally accountable."[3] To be sinless does not mean being morally perfect but rather not committing acts which we know to be immoral. Thus "accountability" is the key word in his system. A just God will hold us guilty for only those acts in which wrong was chosen deliberately.

The concept of sin as transgression of the moral law by people who knew they were doing wrong received wide acceptance among liberal thinkers and greatly influenced the religious education movement in America. The late Harrison S. Elliott promulgated this view of people's basic problem. Perhaps Elliott was extreme in his views; however, his prominence in the religious education movement in America makes it possible to show how closely that liberal view of man was fitted into an educational psychology.

Elliott in his book, *Can Religious Education be Christian?*, rejects the idea that people are by nature sinners. Elliott is in rebellion against authority and vigorously defends the thesis that each generation should decide for itself its concept of truth.[4]

Elliott's concept of sin flows from his concept of God. Christians desire "comradeship with God." He says,

> Certainly Christians should have the right to look forward to comradeship with God in the educational process and in life itself. In such comradeship in meeting the situations of life in this world, human beings would be expected to take initiative, to make decisions, to take responsibility, but all the time in relation to a God whose resources

> they utilize and dependence upon whom they gladly recognize. In such comradeship God becomes a living reality and at the same time man grows in true humility as he recognizes the degree to which he is actually dependent upon God.[5]

He rejects the idea of an authoritarian god, an absolute sovereign, saying that this concept flows from the German mind in thinkers who were raised in homes where the fathers assumed complete authority.[6]

Elliott thinks that with proper education sin can be eliminated. He writes:

> Sin is, to a certain extent, within the experience of all. But many of those with personality difficulties which manifest themselves in what looks like sinful conduct are the victims of our un-Christian social order, and the sin, if there be sin, is more largely that of their forebears or of a ruthless competitive society than of themselves. This distinction is already recognized in juvenile delinquency and some day will be more largely a part of the criminal procedure with adult offenders.[7]

When human nature is examined, Elliott finds no disposition toward good or evil.

> It must be evident that the common assumption that the source of the human predicament lies in anti-social impulses in man is erroneous. . . . The empirical evidence seems to show that there is nothing in human nature with a predetermining influence that the individual will be a saint or a devil; but there are resident within that nature possibilities which will never be exhausted in any lifetime of either or both, and possibilities which are unknown in the animal world.[8]

Actually, to Elliott's mind, the problem is social, for the social situation causes humans to sin and one sins only to the extent that one makes a conscious choice to act contrary to approved social goals.

> . . . it is necessary to make a distinction between sickness and sin; that is, between that sinful conduct for which the individual is responsible and that which has grown out of circumstances beyond his control. Instead of focusing attention upon the individual wrong-doer, there

should be more sense of social responsibility and a larger consciousness of social sin. This gives the basis for a realistic religious education which recognizes fully the limitations of human beings and the seriousness of the human problem, but, at the same time, renders it possible to make a positive attack upon the problem through the educative process, the kind of an attack which will lead to a mature Christian experience in which there is "responsible existence."[9]

We could summarize these views by saying that the human riddle is society; society creates sin; improve society by making life more secure; improve education by making it less individualistic, and sin will cease to be important.[10]

Realistic Theology

Social salvation or an identification of sin with social disease was challenged by Reinhold Niebuhr's book *Moral Man and Immoral Society*, published in 1932. That date is generally accepted as the beginning of what has been called realistic theology. Most American writers in the theological field began to modify their position; and all participated in a vigorous discussion of our basic human problem.[11] By 1942 when the book *Liberal Theology, An Appraisal* was published, almost all American theologians who considered themselves a part of the liberal tradition had reconsidered the liberal concept; and many, such as John C. Bennett, had drastically revised their views.[12]

The modern classic statement of humans as sinners is contained in Chapters 7 and 8 of Niebuhr's Gifford lectures, *The Nature and Destiny of Man*, published in 1941.

Since the old liberalism was most vulnerable at this point and since the tragic events of the past decade have been a constant demonstration that humans cannot control their selfishness and pride, no real challenge of this position has appeared. Rather, the more recent writings have dealt with the connection between psychology and sin and a doctrine of salvation consonant with these new developments. We shall, therefore, examine these newer concepts for they are fundamental to the Christian nurture of children.

What is the distinctive Christian view of people? Niebuhr states it with these words:

> The Christian view of man is sharply distinguished from all alternative views by the manner in which it interprets and relates three aspects of human existence to each other: (1) It emphasizes the height of self-transcendence in man's spiritual stature in its doctrine of 'image of God.' (2) It insists on man's weakness, dependence, and finiteness, on his involvement in the necessities and contingencies of the natural world, without, however, regarding this finiteness as, of itself, a source of evil in man. In its purest form the Christian view of man regards man as a unity of God-likeness and creatureliness in which he remains a creature even in the highest spiritual dimensions of his existence and may reveal elements of the image of God even in the lowliest aspects of his natural life. (3) It affirms that the evil in man is a consequence of his inevitable though not necessary unwillingness to acknowledge his dependence, to accept his finiteness and to admit his insecurity, an unwillingness which involves him in the vicious circle of accentuating the insecurity from which he seeks escape.[13]

Niebuhr acknowledges his indebtedness to Kierkegaard in tracing sin to anxiety.

> Anxiety is the inevitable concomitant of the paradox of freedom and finiteness in which man is involved. Anxiety is the internal precondition of sin.
>
> . . . It must not be identified with sin because there is always the ideal possibility that faith would purge anxiety of the tendency toward sinful self-assertion. . . . Christian orthodoxy has consistently defined unbelief as the root of sin, or as the sin which precedes pride.
>
> . . . Yet anxiety is not sin. It must be distinguished from sin partly because it is its precondition and not its actuality, and partly because it is the basis of all human creativity as well as the precondition of sin.
>
> . . . Anxiety, as a permanent concomitant of freedom, is thus both the source of creativity and a temptation to sin. It is the condition of the sailor, climbing the mast . . . with the abyss of the waves beneath him and the 'crow's nest' above him. He is anxious about both the end toward which he strives and the abyss of nothingness into which he may fall.
>
> . . . When anxiety has conceived it brings forth both pride and sensuality. Man falls into pride, when he seeks to raise his contingent existence to unconditioned significance; he falls into sensuality, when

> he seeks to escape from his unlimited possibilities of freedom, from the perils and responsibilities of self-determination, by immersing himself into a 'mutable good,' by losing himself in some natural vitality.[14]

The actual drive behind sin is pride. Humans refuse to accept their place in the universe, they rebel against God. Instead of admitting their weakness and ignorance and seeking faith, humans try to obscure their weakness and pretend that their truth is final truth. Original sin infects every act, for the will of humanity is defective. This is not caused by a "fall" of humankind in a historic moment but it is the inevitable condition of every person. Everyone has a "fall" because each one's humanity produces anxiety.

Pride, rebellion, will-to-power, and sensuality are shown in their relationship within these paragraphs.

> Man is insecure and involved in natural contingency; he seeks to overcome his insecurity by a will-to-power which overreaches the limits of human creatureliness. Man is ignorant and involved in the limitations of a finite mind; but he pretends that he is not limited. He assumes that he can gradually transcend finite limitations until his mind becomes identical with universal mind. All of his intellectual and cultural pursuits, therefore, become infected with the sin of pride. Man's pride and will-to-power disturb the harmony of creation. The Bible defines sin in both religious and moral terms. The religious dimension of sin is man's rebellion against God, his effort to usurp the place of God. The moral and social dimension of sin is injustice. The ego which falsely makes itself the center of existence in its pride and will-to-power inevitably subordinates other life to its will and thus does injustice to other life.
>
> Sometimes man seeks to solve the problem of the contradiction of finiteness and freedom, not by seeking to hide his finiteness and comprehending the world unto himself, but by seeking to hide his freedom and by losing himself in some aspect of the world's vitalities. In that case his sin may be defined as sensuality rather than pride.[15]

Thelen has made a keen summary of this position by putting "realistic theology" against the older liberal views. Her statement is contained in six points.

(1) In the conception of God against Whom man sins liberal theology has taught that man finds fulfillment in the service of God; whereas realistic theology sees God standing over against man in the double relationship of Judge and Redeemer.

(2) Liberal theology dropped the conception of 'original righteousness'; and various types of liberalism thought that man could secure an easy conscience either by bringing his conduct into closer conformity with the moral law or by reducing the threshold of conscience to conform with behavior which is actually possible. Realistic theology believes that man can neither cure nor evade his uneasy conscience but must seek forgiveness from God within his sin.

(3) Liberal theology believed that the will is free to choose either good or evil and denied the existence of original sin. It saw temptation in man's biological endowment and in cultural lag but left the consent of the will thereto a mystery. Realistic theology believes that sin arises out of man's situation as both free and finite and constitutes a 'bias' within the will itself which makes sin inevitable in every action.

(4) Liberal theology approached sin from the standpoint of moral value and regarded it as equivalent to moral wrong with an added religious reference. It differentiated between big and little sins and had difficulty in taking sin seriously because it was confident that sin was being cured by God in the transformation of lives and in the progress of society. Realistic theology views sin as arising in man's relationship to God and it is appalled by sin both because of its presumption as idolatry and because of the amount of evil and destruction which it causes in the world. In its description of sin realism leans heavily upon the psychological description of neurosis. It is particularly concerned over the 'sins of the righteous.'

(5) Liberal theology found the meaning of Christianity in salvation as transformation; it saw the experience of grace primarily as conferring the power to work the more valiantly for the coming of the Kingdom. Realistic theology finds the meaning of Christianity within our earthly existence to lie in reconciliation to God; it sees the experience of grace primarily as consoling us for the failure of our best efforts and only secondarily as resulting in moral improvement.

(6) Liberal theology found the solution of the social problem in the application of the ethics of Jesus to group life. Realistic theology finds that solution too simple and thinks it necessary to set up a

dialectic between the ultimate goal of love and a realistic social ethics based upon the persistence of power politics.[16]

A full understanding of humanity in the light of the realistic theology and liberalism is yet before us. Dean Sperry of the Harvard Divinity School has recently commented that "Protestant theology needs nothing so much today as agreement upon a credible doctrine of man."[17] His discussion did not doubt the existence of sin but rather the difficulty in knowing just how much sin was in humanity. Indeed, Dean Sperry says,

> . . . if the case is appealed from the theologian to the anthropologist, the sociologist and, in particular, to the psychologist, a stubborn moral malaise seems to persist. Thus one of our Harvard anthropologists has recently said that while scientists no longer believe in 'sin,' they have to recognize in most human beings a baffling 'guilt feeling' which is something more than a matter of social maladjustment. The accepted modern term is little more than a new name for an old and deep awareness of a profound unhappiness.[18]

Anxiety

The root of the unhappiness and the precondition of sin is anxiety. Since the publication of Niebuhr's Gifford lectures, the effort of several writers has been in the relation of anxiety to psychology and theology. Lewis Sherrill wrote *Guilt and Redemption* in 1945.[19] Mary Alice Jones in her 1943 book *The Faith of Our Children* includes chapters on sin and salvation.[20]

1950 was a peak year with the publication of four important books on the subject. Karen Horney authored *Neurosis and Human Growth*, in which she indicated that people were not essentially good but that inherent in people are constructive forces which cause them to strive for self-realization. Human values, Horney believes, arise out of humanity's struggle to arrive.[21] Perhaps the most complete discussion of this basic human problem is found in Rollo May's *The Meaning of Anxiety*.[22] *Psychotherapy and a Christian View of Man* is the descriptive title of David Roberts' new book in which he faces the empirical data of psychology with a dynamic view of salvation.[23] A proper solution of the human problem of sin and anxiety is the focal point of all of Christian education, according to Randolph Miller in *The Clue to Christian Education*.[24]

Even a cursory glance at these writers will reveal that we are dealing with the most basic human problem. Modern psychiatry has developed a working hypothesis concerning anxiety, and American theologians have within recent years turned their attention to the meaning of salvation in the light of these events. Let us take a closer look at the present state of affairs.

Many followers of Freud have approached this human riddle with the assumption that religion is a neurotic symptom developed to allay anxiety. On the other hand, we often find that writers on the religious or theological side of the discussion assume that a person of faith can master anxiety. In order to keep our minds clear, we must recall that in this discussion we have pointed up the fact that anxiety and sin both develop from our common human situation. Humanity has a special dimension of life not enjoyed by any other animal--one can imagine, plan, create, see oneself in historical perspective, and consciously create values for oneself. This gift of freedom places one in a state of unrest, i.e., anxiety, which causes one to sin by striving for security in money, pride of mental ability, etc. But this basic anxiety is not fear. Fear is the human response to a specific threat, to an object that can be defined.

Anxiety is that vague, diffuse uncertainty which hovers over our lives and which is unrelated to any specific event or condition. May uses these words:

> The special characteristics of anxiety are the feelings of uncertainty and helplessness in the face of danger. . . . Anxiety is the apprehension cued off by a threat to some value which the individual holds essential to his existence as a personality.[25]

The value which a person holds dearest may be job, patriotism, love of another person, religion, sense of freedom, or a number of other desirable objects. If these things are threatened, anxiety ensues; for the very core of personality is at stake and what one fears is a loss of one's experience of self. Tillich says this threat of "nonbeing" and the normal anxiety that people have of death are the most common forms of this basic insecurity.[26]

But we must make a clear distinction between normal anxiety arising out of our human situation and neurotic anxiety. Normal anxiety is always with us. The reaction of a baby to hunger is normal anxiety. People's experiences with the power of nature, sickness and death is a source of normal anxiety; obviously these things come to everyone and no special hostility is present. If the anxious strivings of persons are prompted by a force that is not disproportionate to the goal but rather a drive to become successful, they may be entirely normal. If they become compulsive, then they are neurotic. If persons recognize their limitations, their strivings are normal; but if they deny their limitations, then they are neurotic.[27]

Furthermore, normal anxiety has a significant place in the development of selfhood. Normal anxiety starts when the baby feels a threat to the security provided by mother. As children become conscious of themselves they begin to understand the differences between themselves and their parents, especially their mothers. As they move away from the protecting adults into wider ranges of self-expression, they lose some security and create some anxiety. But the new freedom brings a sense of accomplishment and autonomy, thus making it possible for the child to move on toward responsible adulthood. This is a creative and normal experience of anxiety. As Kierkegaard said, "To venture causes anxiety, but not to venture is to lose oneself."[28]

> Neurotic anxiety, on the other hand,is a reaction to a threat which is (1) disproportionate to the objective danger, (2) involves repression (disassociation) and other forms of intra-psychic conflict, and, as a corollary (3) is managed by means of various forms of retrenchment of activity and awareness, such as inhibitions, the development of symptoms, and the varied neurotic defense mechanisms.[29]

Another way to look at the matter is to observe how persons use anxiety when something threatens them. If they seek a solution to their problem, then they are the victims of normal anxiety and their effort is objective. Contrariwise, if they avoid the problem or build up defenses as to why they cannot grapple with the threat, then they are neurotic and subjective in their efforts.

Anxiety is like the temperature of the physical body. Normally, for most people this will be 98.6 degrees Fahrenheit. Tissue is being destroyed and rebuilt; germs are entering the body but they are either destroyed or held in check. So normal anxiety is the condition of everyone, but the psyche is strong enough to fend off threats and fears.

Christian Education and Neurotic Anxiety

Neurotic anxiety we shall label sickness. This part of humanity's riddle is coming more and more under the curative powers of the psychiatrist. Child guidance clinics offer real hope for parents and teachers who observe the outcropping of abnormal anxiety in a child. Our understanding of this phase of the human problem can help us do preventive counseling and can guide us in planning programs for children. This is a psychological and educational problem, and it will not be amiss to indicate the type of mental hygiene that can be brought to bear on this matter. We who work with children in the church have an unusual opportunity to prevent many of the crippling mental diseases and much of the unhappiness that plagues mankind.

1. Leaders who work directly with children must be selected on the basis of possessing the right attitudes toward children. Neurotic anxiety is created by conflict; we should not enlist leaders who are so insecure themselves that they react with condemning, critical attitudes. The leader should be poised, quick to listen, able to exercise control through group activity, and should be as respectful of each child as one would be of an adult.

2. It is very important that children learn to meet threats constructively and objectively; they must be helped to move on in experience rather than to develop an escape device such as avoidance or introspection. Informal group activity and play provide the finest opportunity to help children meet threats to themselves and to develop self-reliance.

3. Adults must recognize that each child grows because of the tension that exists between desire for security and the anxiety that confronts one when one moves out into new experiences. The real self of the child is the factor that should emerge; and adults should allow that selfhood to come to the fore by their acceptance of the individual. Rogers' client-centered therapy rests, in part, on the concept that the real self of persons will not emerge until they are allowed to talk and work with persons who will accept them as they really are. Clinically speaking, Rogers sees a clear movement from symptoms to self when individuals are permitted to be themselves.[30] This desirable condition is created because clients experience a feeling of safety when they discover that the counselor accepts them as they are. Under such arrangements one is able to explore one's feelings, discover one's hostility, voice one's fears, and yet sense the warmth and respect of the counselor.[31]

4. Severe neurotic anxiety is often started in childhood when children are thrown up against dangers and threats before they are able to handle them. These cases may require expert care; but we can redeem a life if we are able to identify the suffocating mood of anxiety and make possible a program of therapy which will release the soul before maturity crystallizes the pattern and makes the person ineffective. Often the quiet, docile, obedient child who gives us no trouble is the one whose spirit is being crushed by threatening parents.

5. Sometimes we observe anxious children so intent on harmony between themselves and adults that they will adopt a very rigid thought system. This can be religious dogma, political or social creed, or fierce loyalty to a person. If one's basic insecurity is not removed, the thought system will harden and life will be one long struggle to defend the authority of the thought system. Although some therapy may be administered at the verbal level, this condition will not be ameliorated until the children are helped through their insecurities and gain inner strength to affirm their own selfhoods.

6. American culture is dominated by a "success-ideal" interpreted in terms of power, prestige and wealth; such an ideal gives rise to the highly desired goal of individual accomplishment. Middle class children soon learn to be acquisitive and competitive. They are literally taught by parents, adults, comic strips and movies to strive for personal success without too much regard for the damage done to others in the process. Davis and Havighurst describe this process adroitly in their discussion of the Washington family in Chicago living in the slums at the lowest cultural level.[32] Below them are the irresponsible bums and jailbirds.

Mary and Paulette Washington, aged eight and one half and six, demonstrate a working, playing, and sharing fellowship that grows out of their communal living. At two years of age the children of this family crossed the street alone and at three they roamed four blocks away. At four years of age they knew how to get their neighbors to feed them. At eight years Mary could run the family, for the mother was gone all day sweeping out the railroad cars on the B. and O. Railroad. In contrast the authors described the Bretts, college graduates, living in a ten-room house with maid and two children. Everything from orange juice to bedtime was carefully controlled, including judiciously selected playmates.

Through this book, *Father of the Man*, we see how the middle class child is trained for a world that demands fast and early attainment. The training builds a desire for accomplishment, or negatively speaking, the parents "instill a deep anxiety in the child that he will be a failure, or will not be loved, if he does not learn early and well the cultural goals of middle class life."[33] The neurotic drive to achieve, or contrariwise, hostility arising from failure to accomplish, is often rooted in the home life of middle class children. It is from this group that we Protestants draw our support and to whom we extend our leadership. Efforts to develop cooperative activity, to diminish the fanatical drive to achieve, to show parents the folly of prestige at any price, and to de-emphasize the value of money will bring healing to this plague of middle class striving.

Christian Education and Creature Anxiety

The distresses of neurotic anxiety can be recognized and treated by modern psychotherapy; these conditions we do not consider sin but rather sickness of mind and soul. However, our definition of anxiety indicated a creaturely, or normal, human anxiety which was the precondition of sin and in which we are all caught by reason of our birth. Humans violate their own nature not because society forces them, not because they are ignorant, but because they want to for their own selfish interests. Their wills are biased toward evil, not because God created them that way but because they had freedom and they abused their power. In short, humanity is alienated from God. This phase of humanity's riddle is not psychological but theological. How can humanity be saved?

It is interesting to note that most theologians introduce their discussion of salvation by indicating that their proposal will not be satisfactory, even to themselves.[34] Realistic theology has so established the doctrine of sin that attention has been turned to a fresh understanding of redemption. The difficulty of the problem can be seen in one statement in Williams' book *God's Grace and Man's Hope* when he observes that Niebuhr's redeemed humanity is not much better off than his unredeemed humanity, for sin has been overcome in principle but not in fact.[35]

The precise matter before us now is the extent of sin. Let us recall Tennant's concept of sin as moral responsibility for acts or choices in which the person consciously follows a lower ethical choice than one should. Under such circumstances salvation would be relatively easy to define, subjective in application and psychologically oriented. But to define, subjective in application and psychologically oriented. But to follow this path means that we must abandon the idea of sin as a necessary condition of human life, which realistic theology and modern experience will not allow. Bennett says he doubts "if theologians will ever discover a formula which will solve this problem."[36]

Paul Schilling offers a solution in his article "How Does Jesus Save?"[37] Accepting the idea (Tennant's) that sin "is disobedience to God through the choice of lower values when higher ones are recognized and possible," he rules out the belief that sin is an inherent part of human nature. An important distinction is made between atonement as faith and theory. Faith in the atoning power of Christ is traced through the New Testament to show how the early Christians found victory over sin through their faith in Christ. All previous theories of the atonement are seen to contain truth; and rather than speculate on a new theory, Schilling catalogues the main truths from each historic view as an acceptable statement of the salvation process. His summary is as follows:

> God acts in Christ to reveal to men:
> 1. The pattern of a perfect life.
> 2. His victorious power over evil.
> 3. The wickedness of sin in contrast to the holiness of God.
> 4. His suffering, forgiving love.
>
> As they respond to God's redemptive activity, men experience:
> 1. Conscientious endeavor to follow Christ.
> 2. Victory over evil through trust in divine power.
> 3. Conviction of sin, repentance, and obedience.
> 4. Self-giving love and devotion to God.[38]

As long as sin is viewed as those acts for which a person can be held accountable (Tennant), it will be hard to avoid a moral or personal concept of atonement such as the one just outlined by Schilling. This view, first formulated by Abelard and then given wide distribution through Schleiermacher and the modern liberal movement, assumes that the barrier to redemption lies in humanity and that the self-sacrifice of teaching of Jesus provide humanity with the ideal pattern of life and the goals toward which they should aspire.

But, if we go back to the concept that sin is a necessary part of human nature, we are reminded of the two great formulations of Greek and Latin thought. The Greek formulation (Irenaeus, Origen, Athanasius) held to a ransom theory by which God in Christ paid the devil for humanity's release from sin. The Latin formulation which was carried over into the Reformation theology was an emphasis on satisfaction and substitution; it developed the belief that Christ as God-man bore the punishment demanded of sinful humanity by a just God, thus making it possible for the love of God to forgive.

Against these two views Roberts reacts unfavorably on the point that they are static.[39] That is to say, he believes a static view of salvation is psychologically and theologically wrong; for it keeps people ashamed of themselves, imposes an obligatory pattern without regard for the needs of the individual, causes a person simply to say the right words of repentance, and reduces humanity's interest in overcoming social sin. Yet Roberts sees the full dimension of sin as a malignant condition of the will as well as a personal and social evil. The solution is, to his mind, a dynamic view of salvation.

Taking as his cue the ability of a religious ideal to resolve conflict, Roberts says,

> . . . this conception implies that its saving purpose is to give men a faith and a mode of life which will make them no longer ashamed of themselves. It cures guilt, not by putting forward ideas which assure men willy-nilly that they are 'all right,' but by releasing a power which removed the causes of guilt.[40]

After rejecting a concept of salvation based on crisis theology (in which the conditions are fulfilled exclusively by God) and a concept of salvation based on humanism (in which the conditions are fulfilled exclusively by humans), Roberts words his concept thus:

> . . . salvation as that condition of wholeness which comes about when human life is based in openness (i.e., with 'self-knowledge') upon the creative and redemptive power of God. This condition is reached by means of man's freedom, and constitutes an enhancement of that freedom. Its initiation, once or repeatedly, may involve 'taking him

freedom. Its initiation, once or repeatedly, may involve 'taking him captive'; but the 'captivation' is releasing and the released person affirms it and desires to sustain it.[41]

When we ask how we achieve dynamic salvation, we find that we are not to assert our own interest but are rather to devote "ourselves in fellowship to a way of life which reaches personal fulfillment along with, and partly through, the fulfillment of others." Christ's relation to this process is in these words:

> . . . Christ (is) the supreme disclosure of what coincidence between human beatitude and divine love means. Christ is Savior as He opens, for each man, the way whereby that individual can move toward such coincidence. This involves moving forward into a deepened recognition of failure, impotence and need at many points. But the divine forgiveness which He discloses always has been and always will be accessible to men. We experience divine forgiveness as that 'making right' of our lives which occurs when we turn away from fighting ourselves, and others, and the truth itself, and turn trustfully toward the divine power which surrounds us and can work through us. This experience of reconciliation, despite past failures and unsolved problems in the present, makes men actually more lovable, more discerning, more capable of devoting themselves to goods which enrich all humanity.[42]

The goal of Roberts' salvation is apparent--it is the abundant life in the good society. It is curious that Christ as a person gets such scant attention in the discussion of dynamic salvation. It appears that Christ was the great object lesson of dynamic salvation; Roberts shows what actualized reconciliation between God and humanity is. This theory fits nicely into the findings of psychotherapy concerning humans; how well it fits into the biblical revelation depends on one's interpretation of Scripture.

The Biblical View of Faith

Edward Waldo Emerson in his biography of Henry David Thoreau tells a story about the naturalist as he was approaching death. His Calvinistic aunt asked: "Henry, have you made your peace with God?"

Thoreau was evidently not too concerned about the matter for he replied: "I didn't know we had ever quarreled, Aunt!"[43] The New Testament assumes there has been a quarrel and is reasonably clear on the idea of salvation. Jesus summarized the whole matter by saying that persons should first love God with all the attributes of their being and that their second love should be toward their neighbor.

Jesus did not get very serious about the sins of externalism which seemed to bother the Pharisees, nor did he observe strictly the legalistic code of holiness. Jesus showed that sin was the attitude that kept one from God. The objects of anxiety such as food and clothing which caused so much frustration and neurotic behavior, were necessary things; but it was the basic anxiety which needed to be cured. That section of the Sermon on the Mount has as its theme "But seek first his kingdom and his righteousness, and all these things shall be yours as well" (Matt. 6:33).

Although we do not ordinarily think of the gospels as theological material, we must understand that they were written for an evangelistic and not biographical purpose.[44] They were not written when the Christian message was new and when simple-minded people were hastily recording the story of Jesus. Rather, they appeared when the faith had taken hold and the church had been established. In fact, Scott believes the gospels were the textbooks of instruction for converts.[45] They were written to explain the Christian Faith. The Gospel of John states as its purpose, ". . . but these are written that you may believe that Jesus is the Christ, the Son of God, and that believing you may have life in his name" (John 20:31). In a real sense that is true of the synoptics too. There is no historical life of Jesus in the New Testament; rather there is the account of a man whom the writers believed to be crucified, buried, and resurrected and in whom God fulfilled the Old Testament expectation of a Savior.

Paul, who systematized most of the theology in the New Testament, certainly had no other purpose than to kindle faith in Christ to the end that a person might be saved. The Christ shown in the New Testament is a cosmic one available for the world, a demonstration of God's love for humankind. Grant gives a general summary of the New Testament statement of salvation in these words:

> At the inmost core of the Christian religion, and an indispensable condition of its true and full expression, lies a type of experience

which can only be described as mystical. These things cannot be stated in words; they cannot be completely described, let alone rationally explained and accounted for. Why all this took place; how it took place; how and why salvation, both as act and as state, depends upon Christ, and especially upon his death--to these questions the early church has no complete answer. The best explanation it can offer is analogy. The analogy which most readily suggested itself--to almost anyone in the ancient world, but especially to a Jew, whose religion was enshrined in the Old Testament--was naturally that of sacrifice.
. . . For the blood was the life (Lev. 17:14), and the presentation of a life was the highest, noblest, completest conceivable offering one could make to God. . . . Thus it was the most natural step in the world--in the world of the first century--for the answer to the question, 'Why did Jesus die?' or 'Why did God's Messiah have to die?' to take the form, 'He died for sins--for our sins--in accordance with the scriptures' (cf. I Cor. 15:3).[46]
. . . God treats the penitent sinner as if he were already righteous--even as a father treats a penitent child as if he were already obedient and responsive. God can do this because he sees more possibilities in the situation than human eye can discern. . . . And the miraculous and unpredictable fact turns out to be that the penitent sinner responds to this treatment--'responds,' we say, as we say that a difficult case 'responds' to proper medical treatment; but the sinner is still saved by 'grace,' not by his own effort. In fact, the response is far profounder, far more radical, far more complete than anything the ancient formula of law-obedience-reward could show.[47]

Rudolf Bultmann in the first volume of his *Theology of the New Testament* gives a detailed critical study of the salvation occurrence; in it he shows that Paul did not think of Christ's death as merely a sacrifice to cancel the guilt of sin but that it also was the means of releasing humanity from the powers of this age: law, sin, death.[48] This was the gospel of the early church, this was the affirmation thrown out in the Acts of the Apostles as the creedal statement of Christianity, "Believe in the Lord Jesus, and you will be saved" (Acts 16:31). Thus it was faith in Christ that brought salvation. "Because if you confess with your lips that Jesus is Lord and believe in your heart that God raised him from the dead, you will be saved" (Rom. 10:9). Often theologians have formed theories of the atonement and have insisted that people place their faith in a creedal statement. Again, churches have formulated a belief which insists there can be no salvation outside their jurisdiction. The New Testament says *the* requirement for salvation is faith in Christ. Perhaps we should rest our case there. There is a difference between faith and theory. The New Testament was written that we might have faith in Christ. Can Christian Education have a more desirable goal?

Notes

1 John C. Bennett, "After Liberalism--What?" *The Christian Century*, 50 (1933): 1403.
2 Mary Frances Thelen, *Man as Sinner* (New York: King's Crown Press, 1946) 13.
3 Thelen 17.
4 Harrison S. Elliott, *Can Religious Education be Christian?* (New York: Macmillan, 1940) 1-62.
5 Harrison 159-160.
6 Harrison 161.
7 Harrison 176.
8 Harrison 196-197.
9 Harrison 176-177.
10 Thelen 32.
11 Walter M. Horton, "Systematic Theology," *Protestant Thought in the Twentieth Century*, ed. Arnold S. Nash (New York: Macmillan, 1951) 114.
12 John C. Bennett, "The Christian Conception of Man," *Liberal Theology: An Appraisal*, ed. David Roberts and M. P. Van Dusen (New York: Scribner's, 1942) 198.
13 Reinhold Niebuhr, *The Nature and Destiny of Man* (New York: Scribner's, 1941) 150.
14 Niebuhr 182-186.
15 Niebuhr 178-179.
16 Thelen 167-168.
17 Willard L. Sperry, "On the Doctrine of Man" *Pastoral Psychology*, 2.15 (1951): 55.
18 Sperry 54.
19 Louis J. Sherrill, *Guilt and Redemption* (Richmond: John Knox Press, 1945).
20 Mary Alice Jones, *The Faith of Our Children* (New York: Abingdon, 1943).
21 Karen Horney, *Neurosis and Human Growth* (New York: W. W. Norton, 1950) 13-16.
22 Rollo May, *The Meaning of Anxiety* (New York: Ronald Press, 1950).
23 David E. Roberts, *Psychotherapy and a Christian View of Man* (New York: Scribner's, 1950).
24 Randolph C. Miller, *The Clue to Christian Education* (New York: Scribner's, 1950) 55-70.
25 May 191.

26 Paul Tillich, *Systematic Theology*, Vol. I, (Chicago: UP, 1951) 189-192.
27 Horney 38-39.
28 Quoted by May 234.
29 May 197.
30 Carl R. Rogers, *Client-Centered Therapy* (Boston: Houghton Mifflin Company, 1951) 135.
31 Rogers 139.
32 W. Allison Davis and Robert J. Havighurst, *Father of the Man* (Boston: Houghton Mifflin Company, 1947) 12.
33 Davis and Havighurst 24.
34 Wilhelm Pauck, "Issues Raised by the History of the Doctrine of Redemption," *The Journal of Religious Thought* 3 (1946): 16.
35 Daniel Day Williams, *God's Grace and Man's Hope* (New York: Harper and Brothers, 1949): 35.
36 John C. Bennett, "The Meaning of Redemption in Personal and Social Life Today," *The Journal of Religious Thought* 3 (1946): 35.
37 S. Paul Schilling, "How Does Jesus Save?" *Religion in Life* 28 (1949): 163-174.
38 Schilling 174.
39 Roberts, *Psychotherapy and a Christian View of Man*, 124.
40 Roberts 129.
41 Roberts 132.
42 Roberts 135. Cf. Otto A. Piper, *The Christian Interpretation of Sin* (New York: Scribner's, 1951) 194.
43 Bernhard W. Anderson, *Rediscovering the Bible* (New York: Association Press, 1951) 180.
44 Ernest F. Scott, *The Purpose of the Gospels* (New York: Scribner's, 1949) 74-100.
45 Scott 77.
46 Frederick C. Grant, *An Introduction to New Testament Thought* (New York: Abingdon-Cokesbury, 1950) 251-252.
47 Grant 253. Cf. Paul Ramsey, "God's Grace and Man's Guilt," *Journal of Religion* 31 (1951): 21-37.
48 Rudolf Bultmann, *Theology of the New Testament* Vol. 1 (New York: Scribner's, 1951) 297-298.

4

The Role of Theology and Education in the Christian Nurture of Children

Living in a university community has shown me how easily an academic discipline can become isolated or even lost in the never-ending struggle to keep up with our increasing knowledge. Home economics, for example, struggled to secure itself in the college curriculum and did so by including vigorous courses in food chemistry and other "respectable" fields. But as a course of study it lost sight of its objective. Women who were mainly interested in learning how to establish homes resisted degree programs in home economics with the stiff technical courses in chemistry. A national association concerned with home economics instruction appointed a special committee to investigate the decline in enrollment which in the decade of the 40's was nationwide. Now the trend is toward "homemaking"; the curriculum has been changed in many colleges to prepare a woman for marriage, motherhood, and management of a family, while the chemical analysis of food is left for the few who desire to become technical experts in dietetics.

Old Testament critical scholarship is another illustration. Introduced in the United States during the first half of the 19th century, it was centered in several theological seminaries. The field of study expanded to include archaeology, oriental languages and the antiquity of humanity. Soon the large universities set up departments in oriental languages and literature; and by the turn of the twentieth century most of the work was being done by and through the large universities. Thus, the field of study became concerned with historical growth, comparative religions

---

Lecture given to the Children's Work Session, Division of Christian Education, National Council of Churches, Columbus, Ohio, February 10-12, 1952.

and language science, while the needs of the church were largely unattended. Wright in his survey of the problem says that the field of Old Testament studies so declined in importance that the "great generation of biblical scholarship before the first War was actually unable to reproduce itself."[1]

Religious education has in a measure followed this same path in tending to become separate from the church. Of course, religious education is not really new, for the Old Testament gives a high place to education and in the New Testament we find that teaching ranked with preaching as a means of spreading the gospel, and it has never, in fact, left the church. Our concern here is with the tendency of religious education in recent times to develop into a separate "field" of study and activity. The Sunday School movement had its great expansion in America from 1824-1872 when it functioned as the teaching arm of the church. It was during this period that denominations formed "boards" or "committees" on education, thus creating the specialty of education within the church. By the end of the past century this specialty had created the Uniform Lessons, given birth to a powerful youth movement, designed graded materials for children, and started leadership education.

At the turn of the century the specialty had become a profession and a field of study. At the same time the secular educator was becoming conscious of the uniqueness of his/her position with the development of educational psychology by Edward L. Thorndyke, the child-study movement by G. Stanley Hall and the concept of social education by John Dewey. The two movements were almost literally born together and they spurred each other to greater accomplishments. The professional religious educational forces sensed the uniqueness of their position and sought to consolidate their gains and make greater plans for the future by forming the Religious Education Association in 1903. Thus a "field" of knowledge was recognized as separate from the sponsorship of the church, and in the next few decades the movement looked to the educators in the large universities for inspiration, direction and training. Many good things came from this alliance--such as the quick adoption of better teaching methods, a clearer understanding of human personality and an insistence that Christianity be meaningful to life and applicable to social problems. However, religious education was inspired largely by the tenets of the educational philosophy in vogue during those years, even though the movement functioned largely with church sponsorship. It was a case of the movement being *in* but not entirely *of* the church.

During the past ten to fifteen years the religious education movement has begun to appreciate its position in the church and to become more a part of the church. This is due partly to the revival of theological interest generally, particularly biblical theology, and partly because the understanding of humans and their problems developed by realistic theology has brought an awareness of sin. This search for surer foundations first became apparent in the work of the International Council of Religious Education (I.C.R.E.) through a committee seeking a common statement of principles. Published in 1940 under the title *Christian Education Today*, this booklet was the product of three years work, and it turned the corner from religious education to Christian education. The issues were sharply drawn by Harrison Elliott's book *Can Religious Education* be Christian?, published in 1940, and Shelton Smith's book *Faith and Nurture*, issued in 1941. *The International Journal of Religious Education* helped publish the conflicting views through several articles published soon after these two books were printed. Mary Alice Jones published *The Faith of Our Children* in 1943 to show the need for proper theological orientation in children's work. *The Rise of Christian Education* by Lewis Sherrill (1944) is an effort to show the historical basis for education as a function of the church.

During the early part of the decade of the 40's the *International Journal of Religious Education* published a number of articles on evangelism, proper methods of Bible study, "Person of Christ," and "Working with the Holy Spirit." However, the main impetus to a more theological statement for Christian education was the study of the whole program of education conducted by the I.C.R.E. in 1944-46. During this two-year period representatives from all the participating denominations helped formulate a statement entitled "Foundations of Christian Education," which is an excellent summary of theological belief.[2] Perhaps this statement is the historic mark by which we can say that Christian education was again brought wholeheartedly into the main stream of Christian thought.

If Christians had no knowledge of the relation of theology to education except that which they could obtain by reading the *International Journal* from 1941-51, they would realize the educational forces of the church had a real concern for the important theological beliefs. In addition to the articles cited above, one would find in that ten-year period articles on salvation, prayer, death, evangelism and a series by Roy L. Smith on a variety of topics such as "The Meaning of the Reformation," "Roman Catholic Beliefs," etc.

Randolph C. Miller's new book (1950) *The Clue to Christian Education* continues the quest for a working relation between theology and education. Sherrill's inaugural address as professor at Union Theological Seminary in New York in 1950 was on "Theological Foundations of Christian Education"; in it he promises that, as Christian education returns to the church, it will gain strength and broaden its service.

Granted, you might say, there *is* a renewed interest in theology and a general return to the church for guidance. But what problems does this pose and especially what does it mean to one who works with children? First, let us define terms and then seek a relationship between theology and education, since we will be facing this matter more urgently in the years that lie ahead.

Authority and Function of Theology

Theology is the knowledge of God. Its authority is the Bible (revelation) and reason. Its function is to systematize the knowledge of God, to defend the faith, to guide the church and to seek God's will for our day. Theology can do three things for education.

A. Theology by reason of its authority and function can help us establish the general purpose of Christian education. When religious education was under the influence of secular education, the goal was once formulated by George A. Coe as "Growth of the youth toward and into mature and efficient devotion to the democracy of God, and happy self-realization therein."[3] Today we see a move toward a general purpose in terms of the church, such as "helping people to know Jesus Christ as Lord and Savior." Three reasons appear for this current state of affairs.

First, the development of biblical theology which has focused our attention on the fact that our whole Christian tradition is built on the drama of God's redemption offered in Christ. The Bible has no other doctrine; and for us to substitute a different goal is to take ourselves out of the Christian tradition.

Second, the optimistic views of humanity have collapsed, showing the sin of humanity, especially the brutality of humanity when vengeance is expressed through society or nation. Furthermore, we see that sin operates at every level of human existence from the intellectual efforts of the trained scientist through the simple day-by-day relations of ordinary people.

Third, the precarious basis on which we live today convinces us that we have little security in the world. Although we devote resources to a development of treaties and political arrangements that tend to make us secure, we realize we are up against a world where the forces of evil are not chained but are only held temporarily in check by force.

B. Theology stands ready to help the educator evaluate the goals of Christian education. Perhaps the first effort to codify a set of goals for religious education was done by Paul Vieth in 1930.[4] Almost every textbook in the field has included Vieth's formulation of goals, and many denominations have worked them over to bring them in line with their own beliefs. Curriculum writers in many denominations have used this set of goals as they prepared a "balance" of materials for various lesson cycles, adapting the goals as necessary for the age group involved.

My question does not concern the goals themselves. It would be hard, if not impossible, to conceive of a set more comprehensive than the set we have all used the past twenty years. My question concerns the desirability of ranking the goals in order of importance. Are some goals more important than others? Our carefully prepared statement of goals is like a boy dressed for church school on Easter morning. His attire is complete, harmonious and fresh. But when you turn that boy loose Easter Sunday afternoon, he will strip himself down for the real business of a boy's life. Hat, coat and tie come off. The white shirt is replaced with a cotton pull-over, and the blue jeans he slips on may be reinforced at the knee. Theology stands ready to help us review our goals and arrange them in order of importance, thus setting our emphases. In a real sense, the "Study of Christian Education" did this for us in the middle of the past decade; and Vieth's book *The Church and Christian Education*, which summarizes the findings of that group, has shown by its reception (seven printings from 1947-51!) how eager the educator is for this type of evaluation. Such consideration of theological and educational foundations should be reviewed every five or ten years to keep our forces together.

C. Theology is constantly seeking the will of God for our time and culture which results in studies in Christian ethics. Since we educators must do our work in a world of conflicting values, among people whose attitudes vary according to social class and individual background, we need the guidance of Christian ethics. Through our study of psychology we develop a "clinical" approach to people, applying the Christian truth to individual cases; in this process we tend to become relative in many of our ethical judgments. A closer walk with theology will help us understand the will of God in our shifting social scene.

Authority and Function of Education

Education is an application of all knowledge of humanity to the problem of guiding growing individuals into an intelligent and satisfactory participation in society. The authority of education is knowledge of humanity which it derives from sociology, psychology, anthropology and medical science. Education, in adapting the knowledge of humanity to its own goal, develops areas such as "methods of teaching," "theories of learning," "counseling," "reconstruction of personality," "psychometrics," the charting of physical, mental and emotional growth, and principles of curriculum planning. All of these functions have a bearing on Christian education. The latest and most effective methods of teaching are needed in thousands of schools sponsored by the church. Theories of learning are needed for the adequate preparation of curriculum materials. Those who work with children in the church are conscious of their indebtedness to modern psychology for their understanding of the child and for providing an empirical basis on which to plan their work.

Theology, Education and Christian Education

Having briefly described the field of theology and education, each of which has an authority, function and noble history, what then can we say as to the relation between them as they form our field of Christian education? What is the relation of theology to education in the Christian nurture of children? During the past ten years that question has been uppermost in our minds and a variety of answers have been given. All signs indicate that this question will continue to occupy a prominent position in our thinking for the next decade, for we are obviously in a period when the educational work of the church is seeking to become more consciously a servant of the church.

Let us look at three answers that have been proposed.

First, some people say that theology must be depended on to set the framework in which we operate and that the main function of Christian education is to provide the methods by which we help people arrive at these beliefs. There is, of course, an element of truth in this answer; but actually it reduces Christian education to a position as servant of theology, rather than of humanity. Unfortunately this answer has been proposed by some who are very conscious of the cultural and religious crisis through which we are passing, yet who at the same time are not so aware of the positive contribution that education has made. But if we want to see how this answer will work out in practice, we will not have to theorize. We can observe certain dispensationalist groups which in recent years have developed a church program. Rejecting the process of education, they set their beliefs before their people as the test of Christian faith and require that all programs for children and youth be formed to introduce the dogma. Invariably the program for children becomes a matter of object lessons or other devices to illustrate adult theology simply.

Secondly, others who have grown up in the religious education movement are convinced that education has so proven its ability to understand human nature and provide methods of coping with life's problems that we should follow the lead of education. Contrariwise, they see the church as a class institution captive to American culture and relatively powerless to attack the major ills of our day. Feeling that the progress of humankind has been gigantic during this scientific age, some leaders think that in the long view of history the most dependable guide is the empirical knowledge of human beings; and they are equally confident that leaders can learn to apply their skill for the benefit of all. However, this position is increasingly difficult to maintain and probably will not be productive in the next few decades, for the devotees of this answer must dedicate a good portion of their efforts to a defense of their position.

Third, friends of Christian education seeking to guide the movement as it reconsiders it basic foundations have advocated a mixture of theology and education. The usual procedure is to identify certain fundamental Christian beliefs and then apply developmental psychology, with a view to establishing how much of a particular doctrine can be inculcated at a certain age level. If an educator works out the combination, the theologian often feels that the proper mixture was not obtained; and if the theologian produces a mixture, the educator often charges that he does not understand children. But the "mixture" idea will appeal to many, for it seems to solve the problem without disturbing either field too much.

A fourth answer seems more desirable. This would be a *union* of theology and education. From that union would issue Christian education which would be a part of both but separate from each. In fact, the analogy with family is helpful. Husband and wife are individual people and will remain so; yet something new is created between them in terms of relationship. The offspring is a part of each parent but there is no rigid distinction of the contribution each will make in the rearing of the child.

"Mother Education" will not conceive of her task as the careful bringing up of "Baby Christian Education" in order that the child might understand "Father Theology!" No, they both work at the job. Father Theology might have to warm a bottle on occasion; and when he is absent, Mother Education might have to mow the lawn. The two parents are united and each functions according to the needs of the child and the household at any given time.

The old issue of indoctrination versus creative education is never solved as long as each is argued against the background of theology or education. The issue might fade in significance if we could see both in relation to specific human problems. In some situations we must make a clear statement of fact that borders on indoctrination, even for a four- or five-year-old. At other times we might prepare a child mentally and emotionally for a great theological truth, which itself may not be introduced until later. But in every case we judge on the basis of a union of theology and education in the light of the situation that faces us.

A few years ago I was Director of Youth Work for the Presbyterian Church, U.S., and one of my duties was to be chairman of a curriculum committee planning a new course of study for high school youth. I remember how carefully we selected the committee which was to work on the task for a two-year period. We included directors of religious education, pastors, specialists in youth work, a professional psychologist and a highly-trained supervisor of high school teachers; but it never occurred to us to put a trained theologian on the committee. If I were doing that over again, I would find a competent theologian who was successful in his own family living and ask him to help create a bond of union between his field and ours.

Incidentally, a good illustration of what I am talking about is Mary Alice Jones' book *The Faith of Our Children*. In that book she talks like an educator and a theologian all at the same time with a compromise of neither. Let us look at a few illustrations. In each case we will see that there is a "logic" arising out of the situation that cues off the proper relation between theology and education.

A. Death. Children come in contact with death at an early age. They know what it means to kill a bug or to see a flower die. Often a pet is killed and they face the grief of a world without the animal friend. They sometimes mistake a parent's absence as death or a relative's death as absence. We cannot avoid death. We cannot avoid an honest direct affirmation about the meaning of death even to a four-year-old child. This is indoctrination. We do not discuss the fact; we do not let him discover its significance. We tell children kindly and affectionately, but we tell them; and they accept because they love us and because we stand with power and prestige in their eyes. In this case, theology supplies the answer, psychology tells us how to explain it to a small child. So, we often say a person's body is like a house; if it is a man, when he dies he leaves his body and goes to live with God just as a person leaves his house to live elsewhere. Actually, according to the New Testament, the death of the spirit is more important than the death of the body; but this is an adult concept. We must not trace cause of death to God or link it with sin, for this, too, is an adult problem. We must build trust in God and help a child to realize that being with God is a very desirable state.

B. Salvation. Here is a different problem. We do not seek to mix theology and education by gradually introducing the doctrine of salvation. Rather, we see all of our work from the first day of a child's life as preparation for the day of responsible commitment to Christ and his church. We will not dwell on sin in our work with children, but we will not avoid it. We will help children recognize sin when it emerges and trace it to the freedom God has given us. We will, under those circumstances, always emphasize forgiveness, a concept the child readily understands.

Children are not too keen on abstract concepts, but they can see the difference Christ makes in the lives of those with whom they associate. They can learn the story of Christ, the stories of God's love for humanity and the concept of sharing what they have. Songs, prayers, group activity all breed confidence in life and love for Christ's church. As children grow older, they will see more clearly the gap between what they are and what they ought to be; they will know temptation; they will see the need for a way to escape the power of sin and thus be prepared to make their confession of faith in Christ and commitment to the church. Shall we teach the "plan of salvation?" Yes, in the sense that the child's teachers and parents have it in mind as the goal toward which they work but not in the sense of a formula that must be memorized. Christian education is seeking to help a person stand in a redeemed relation with God, of which the theological statement is an adult formulation.

What do we do when pressure is put on us to engage in efforts to get children to make a commitment before they are ready? The educator in us arises and asserts its authority. We declare such procedure would violate the person, develop a false idea of salvation and be almost meaningless to the individual. In this situation education takes precedence over theological statement but not over theological truth, for the Christian educator is seeking to develop the relation with God so that the person will affirm the statement as truth for his/her life.

C. Christ. All church-sponsored education would agree that Jesus looms large as a topic of school lessons. Some would tell his life story with so many references to other great men that the child will begin to understand Jesus as a kind of Abraham Lincoln. Others would so develop the mystery and miraculous elements that Jesus would be God. Most of us would show how Jesus helped others, how he prayed, how he did his Father's will and how he met everyday situations with faith and courage. As children grow older, they will understand more of the ethical teaching of Jesus, face the fact of miracles and begin to grasp the cosmic significance of Jesus as the Christ. After all, if we never get beyond Jesus to the reason for his life, the child will never know why we spend so much time talking about him and praying in his name. Children can learn the facts of incarnation before they are ready to declare their commitment to Christ.

Evangelism

Earlier we said that one of the first functions of theology was to help set the general purpose of Christian education. That purpose was suggested in evangelistic terms. The central thing is not education nor theology but a relationship with God through Christ. To show how theology and education combine in a statement of this type, let us use the definition of evangelism that is found in the book *Towards the Conversion of England*: "To evangelize is (1) so to present Christ Jesus in the power of the Holy Spirit, that (2) men shall come to put their trust in God through Him, to (3) accept Him as their Savior, and (4) serve Him as their King in the fellowship of His Church."[5] Note we have a theological concept, (1) the "given" of the gospel. Then in (2) we have the relation of faith which is the goal of Christian education. Acceptance of Christ (3) is an act of faith, theologically explained and (4) the person is nurtured and given opportunities for service in the society of believers, an educational process. Thus we set up not the superiority of education, nor the claim of theology over education but a union of the two as each contributes its part to the end that people might believe. This is the spirit and intention of the New Testament and it will be ours if we choose to function together with theology as servants of Christ's church.

Notes

1 G. Ernest Wright, "The Study of the Old Testament" *Protestant Thought in the Twentieth Century*, ed. Arnold S. Nash (New York: Macmillan, 1951) 23.

2 Paul H. Vieth, ed. *The Church and Christian Education* (St. Louis: Bethany, 19947) 52-87.

3 George A. Coe, *A Social Theory of Religious Education* (New York: Scribner's, 1917) 55.

4 Paul H. Vieth, *Objectives in Religious Education* (New York: Harpers, 1930).

5 Commission on Evangelism, *Toward the Conversion of England* (Westminster, S.W. 1: The Press and Publication Board of the Church Assembly, 1945) 1.

5

The Contemporary Mind

The Gospel comes to us from ancient cultures. One of the major tasks of the biblical scholar is to disentangle the timeless from the time-bound, the eternal word of God from the temporal housing of Hebrew, Greek, and Roman cultures in which it has lived. Although this is a formidable task and never done with finality, it is matched in importance with the necessity of understanding the contemporary mind to which the good news of God in Christ is directed. In some ways the contemporary mind is more difficult to assay than the biblical message, for we are inescapably bound to our culture, especially to culturally-influenced modes of thinking. Furthermore, we are warned in the Bible that God's message to humanity is so contrary to normal human expectation that it is more readily understood by a trusting child than by a worldly-wise adult; that it will be a stumbling-block to sign-seeking Jews and foolishness to wisdom-seeking Greeks (1 Cor. 1:23). Thus all of us who work in the practical field must understand not only the Gospel but also the generation to which we would communicate the good news.

Culture

Perhaps the most important factor in shaping the contemporary mind is culture. This abstract but ever-present reality provides a mold into which a person is born. The extent to which a person fits the detail of the design in the cultural mold will vary considerably. Some people struggle consciously against conformity, but even those who struggle must do so in a social context over which they have little control.

Prepared for a seminar on "The Contemporary Mind" as a part of the inauguration of five professors (including C. Ellis Nelson) at Union Theological Seminary, New York City, October 23, 1957.

There are many ways we can examine culture. The most fruitful for our purpose is to think in terms of values. Culture is hung together by a value-system which is propagated to the children by family, institutions and customs. In a sense cultural values are religious, for they are explanations of existence and, as such, represent the "good" with which persons associate their well-being. Culture, therefore, is both a conditioner and an enemy of faith.

In a highly industrialized, technical, western nation such as the United States, the culture is made up of many groups with varying value-structures. However, the heterogeneous groups are held together by a common core of values to which almost all people give assent. Two over-arching social values are described by W. Lloyd Warner: (1) the American dream, rags-to-riches, log-cabin-to-president idealism and (2) the American social solidarity based on sacrifice of the individual for the nation's security.[1] Paul H. Furfey, a Catholic sociologist, thinks the main values in American life are summarized in the "success-ideal," i.e., the business community with its prestige and its ability to measure tangible evidence of accomplishment has so permeated our common life that success has become the major value of our day.[2]

Most writers about American culture seem to agree that vast changes have taken place in the past half-century from a moralistic-individualistic value structure to relative morality and group-approved conduct. This judgment is given support by three studies of the current youth generation which indicate that they are comfortable in their conformity to current ethical and moral conduct. Such a shift in values makes our problems more complex because it means that within the church we have an older age group which usually has a controlling voice in policy-making decisions and which operates on one morality and a younger age group developing a new morality on a different value-foundation.

The Christian educator must appraise the elements in society that help to inculcate belief and those that are contrary to faith in God. Among many specific American values, four seem to create our major difficulties in communicating the Gospel to our generation.

(1) Accumulation of wealth. Hardly any area of our life is inoculated against the value of money. Along with the high value given money there is a glossing-over of the ethics by which it is obtained. The rewards of our society go to those who have or can command money. In contrast we have in the Christian faith an emphasis on the proper use of money and the value of service and sharing. "Do good and share"

would be the substance of what most of our children get out of Sunday School; but all other influences, and some of them quite powerful, instruct the child to "Get money and what money will buy."

(2) Competition. This is one of the most accepted of American values, essential to our methods of business. It has been proven useful if not indispensable in what we call the "American way of life." Yet, the gospel professes to lift up the motives of "love," "goodness" and "cooperation." The culture says "move against people;" the Christian faith says, "move with people."

(3) Success in terms of accomplishment. This is certainly a desirable and sought-after status. In every field it is assumed that a person is success-minded and will do whatever is necessary to obtain this distinction. So powerful is this value that we have been in danger of "selling" the story of our Lord's life in terms of the log-cabin-to-president motif of Lincoln. More commonly we evaluate our success in church work by the size of the budget, the number of members obtained, the size of the crowd in the evangelistic meeting. There is a success in Christian terms, but it is to be found in obedience to our Lord; and most New Testament illustrations of obedience show that the heroes of faith were seldom supported by an enthusiastic rooting section.

(4) Pleasure. As a general goal this is assumed by all; and the church, too, is wrapped up in its demands. Within limits one would not decry pleasure in the name of faith except that today we tend to forget the tragic elements in life--the suffering and the needless misery. Pleasure for good times' sake is what most people want rather than the deep relaxation from work that is significant and creative.

These four specific American values all struggle to some degree with the values of the Christian faith. However, these and other cultural values are interpreted differently according to the class with which persons identify their interest.

Class

The last twenty years have seen the development of a whole series of studies of the class system in America. In general these studies show that the lower class in America is relatively stable. These people are stable because they know they are lower class; they cannot go up because they do not have the skills or education to rise in the social order. Child training, education, sex, work, religion and recreation are all viewed, managed and utilized differently by the lower class. Generally, the lower class does not defer gratification of bodily desires because it has never learned that deferment properly handled can help bring a rise in class status. Socially and economically, these people are dependent on other people's planning, for they have never learned in their social setting the rewards of planning.

Strange to say, the leisure class resembles the lower class in some important attitudes. The lower class does not strive because it cannot arrive; the leisure class does not strive because it does not need to arrive. Education in its advanced forms and on its professional levels is not too important to the leisure class, and is not unimportant to the lower class. Both groups are reasonably free from anxiety about money; the lower class, because it lives from day to day without much money, the leisure class because it never had to worry about money.

The middle class is the anxious class. The whole range from lower class to secure leisure class is beset with anxiety. The anxiety is caused by fear of slipping lower in the social scale or of not being able to advance in the social order. "I want my child to have what I didn't have" is the cry of the typical middle-class parent. Education is the means of achievement, so great stress is put on educational goals.

A look at two families by way of contrast will show the way anxiety is a necessary part of the middle-class social structure. W. Allison Davis and Robert J. Havighurst describe the Washington family, a family as low in the social scale as one can go and still be respectable. The parents are "good" but both work. There are ten children. The family lives upstairs in an old house which contains a store on the lower floor. Mary keeps a record of the number of men who have been murdered in their block. They talk freely about sex. Everything is shared. Children await their turn for food, for sweets or for gifts; for each child knows that all will get an equal part. Everything is owned in common and seldom do children have anything they can call their own. There are almost no toys. Meals are served at any time, and when there is no food they do not eat. They sleep three or four to a bed and they go to bed at any time and to a movie when they have the money. At two years of age the children cross the street alone, at four they are almost on their own, and the eight-year-old daughter has complete responsibility for four young children while the mother works.[3]

Contrast the Bretts. They live in a ten-room house of rough gray stone; the two children play in the yard. A full-time maid answers the door. The house is well kept, full of antique furniture. Each child has a room, goes to bed at nine o'clock, has toys in his room and receives a regular allowance. The children have cod liver oil and orange juice daily and all meals are served on schedule. These Brett children are being trained in a world where fast and early attainment is necessary. The parents by many processes instill deep anxieties in their children: that they will be failures, that they will not be loved, that they will not achieve the goals set for them by the parents. In the Washington family the children learn to gratify their desires immediately without much anxiety and thereby develop a style of life containing little ambition or sense of social responsibility.[4]

The contemporary mind influenced by lower-class values is exceedingly difficult to reach with the Gospel in a meaningful way. If we start with Protestantism as it is known today, we find ourselves with a religion so intricately intertwined with middle-class morality that it is rejected by the lower class. The failure of the middle-class Protestant mind to communicate the Christian faith to the lower class is not only historic but is widespread today. Perhaps we will not succeed until we are able to live with the lower-class mind, identify with its problems and style of life, and then create, by the spirit of God, new forms of faith. If we look at how the lower class has sometimes appropriated the Christian faith, we are struck with the excess emotionalism, the superstition, the ignorance and lack of leadership that characterize it, thus compounding our problems in sharing the Gospel.

One of our major problems with the contemporary middle-class mind is success. The cultural definition of success has been appropriated by the church so that today we prove our faith not by our ministry but by church attendance, membership and record budgets. These means of evaluation betray our orientation; Christianity has in many cases become a religion to placate class anxiety. This judgment is partly confirmed by the way in which a critical examination of society has quietly dropped out of the interest of many Protestants; and this in turn eliminates the note of sacrifice and obedience which historically has marked those who have sought the City of God.

Family and Conscience

Cultural and class values are instilled in the child by the family. From the day babies are born they are faced with the realities of life and an interpretation of what these realities mean. The result is the formation of conscience which has an enormous influence on the type of personality the child develops. Conscience then, as a regulatory mechanism, is one of the most important dimensions of the contemporary mind as far as religious conduct is concerned.

The conscience develops in prohibitions and not in a reasoned understanding of what is the best course of action. Children have no innate way of knowing the rightness or wrongness of their impulses or emotions; this "moral" content to behavior comes from without--from their parents. So the memory of what we were denied is often our earliest personal memory.

Children slowly begin to organize the different experiences they are having and to sense that there is an "order" back of all authority that must be obeyed. If one doesn't obey, one feels fearful; for one is most often punished for disobedience. Even if not punished, one feels fearful of expected punishment in some form. When we see small children doing something they know they should not do, we observe how anxious they are and how they reassure themselves. It is in this situation of punishment that generalized guilt develops as well as a sense of unworthiness; for children often think they are being rejected when they are punished and don't separate themselves from the act as their parents do. Thus we lay the foundation for a moralistic religion based on current cultural and class values as they are transmitted to the child by the parents. Many people never advance beyond their negative conscience and later transpose their inner inadequacy onto the Christian faith by making it a moral code of things they may not do and by making their religious life a struggle not to be "bad." It is for this reason that the Apostle Paul considered conscience an unreliable ethical guide and indicated that conscience must be purified and guided by the Spirit of Christ.

Thus we are reminded by the Apostle Paul that we are not the victims of our culture, we are children of God, capable, with God's guidance, of creating the kind of life God desires. We can look back over the long history of Christendom and see how cultural values have been influenced by the Gospel. We can read from Paul that in Christ "we were all baptized into one body--Jews or Greeks, slaves or free--and all were made to drink of one Spirit" (1 Cor. 12:13). We can help transform the contemporary mind into the mind of Christ. Through our ministry we can help people develop a positive conscience which causes them to serve in the kingdom of God out of a motivation of love, a love that is present because God first loved us.

Notes

1 W. Lloyd Warner, *American Life: Dream and Reality* (Chicago: University of Chicago Press, 1953) 3, 104-107.

2 Paul Hanly Furfey, *Three Theories of Society* (New York: Macmillan, 1937) 3-16.

3 W. Allison Davis and Robert J. Havighurst, *Father of the Man* (Boston: Houghton Mifflin, 1947) 11-20.

4 Davis and Havighurst 21-29.

6

Growth in Grace and Faith-Knowledge

Lecture 1
Communication Through Event

The Christian faith affirms that God has shown Godself to humankind. This does not mean that we claim to know all about God, but it does mean that we believe that God has been and continues to be active in human affairs. The way God elected to disclose Godself and God's will is of crucial importance because God's way of communication must be congenial to the faith God grants and fosters. If we can understand God's method of communication, we shall have a valuable paradigm for sharing the Christian faith.

We must be careful not to give the impression that there is a single, clearly defined, step-by-step process that can be certified as God's way of communication with humans. To do so would be to imply that God is the prisoner of a particular method. God is free; God can use any method to communicate with humans. However, the biblical record of God's revelation gives a discernible pattern; and this pattern itself gives us an indispensable understanding of the nature of God. Indeed, some of our major beliefs about God--for example, that God does not violate freedom of choice so that a person remains a responsible moral being--are derived from the biblical description of revelation.

The biblical description of God's communication with humans, therefore, becomes our clue to the nature of the Christian faith and the process by which that faith can be known and shared.

Lectures prepared for discussion in the introductory course in Christian Education, Union Theological Seminary, New York.

Biblical Mode of Communication

When we read the Bible to discern the pattern of God's revelation, we are struck at once with the uniqueness of the Christian faith. God did not set forth a series of ideas about Godself nor did God seek to prove God's existence. Rather, God elected to show Godself to people through events of life. The biblical account of God's revelation is a description of these events which we might term "holy events" in that they became the media through which God's will for God's people was made known. In the Old Testament it was the covenant with Abraham that formed the people of God. The standard description of God was that God was "the God of Abraham, Isaac and Jacob"--that is, the God who had a practical and clearly discernible relationship to the event that formed the Hebrew nation. The great historic event that molded the various tribes into a nation was the Exodus, in which the covenant made by God was kept and the promised land was delivered to the children of Israel. In the New Testament the event was the birth, life, teachings, death and resurrection of Jesus Christ; and the oldest Christian creed, the only one that is repeated by all Christians, affirms that Jesus Christ was "born of the Virgin Mary, suffered under Pontius Pilate." Thus we affirm the historicity of the event. Although the New Testament does not make a fetish of dates, Luke is profoundly right in his effort to date the life of our Lord with phrases such as these: "In the days of Herod, king of Judea, there was a priest named Zechariah. . . . " (Luke 1:5); "In those days a decree went out from Caesar Augustus that all the world should be enrolled. This was the first enrollment when Quirinius was governor of Galilee. . . ." (Luke 2:1). The Gospels follow the Hebraic tradition of insisting that events actually happened, in this case that Christ was a real person and that the resurrection was a real event. For they are saying through these events that God has broken through time and space to send God's son; and the historical accuracy of the date and description of the event are important.

Dates are profound in the Christian faith because they proclaim a major characteristic of God--that God works in the human situation. Perhaps it is for this reason that we instinctively try to protect the dates in the Bible and defend the accuracy of the record. In truth, we are fighting for the idea that God can, does and has communicated with humans. If we lose that affirmation, we lose our Christian God; if faith becomes disassociated from history, we no longer have spiritual authority for our lives.

Yet we do not defend the authority of holy events on the accuracy of dates or other empirical facts. In the Old Testament, especially the older sections, we do not find historical accuracy; these writings came out of a culture that did not value "factual" reporting as much as "meaningful" narrative. The Hebrews were above all intensely concerned with the meaning of history. But the vast array of archaeological data of recent years plus the scientific ability to date pottery and other artifacts of Palestine show a remarkable similarity between Old Testament history and dates obtained independently of the biblical record. But this is a detail; *accuracy of record* is not the same as *truth of narrative*.

Event

Perhaps we should at this point note some of the major characteristics of an event.

It is specific. An event is something that happens. The occurrence takes place in a rather definite time and place, enveloped in a cultural setting as specific as language and as elusive as mood.

It is unique. It happens once and it will not happen again in just that same way. Although one event may impinge on another or blend into another, an event is separate enough from the main stream of life to be reported, analyzed and remembered.

It is inclusive. It is the sum of a myriad of acts, thoughts, words, responses and, in the biblical record, God's will. And these elements are hung together and interrelated.

It is dynamic. An event involves people--an event cannot be individual. A person caught up in an event cannot be a spectator even if that person is a bystander; for the nature of the event involves our deepest sentiments, our values and our judgments, and these elements in our life participate in events even if we are not actors. Perhaps it would be better to say that an event is something which so involves us that we must act, speak, or respond in some way that commits our whole being.

The above statements are not suggested to be criteria by which to judge an event, least of all a biblical event, but rather characteristics that point up the features of an event and at the same time indicate some of our difficulties in understanding a human event.

Event and History

If revelation has come through event, we are immediately faced with the matter of our record of these events. These records do not claim to be history in an empirical sense, yet they are historical because they represent events that happen. For example, the momentous event of the Exodus, though holy and charged with meaning to the Hebrews, was hardly a revelation to Pharaoh; indeed, the biblical account acknowledges this by saying that God hardened Pharaoh's heart. The biblical event is both an occurrence and interpretation intermingled, with each factor conditioning the other. In biblical records some facts of events are selected and emphasized, others forgotten or explained in order to convey truth. Biblical history is verisimilitude--the use of facts to demonstrate truth.

The necessity of interpretation as a part of presentation of facts in historical studies applied to the New Testament is carefully delineated by John Knox in these words:

> Christianity grew out of an event, or better perhaps, a closely knit series of events; it was not the elaboration of an abstract idea or ideal. That event, or the center of that series of events was the person whom we know as Jesus Christ. All distinctively and authentically Christian ideas are inferences from 'the thing that has happened among us,' are attempts to explain and interpret it. But although there can be no question that in the last analysis fact is more important than explanation, actually they cannot be separated, for some measure of explanation and interpretation--adequate or inadequate, accurate or inaccurate--is part and parcel of any knowledge of objective reality it is given us to have. If there is such a thing as a 'bare fact,' certainly we cannot know one. If there is such a thing as a merely objective event, certainly we can have no knowledge of it as such. History and interpretation, distinguishable in idea, cannot in fact be separated.
>
> What is not so clear, but is equally true, is that there can be no historical understanding of the Bible which is not also devotional, or religious, or theological. For the books of the Bible are not primarily concerned with facts in some hypothetical 'bare' sense, but with meanings in the concrete sense of the term. Now such meanings cannot be apprehended with the same degree and kind of objectivity

as formal facts can be. One cannot understand such meanings from the outside; one must see them from within. This involves the likelihood, perhaps the necessity, of subjective mistakes; but that risk must be taken, although only with all possible caution. The historian who steadfastly keeps himself as a person out of his study of an epoch may avoid certain subjective errors, but he misses most of the epoch. Purely objective historiography would be neither truly objective nor history. Historiography has to be somewhat subjective in order to be as objective as it can be. This is true because the *objects* of historical study are events, which are in no small part *subjective* objects; for events do not simply happen, as in a vacuum: they happen in connection with persons--they happen not only among persons and to persons, but also in considerable measure within persons--and only persons as persons can even begin to understand what any historical event in its concreteness is. The true historian is artist and philosopher, not scientist only. A good piece of historical writing is a picture, not a map; a living body, not a diagram; a full-length portrait in color, not a list of dimensions or a thumbnail description.[1]

Event and Interpretation

The biblical record carries both a description of events through which God reveals Godself, and interpretations given those events by individuals. Both the event and interpretation of event were given significance by the community of faith--the covenant people in the Old Testament and the church in the New Testament--for interpretation of event would not have endured if it had not been given meaning by a community. Each experience of revelation described in the Bible arises out of specific situations. Putting these experiences into words, fitting them into the affairs of the moment makes them epical, discrete, personal, illuminating but not necessarily consistent or related to logical order. So, one of the major characteristics of the Bible is the lack of system in the revelational events reported, the highly specific and sometimes extremely personal context of the revelation, and the lack of interest on the part of most biblical writers in developing a systematic theology.

But matters are further complicated by the way the community of faith interprets the original event. As the community lives, new problems emerge, new friends and enemies press from without, and the community reinterprets or reapplies the original event and its meaning to new conditions. For the sake of clarity, let us label this part of biblical interpretation "systematic theology" for it has two important differences from interpretation found within the biblical record. First, the writers of systematic theology are separated from the holy events through which revelation came, so that they are able to recapture but a part, although perhaps the essential part, of the original meaning of the event. Secondly, systematic theology must contend with new conditions, modes of thought, or socio-economic structures of power which are not involved in events reported in the Bible. For this reason most systematic theology also is a defense of the Christian faith, seeking to re-establish its heredity in a quite different environment. One has only to read the Nicene Creed (381 A.D.) and compare it to the letters of Paul to see how the interest of the church had changed and how the problem of the nature of Christ absorbed the energy of the church in the fourth century.

This description of the function of systematic theology is not a criticism. Rather it is a recognition that theology is different from revelation. Theology is a reflection on revelation; it is a systematic, logical, seasoned explanation and defense of Christianity. The process of developing a theology removes it from life, for life is not orderly, systematic, or logical in the same way as a system of thought. This remoteness of theology to life is not only characteristic of systems that have long endured, but it is to a certain extent present when one makes a logical system out of one's own experience. When systematic theology becomes formalized, it may even become official so that a church will approve its content by vote. Although this consensus serves a valuable purpose, it cannot be said to reflect faithfully the Christian experience of every member of that denomination. Indeed, most denominations which have creedal statements also have a provision whereby they can be changed, showing at least in principle the subsidiary position of creed to experience of God in the community of faith.

Event and Personal Experience

However, when we say "the experience of God in the community of faith," we are not making a person's experience the norm for Christian faith. Life as it comes to an individual is an educational process, and an educational philosophy can be made out of life's experiences. Indeed one's own life is so real and one's problems are so immediate and important that motivation and goals of learning arise spontaneously. This is particularly true of children, for almost day by day they are able to increase their power to control their environment and add to their pleasure. For example, teaching children to control the faucets in a bathtub is an easy and rewarding matter. The children's confidence in themselves is strengthened as they control their environment in an activity that gives them pleasure. The goal of experience-oriented education is growth in the individual and an increasing utilization of one's abilities to manage life.

Christian education is centered in the person, as we shall elaborate in another lecture, but its goal is not individual growth alone. Rather, the reality of faith must be appropriated within the peculiar and particular situation of a person; but the object of faith and the source of guidance is the God who has revealed Godself in biblical events most clearly seen in Jesus Christ. So, personal experience cannot be the setting of Christian education; it can only be a factor, however important a feature in the appropriation of faith.

Communication and Event

We have said that revelation comes through event. These mighty acts of God, as recorded in the Bible, contain fact and interpretation intermingled to tell the story of God's redemption of God's people. The meaning of God's disclosure of Godself is preserved in, and as time passes or conditions change, is reinterpreted by the community of faith which was called into being by these historic episodes. At the beginning of this lecture we said that the biblical mode of revelation would not only help us understand the nature of God, but that the way God revealed Godself must be consistent with God's nature and therefore be the model by which we would be God's agents in sharing our faith. From this brief description we would indicate the *motive* and *purpose* of Christian education.

God's *motive* in revelation was God's love for God's creation. In God's freedom, God could have abandoned the world and humanity, but God's nature is love and love always seeks to create or recreate that which is damaged. Love led God to create humankind in God's own image; love led God to care for humans and guide human destiny. In the Old Testament God's love is seen in God's many acts of forming the nation Israel and in God's covenant to be their God, so that through them all the world would be blessed. Although many citations can be given, the book of Hosea perhaps summarizes the Old Testament's witness to the yearning, forgiving, and guiding love of God for God's people.

In the New Testament the love of God is seen in the life, ministry, death and resurrection of Christ. It is in the New Testament where the Greek word *agape* is coined to express afresh the sacrificial outgoing love of God for all people so that the latest books of the New Testament, those that represent the mature theology, can say "God is love" (1 Jn. 4:8). Or, "For God so loved the world that he gave his only Son. . . ." (Jn. 3:16). But let us not think the Johannine literature, because it was written about seventy-five years after Christ was crucified, presents a glorified remembrance of Jesus. Actually, the greatest description of divine love is given by the Apostle Paul from the first generation of Christians. Seeking to guide the newly converted Gentiles in Corinth, Paul speaks to them of many practical matters including the meaning and proper form of celebrating the Lord's Supper, the matter of eating meat offered to idols, the use of one's talents in the church; then he goes on to show the uniquely Christian motive in all that we do when he says, "I will show you a still more excellent way" (1 Cor. 12:31b). Then follows the poem about love, showing that, unless love is the motive, even good works amount to nothing.

However, we must note that Paul's use of love is not exactly the same as that in the Johannine books of the New Testament. Whereas John uses love as the outgoing concern of God to humanity in Jesus Christ, he also uses the word love to designate humanity's response to God. "We love, because he first loved us" (1 Jn. 4:19). This response of love in John's language is tested, proved and perfected in service. "Beloved, if God so loved us, we also ought to love one another" (1 Jn. 4:11). Paul is more inclined to use the word faith to show a person's response to God's love. God's love is shown in words like these ". . . while we were yet sinners Christ died for us" (Romans 5:8). Faith then becomes our response to God's love in Christ. To Paul faith means not only the acceptance of God's love in Christ but also a commitment of oneself to God in a mood of gratitude and a life of obedience.[2]

The impulse of love is to create and recreate. Love is the effort to actualize the good in another person. One who experiences God's love has a constraint to share one's experience and a restlessness to demonstrate one's concern for others. The motive for Christian education, indeed for all the ministries of the church is the same as that of the Gospel, "For God so loved the world that he gave. . . ." (Jn. 3:16). This is the only authentic reason for education or evangelism in the church.

Without the motivation of love no method of education can be Christian. With passionate, intelligent love any method can be used to share faith in God. Christian education is not independent of the Gospel nor of the community of grace in which Christian education is exercised. Indeed Christian education as such can be no more effective (regardless of the quality of the program, curriculum, or equipment) than the spiritual level of the church or individuals sponsoring the enterprise. When we use educational programs to build up institutional health in terms of financial support and organizational strength, when we appoint teachers who have not experienced the love of God, when we employ non-Christians to supervise programs for children, we are creating conditions that are foreign to a Christin style of life. With these conditions it is no wonder that very little happens to cultivate growth in grace.

Closely linked with motive is *purpose*. Why did God reveal Godself, and how can we be associated with that enterprise? God's love created the world and God's love came to heal, to redeem God's creation. God's revelation comes in concrete human events to show God's will for God's people. Indeed, revelation through human event leads logically to the incarnation--God making Godself known in a human being. Christ came to actualize the love of God and to initiate the new covenant. Although many things about God can be known through biblical record, God's revelation is primarily of Godself and of God's will. The content of revelation is the will of God.

If these summary statements be true, then all the processes of the church, including education, are subordinated to learning and doing the will of God. The revelatory events recorded in the Bible become norms by which we shape our conception of God; and the biblical record at the same time become a channel through which the living God actualizes Godself anew in contemporary human events. Therefore, our purpose is to understand and lead others to understand the nature of the God of the Bible and to obey God's will for our lives.

Let us grant that this is an exceedingly general statement and that the difficulties come when we become more specific and practical in our discussion. At this point, however, the only intention is to show that

Christian education has the same purpose as any other ministry of the church. Moreover, this general purpose is indigenous to the Gospel and is not dependent on a philosophy with an alien conception of God. For example, this general purpose--"learning the nature of God and doing God's will"--separates us sharply from those who see education largely in terms of individual growth, training for church leadership, or acquisition of doctrinal information.

Notes

1 John Knox, *Jesus, Lord and Christ* (New York: Harper, 1958) 61-63, 64.
2 A. T. Mollegen, "The Meaning of Love in Christian Thought," *The Christian Faith and Youth Today*, eds. Malcolm Strachan and Alvord M. Beardslee (Greenwich, Conn.: Seabury Press, 1957).

Lecture 2
The Receiver: A Self-Activating Person

Affirming that God is known through human events begins to describe the nature of God. Since the Bible assumes the existence of God by describing God's revelation to humanity, we will also assume that God as a living spirit can enter our experience. The God of the Bible is not described as an isolated, solitary being with a long list of attributes or characteristics. These descriptions of God have all come after the canonical books of the Bible were written, when Christians began to reflect on the nature of God in the light of what the biblical record disclosed about God's action in human affairs.

God, then, is not reason nor the result of our thinking; else our mind would think in series with God and we would find God through cognition. Our reason is so culture-bound, so interlocked with the range of ideas and assumptions that are current, that it is not and has not been a reliable path to God. Reason, which claims to find God, turns out in the final analysis to be based on hope or hunch, not on reason itself; for every reason or proof for the existence of God that has been advanced there has been a corresponding argument that logically denies God's existence. Moreover, if reason could take us to God, we would in a sense control the path to God and by implication, God's self. For this type of knowledge of God would lead us to general principles of how

God would act; and the mystery and power of God would evaporate as we increasingly used our knowledge of God just as we use our knowledge of electricity to make our life more pleasant and efficient. These statements do not rule out the use of reason to understand faith, to make more meaningful our experience with God, or to communicate more clearly and incisively our conception of God. The only thing being denied here is the human effort to learn about God through the most fascinating and Godlike faculty--reason. A prophet used these words to state the discontinuity between God and humans: "For my thoughts are not your thoughts, neither are your ways my ways, says the Lord" (Isa. 55:8).

The Apostle Paul faced this specific problem when he established churches in the Hellenistic world influenced by Greek philosophers who viewed the world as a fixed cosmic order. The wisdom of the Greeks presented a well worked-out scheme in which the work of the gods was seen in a moving cycle of nature (the sun, moon, seasons, etc.) and history, wherein life was seen as duplicating and reduplicating the past.[1] The Greek philosopher could use his reason to analyze these cycles and bring order out of disharmony or disarray. He developed the idea of the immortality of the soul by separating the soul from the body, thereby relating the soul (which was primarily one's ability to reason) to the reason of God and concluding that at one's death one's soul would naturally flow back to the pure body of reason and ideas, God.

But Paul did not accept the Greek philosophers' view. Paul accepted the world as known through biblical revelation--that the world itself did not include God, but was rather a creation of God. Indeed, Paul was not greatly concerned with the cosmos and certainly not worried about developing a coherent, consistent thought system about the universe. He considered the Greek wisdom a "foolishness" (1 Cor. 1:19-20). God, to the Apostle Paul, was separate from the world of humanity. God was seen through the moving events of life, which included not only the dynamic conversion of Paul himself but the broad sweep of Hebrew history. The locale of faith was within a person as one faced the circumstances of one's life. The active agent of faith was God-in-Christ, who was the power and wisdom of God (1 Cor. 1:24). These views, as opposed to Greek wisdom, together with the thought of the unity of body and mind which he inherited from the Old Testament, caused Paul to affirm the resurrection of the body rather than the immortality of the soul (1 Cor. 15).

When we say that God's communication with humanity was not through human reason but through history and event, we do not mean that God's self-disclosure was impersonal. On the contrary, the revelation was first personal; for it came to a person and was mediated and explained by a person to the people of God. The larger inclusive channel of revelation was event, but the principal agent was always a person who performed in the event like an actor or actress in a play.

Self-Activating Person

Paul Minear in his book *Eyes of Faith* uses the illustration of a drama to illustrate the person responding to revelation in this fashion: You are at a theater with a group of friends, sitting in a box. You are absorbed as a spectator of the drama which is taking place on the stage below. Suddenly the author and director of the play steps out from the wings and, while the drama continues, shouts your name. "John Smith!" he calls. "Come down here on the stage and get into the act; I have a part for you." The peculiar thing is, no one else hears him shout your name and no one else moves or looks at you, for they are intently following the drama below. Now you are aroused and you feel compelled to respond. You are embarrassed to leave your friends without a sensible explanation, but there is no logical reason for entering the drama except the compulsion from within. You begin to feel a panic, perhaps a cold sweat. What will you do? Will you suppress this urge to get into the play? Will you argue with the director? Will you get up and leave the theater? Will you get up and throw yourself into the drama and try to influence the course of action according to the impulse that urges itself upon you?[2]

This is an excellent illustration of the responsible selfhood assumed in the Bible. We do not mean by this illustration that a person is absolutely free and rationally capable of desiring the good and doing it. Rather, we shall see in succeeding lectures that one is bound to one's culture, restricted by one's perception of reality, and inevitably a victim of anxiety and hostility. Perhaps we should say that one is reasonably free or capable of self-direction and that one is responsible for one's actions within the range of the conditions one faces and that we know one in the light of one's meeting of these conditions. Certainly we know conditions as a person enters them as an actor or actress to influence the course of events.

Perhaps it is for this reason we have almost no biblical examples of revelation coming to children. This is not to say that children are unimportant; Jesus forever enhanced their worth when he said "Let the children come to me, and do not hinder them; for to such belongs the kingdom of heaven" (Matt. 19:14). Rather, children are not the receivers of revelation because they are not capable of responsible self-direction. Perhaps the story of Samuel (1 Sam. 3) is the only exception to this general rule and, if it is an exception, helps to prove the rule. Yet the story of Samuel itself states that the boy Samuel did not know that the words he heard were the words of the Lord until the elderly Eli was able to identify the words for him and instruct him as to how he should respond to the words of the Lord. However, if we continue to read the story of God's call to Samuel, we will see that the story simply records that God was pleased with Samuel; and the story serves as an announcement that he was "established to be a prophet of the Lord" when he became a man. Even the one episode we have in the life of our Lord between his birth and his ministry (Luke 2) shows our Lord in training for his divinely appointed task.

Responsible self-direction on the part of biblical characters does not mean that they are heroes. Perhaps we have done more damage to true faith by the way we have sentimentalized and idealized the actors and actresses in the biblical drama than by sheer neglect of God's word. Even the biographies of the patriarchs that come out of the remote legendary past contain accounts of their wickedness and sins. Cain slew Abel, Noah shamed his sons with drunkenness, and Joseph was tricked by his brothers. Moses is shown as a rebel against God and David is clearly portrayed as an opportunist, adulterer and murderer. Our Lord had his denier and betrayer. The early church contained embezzlers such as Ananias and Sapphira. Yet through all the vicissitudes and calamities, in spite of sin and uncertain leadership, the biblical report of revelation is to a person who heard the word of the Lord and stepped onto the stage and entered the drama. In spite of the actors' and actresses' human frailties and sin, they took charge of themselves and assumed responsibility for the area of human activities where they had a measure of control and influence.

Personal Time

Only God is free in the sense that God can do what God really wants to do and is not caught in the clutches of time. We creatures of God are limited in our freedom, both from the standpoint of our sin and disobedience to God, which we shall examine later, and also from the limitations of time by reason of death, which itself is a limitation occasioned by our corporate guilt. These limitations imposed on our human condition are perhaps some of the reasons why the biblical writers are not careful about the precise dating of historical events. Perhaps Isaiah's vision (Isaiah 6) is a good illustration of biblical time. "In the year that King Uzziah died I saw the Lord. . . ." The event is historical and factual--the year that King Uzziah died--yet the writer did not attempt to date it chronologically as a modern historian would because that was unimportant. Revelation is concrete, in that it really happened in a specific time and place, but the physical time and place are important only as vehicles through which God speaks. So the writer continued with his vision of God's holiness, a confession of his own sin and unworthiness, a statement concerning the forgiveness offered by God, and finally a consecration of life, "Here am I! Send me." This experience with God was concluded by a declaration of God's will for the prophet in that situation, "Go, and say to this people. . . ." The time that mattered was the personal time allotted to the prophet by God and the task the person was expected to do for God in that allotted time.

Self-activation towards God's purpose takes place because a person realizes eternity has come into time: God has visited a person. When this happens, time assumes a different characteristic. "*Chronos*," clocktime, that comes and goes according to human's machines for calibrating the cycle of the planets around the sun becomes less important than "*kairos*," God's time for a person. A time that matters is the time God has given us. When we experience God in our lives, we are excited by the possibilities that lie ahead and cast our whole being into that future. The future with God directs the present and helps us to come to terms with the past. We control our present only with a future, and this future has precedence in our thoughts, hopes and plans.

From the Christian point of view the Apostle Paul gives a more explicit version of biblical time in Philippians 3:13-14: ". . . forgetting what lies behind and straining forward to what lies ahead, I press on toward the goal for the prize of the upward call of God in Christ Jesus."

Here we have reconciliation with the past, for the past of a person is never gone; it is ever-present--ask any clinical psychologist. We have the compelling power of the future that gives hope, reward and confidence; after all, we are never far from the knowledge of our death and our destiny, a future that shapes our present. Also in the Apostle Paul's statement we have a demonstration of what a person's attitudes toward the past and the future mean for the present--they organize life about a divine purpose.

We understand the importance of personal time when we consider what happens to people who lose control over time. Some people are so loaded with guilt from past deeds they cannot live comfortably in the present. Yet the elimination of the past is no solution to this problem; for, if we lost our memory, we would be disassociated from life and unable to function in a meaningful way. Surgical efforts to excise portions of the brain that may be the physical location of mental illness have produced a post operative adult without a past who has had to be trained again like a child. This grotesque experiment shows the meaninglessness of trying to solve the past through surgery. Or again, look at what happens if the future loses its allure and no longer holds possibility of self-fulfillment. Life for a person becomes dull, routine; suicide often seems the logical way of escape.

So, God's time for a person is related to God's purpose. When a person is touched by God's spirit, one's whole life is quickened and time becomes precious, not to preserve life but to be the means whereby one can serve God. Although chronological time clicks off minutes at sixty-second regularity, God's time is more a sense of the sacredness of God's purpose and a holiness of life when we are confident that we know God's will. In this sense God's time has a tempo all its own and is given value in a person's life according to the manifestation of God in the events that make up one's personal history. Thus, one will date one's spiritual life by events that to others may seem trivial or uninspiring, but to the person they are the means of one's understanding that "God loves me and sent God's son for me." One is tempted to enumerate the great religious experiences of Augustine, St. Francis, or Luther to illustrate God's time and its profoundly personal meaning; but the readers would be better served if they put down this paper for a few moments and took an inventory of their own life and God's time for their life.

Chosen by God

God's wisdom, then, comes to us in our time and times so that personal history becomes our holy history. This is subjective, an inward introspective finding of one's real self, but the truth about ourselves is objective in the sense that it lies beyond us and is not subject to our control. "You did not choose me, but I chose you" is the order of one's experience of God's word according to John (Jn. 15:16). As indicated in the opening of this lecture, God's wisdom is of a different order of truth from a person's effort to form a rational, operating order for the world of nature and humanity. The truth that seeks us is in a person, Jesus Christ, and it comes through persons who have actualized this Word of God in their lives.

The objectivity of God's communication to humanity is a universal characteristic of biblical humanity--the voice is not that of the community, it is not humanity's conscience nor humanity's idealized concept of what ought to be. It is the voice from beyond time that makes personal time meaningful and precious. A distinction of God from the person who receives the message from God is the very quality that produces holiness, for then one can explain "God loves me." God is known not as having a concern for persons in general, nor as an operating procedure or general rule, but in having a care for me in my time and my condition. This radical affirmation of God defies logical reason. The receiver never knows why he or she has been visited, is never able to justify God's gift of grace. The experience is so shattering of complacency that one's previously held self-image is destroyed; the receiver either suddenly or slowly begins to understand himself or herself in a new light; one's old life with its fears and frustrations is dissolved, and a new being begins to grow toward the object of faith, God. It is the same world, to be sure, and the person is still held within the same body with its appetites and glandular needs, but the view is different. One becomes reoriented, the center of one's life is Christ, and all that radiates from that center is reorganized and charged with fresh significance. Paul expresses the experience with these words, ". . . if any one is in Christ, he is a new creation, the old has passed away, behold, the new has come" (2 Cor. 5:17). This is the miracle that makes all other miracles possible and probable.

When we are chosen by God, we know God beyond ourselves. We experience God outside ourselves in order to find the meaning of life within our own time and times. The profundity of the change in orientation is sometimes demonstrated by a person's change in name. Simon becomes Peter or Saul becomes Paul. In the Old Testament we do not have the change of a name as often as we have the selected name of a person which best expresses the role one played in God's drama or redemption. Moses, for example, was so named because he was drawn out of the water (Exod. 2:10), as an indication of God's protection against Pharaoh's orders to kill all Hebrew baby boys. Name-changing is, of course, not proof but only an indication of a deep change that has taken place within a person. Name is equivalent to person. We cannot communicate about a person without a name. A name represents what one thinks one is or a total of all impressions a person has made on us. Thus, the profundity of being known by God sometimes causes a person to dramatize the difference by change in name. But whether name is changed or not, the truth to be maintained is the intensely personal knowledge that comes to those who are confident that they are known by God.

Language

1. God and the Psyche. If revelation is intelligible and a message communicable, then language must be a central feature of God's activity in revelation. Remember the thesis of this course is that there is an affinity between the nature of God and the process God chooses to reveal Godself. How can God speak to humanity since humanity is so separate from God, so intertwined in the contingencies of the moment, so unworthy to claim God's favor? More precisely, through what specific channel can God reach humanity when we have already said that the experience is quite subjective, even to the extent that one who claims to hear God through an event is not often able to get a single person to substantiate that claim? Somewhere within a human there is a receptor capable of distinguishing a word from God. At the beginning of this lecture we ruled reason out as the principal pathway to God. Perhaps the correct answer is to say a person's whole being is involved, with reason assuming an important but secondary role. Although such an answer has the merit of comprehension, it lacks the precision that we expect in the light of modern psychological understanding of humanity's inner life.

One answer today comes from those who understand the deep, powerful and nonrational forces that churn ceaselessly in the unconscious mind. Having seen these impulses and tradewinds of the deep influence humanity in countless ways and through various cultures, some people would say God is in a person's unconscious mind, lower than the lowest explored territory. Specifically, they would say that there is racial unconscious mind that is peculiar to human beings, timeless and culture-free. The archetype of God is not God nor the source of our knowledge of God but rather a pattern that indicates the reality of God or the foundation that makes possible the building of a conception of God. Thus, in humankind generally there is a built-in disposition toward religious beliefs. The usual method of explaining this point of view is to show the similarity between Christian symbols and those of other religions, often symbols of a circular design, indicating the archetype of "wholeness" which all people desire. Indeed, salvation is defined as an approximation of wholeness within a person, meaning one's ability to harmonize the various levels of one's mind, one's appetites and one's capacities. This might be called self-realization in distinction to self-activation referred to earlier in this lecture.[3]

It is at the point of God-human communication that we can see more clearly the conception of God involved in this view. Finding the foundation for belief in God in humanity's unconscious means that the most profound communication between God and humanity is in symbols, not through language. It would be more accurate to say that the language of God in this view is in geometric symbols not words, for actually words are themselves a type of symbol. It is thought that the religious symbols that have emerged in various times and cultures show that there is a prepared field in which the image of God grows. Words are held to be but a feeble and inadequate effort to relate to a person's conscious mind a suitable knowledge of God. Oriental religions are usually examined to provide data, and Buddhism is the favorite oriental religion in this search. This affection for oriental religions indicates an affinity between the conception of God in oriental religions and the conception of God inherent in a God-human communication process through the nonrational unconscious area of a person's inner life.

Oriental religions, particularly Buddhism, are introspective and tend to separate the individual from society by focusing one's attention on one's own inner needs. God is a principle of life one seeks but not a spirit who by separateness has freedom to influence the course of human events. Likewise, the god known primarily through the nonrational elements of humanity is really a general explanation of what is, an affirmation of the mystery toward biological life, and an attitude of reverence toward the forces that well up from within to domesticate and harmonize our interests and our culturally-oriented desires. The battle of the religious life is fought on the ground between one's urges deposited by nature to preserve and procreate life and the self that is socially known and oriented. Persons who hold this point of view in the West are usually concerned more and more with the clinical details of how one is faring in this struggle and are reasonably unconcerned with one's responsibility toward the welfare of society generally.

Certainly we cannot deny there is a battle between one's conscious self, one's biological drives, and the demands of society. But there is a vast difference between being a soldier struggling with all of the common problems of soldiers, and being a soldier engaged in a struggle for a purpose that can give direction and meaning to the warfare. In the latter case the struggles of the individual soldier are important but subsidiary to the outcome of the battle itself. From the first chapter of Genesis on, we are told that we are to subdue the earth and have dominion over everything that moves on the earth (Gen. 1:28). The issue is not a difference in attitude toward the forces of nature; rather, the difference concerns the area of our psyche through which the communication of God comes and the conception of God that such a communication process implies. That it is intensely personal, subjective and rooted in personal time we have affirmed, but we cannot agree that the God of the Bible can be known through the nonrational areas of a person's being because (1) the communication process seems to be limited to pictorial symbols which are open to diverse interpretations and (2) the communication seems to be exclusively to the person about their problems. The biblical conception of God is related to a communication process that includes words. However mystical and vague the experience was that is described in the Bible, the receivers of revelation are finally able to form it into words in their own mind; and they are able to communicate at least its essential features to other human beings with words. To deny the possibility of forming words about revelation is to deny rationality and to disassociate us from Scripture.

The problem as to the more precise area of one's psyche through which God speaks remains. It would be a convenient solution if we could, like some theologians of the past, say God comes to us through conscience. We shall see, however, in another lecture that this is impossible with our modern knowledge of the super-ego. Perhaps in the "ego ideal" or the positive conscience we have the proper area of the human mind for God-human communication. Here at least we can work with the rational word as well as the nonrational sediments that have been deposited in our being by our parents and our community. At this point we simply indicate this possibility in order to continue the discussion of the centrality of language in God-human communication.

2. Mind to Mind. Language is, of course, only part of a symbolic process people have built to communicate with each other. Signs, gestures, painting and music also serve as means of communication. Not only must these symbols be observed; they must also be understood, so that communication is sharing of meaning between mind and mind. The more nearly there is shared meaning, the more quickly the symbols of communication are interpreted and understood. Unless there is shared meaning, communication is awkward, inaccurate and false. For example, a shared experience between parents over the loss of a child may be most profoundly expressed by a cry, a clasp of hands, or silence. However, if they ever hope to convey the meaning of that event to others or even in its fullest form to themselves, they must use words. So a religious experience is more profound than any set of words we could assemble to describe the event. The receivers of revelation actually share their life, which is more profound and dramatic than words and that sharing of life is limited to the life span of the receivers. The only way in which human experience can be communicated to succeeding generations and in a sense understood by the contemporary generation is through words. Words are used because if there is really shared meaning, then words have the power of creating a mental experience that can permeate another person's being so that one can approximate the meaning being shared. It is natural for all biblical characters to have a compulsion to talk because word is the closest approximation to inner experience that we have.

Again, we may be helped if we look at this point negatively. Some of the great mysteries of the world stand as locked treasure chests because we have the sign but we do not have the meaning of these signs. For example, the great stones at Stonehenge, 8 miles north of Salisbury, England, stand in a circle in such a fashion that we know they had significance to the primitive people who inhabited that island about 1800 years B.C. However, lacking words to explain this creation we lack understanding and can only guess as to what these stones mean. So, to have a religious experience and not be able to express it in words is tantamount to not having the experience, at least as far as any other person is concerned.

3. Selfhood and Language. To say that a mind can communicate with mind only by symbols in which language is the principal mode is also to make a declaration about the personal aspect of words. We cannot communicate directly with another mind; therefore we do not know exactly how another mind receives our message. Persons are autonomous--self-contained--and use words to reveal, conceal, or alter their real feelings. The very necessity of having to use word-symbols is a reminder that we are self-conscious persons with a rational structure of living expressed in language. We are most conscious of this when a person by a slip of tongue reveals what we know that person was trying to conceal; by that momentary loss of self-control we are all embarrassed. Or again, if a person with whom we are associated is unable to converse intelligently or coherently or begins to degenerate in the capacity to "make sense," we have our first mark of mental illness. One of Freud's first scientific papers was related to this intimate connection between language and selfhood and we are all aware of his monumental discovery of the unconscious mind through psychological blocks that prevent a person's remembering or speaking.[4] The connection between selfhood and language is so close that we cannot touch one without getting a response from the other. George Bernard Shaw turned the matter around by showing in his play *Pygmalion* how a speech teacher could take a poor slum flowergirl and change her into a princess by teaching her to speak correctly.

4. Particularity of language. To insist that language is the hallmark of a responsible individual is not to deny the social nature of language. We have already said that there must be shared meaning for accurate communication to take place. We can go further by recalling that there is a remarkable parallel between the particularity of revelation through event and the concreteness of language. An event is a specific historical episode made up of human actors and actresses who are deadly serious about the cause and outcome of the affair. Language, too, is concrete. It is always a particular language. Although several artificial "perfect" languages have been invented, none has ever been taken seriously because they are divorced from living people and culture. Language is always spoken at a particular time and it has its meaning at that time. In King James' English it was complimentary to call a girl "homely," but today the meaning of that word has changed drastically. Moreover,

language has meaning to a group where words are sometimes used with specialized meanings growing out of their living experience. Thus, the word for martyr, one who gives one's life for a cause, meant in post-New Testament times a witness at a law court. But so many Christians came before the law court to "martyr" (witness to their faith) and were executed that the word came to have the special meaning of one who witnessed and then gave one's life.

There is a real sense in which language is related to culture in somewhat the same way that language is related to a person. All is part of a human matrix identified in time and geography, providing both opportunities and certain limitations. What does it mean that a people do not have a certain word in their language or a suitable synonym for a word? For example:

> The Marshallese have over sixty terms just to describe different parts of a coconut tree and its fruit. The stages of growth and maturity of the coconut are described by twelve different words. Equivalent terms are not to be found in an English dictionary, while conversely the Marshallese have no words for the numerous parts of horse-drawn carriages, though on some of the islands they have borrowed or made up words for parts of automobiles, trucks, and airplanes.[5]

Since the coconut tree is an incidental part of our life, our language is unable to convey the full meaning of the coconut tree. Since machinery is new to the Marshall islands, the natives must create words to identify the new reality and to convey ideas about its place in their society.

Can a person think a concept without a word for it? Viewed in this way we see the necessity of communication through rational processes and the indispensable function of language both to form and be formed by mental concepts. We also comprehend at once the *limitations* and *complications* of revelation that is rational in the sense that it is bound up with language in a cultural epoch. Thus, we can understand John Calvin's formation of a doctrine of "accommodation" wherein God adjusted to the cultural conditions of the day in order to communicate God's purposes to humans.[6]

Notes

1 John Wild, *Human Freedom and Social Order* (Durham: Duke University Press, 1959) 83.

2 Paul Minear, *Eyes of Faith* (Philadelphia: Westminster Press, 1946) 19. See also Karl Barth, *Church Dogmatics* (Edinburgh: T. & T. Clark, 1936) Vol. I, 1, section on "The Word of God and Experience," 226-260.

3 For a Christian (Catholic) application of Jung's psychology, see Josef Goldbrunner, *Individuation* (New York: Pantheon Books, Inc., 1956).

4 Sigmund Freud published "On the Psychical Mechanism of Forgetfulness" in 1898 and expounded this idea in a popular book *Psychopathology of Everyday Life* (London: Ernest Benn, 1914).

5 Eugene A. Nida, *Customs and Cultures* (New York: Harper, 1954) 198.

6 John Calvin, *Institutes of the Christian Religion*, ed. John T. McNeill (London: S.C.M. Press, 1960) I.17.13; I.14.3; 3.18.9; 2.16.2; 2.11,13.

Lecture 3
Spiritual Reality: Person-in-a-Situation

Revelation coming through event is a complicated matter: the factors involved are so intricately interrelated and so relative to each other that when we stop to analyze one factor the others get out of perspective. The problem of understanding an event that is in progress is akin to understanding politics; the matter is highly specific in that we are dealing with things that are happening, can be seen and discussed, and yet all the while these things have an inner meaning that is unclear or elusive. After the event has happened and the participants are able to trace the hand of God in the events through which they have lived, then the meaning is not so elusive and can, in fact, be stated with remarkable clarity. Thus with scripture we are able to understand, evaluate and learn from the events reported. So we must reiterate that an event is not an occurrence that can be reported by a journalist who reports the "happenings," because a helpful report must also contain the dynamic, pulsing stream of historical facts and conditions that create the situation in which the principal characters function.

A biblical event is not necessarily a momentous historical deed, although some of these events are likewise a part of the biblical record. The significance of an event is not its importance from the historical point of view; but it is valuable in proportion as God's will is revealed to humankind. The event can, by historical standards, be relatively insignificant, such as Paul's relation to a runaway slave; yet the book of

Philemon is valuable for understanding just what the spirit of Christ led Paul to do in that case. Biblical reports of revelation do not contend that it is an "insight" into the nature of history or a general precept about the conduct of human affairs. If this were true, then revelation would be limited to the learned, and an understanding of revelation would conform to rational processes of the mind. This point is illustrated in Luke's gospel when our Lord selected seventy to preach and teach in his name. After briefing them on how to conduct themselves in this capacity, he sent them forth. They returned with remarkable stories of their experiences and Jesus turned to God in prayer saying, "I thank thee, Father, Lord of heaven and earth, that thou hast hidden these things from the wise and understanding and revealed them to babes. . . ." (Lk. 10:21)

Although there were remarkable minds in some biblical characters, they are not remembered because of their scholarship or their social position. There is a tendency in the New Testament to assume that God's revelation can best be apprehended by the workaday person, such as the disciples who were in the main laborers. There is a profound implication here; the type of reality one sees in the Bible is like that of the reality of the wage earner. It is not speculative or esoteric, needing special intellectual training or competence. It is the reality of a carpenter or fisherman, where direct experience shows the fitness of one's action and where a pragmatic test of results is final. Our Lord's speech displays this directness when he invites his disciples with the words, "Follow me"; it is also seen when he suggested the testing of the truth of a prophet by saying ". . . you will know them by their fruits" (Matt. 7:20).

A revelatory event is a situation shaped by historical circumstances wherein persons must make a decision--must put their lives one way or another. A situation makes a claim on the person's being. We might say that a very important part of the event is the awareness that a decision is crucial, that to put one's being on one side or the other makes a difference to God and the church. Historical conditions are shared by many persons, but situations are shared by a few because a situation is what is energized for us out of general conditions. Another way of stating the matter would be to say a situation is that to which one feels one must respond out of general conditions that prevail at the moment. Stated in this way, we will remember that a person is always in a situation. Whether it becomes a revelatory experience or not is a matter which cannot be decided. As far as revelation is concerned, we cannot think of Noah without the flood, Moses without the Exodus, or Peter without the denial of his Lord. Persons are not really known except as they are known in relation to the reality they have had to face. The greatness and importance of persons are judged by the conditions in which they have had to make decisions and live out their life. We can go further and say that a person does not know the deeper levels of the self except in relation to decisions they have had to make.

Specific Historical Situation

As we look back on the revelatory events recorded in the scriptures, we are impressed by the absence of revelation in general. It always comes to a specific person, never to people in general. Some of the truths about God are for people in general, but a historical person enunciates them out of the specific situation. It is for this reason that Scripture does not exist for itself; it reflects the time and place of its composition and exists as a testimony to God's disclosure of Godself. Out of the contingency and uniqueness of each episode comes "thought, word and deed" concerning God's action for God's people. Revelation is therefore rooted in situation, for the plan of action is conditioned by the situation at the moment. It is for this reason that organized Christianity has given so much of its scholarship to a sifting of facts and an understanding of language and social customs of the biblical era. We are confident that the more we know about the creaturely framework through which the revelation came, the more completely we will understand the nature of God. Language is the principal area of research because every translation of the Bible is in some measure an interpretation; and we Protestants are dependent upon accurate rendering of the original meaning of the Bible. Until we have a clear idea of what God's revelation meant to the receivers in their situation, we cannot safely assume we have the beginning of God's wisdom.

Here we must be very clear about our principle of interpretation. We are not saying that the historical event through which the revelation comes is simply a framework and that the content of revelation was a gradual insight into God's purpose which people developed. This view, built on the model of the evolution of ideas, makes people the judge of revelation and results in little that is really new or even distinctive about the Christian faith. On the other hand, we are not saying that the content of revelation is related only to the specific historical situation in which it occurs. Actually, the revelation was to a person in a situation and about God's plan for God's people. We shall examine the content of revelation and Christian knowledge in the next lectures. At this point let us indicate that God's revelation, most clearly in Jesus Christ, is about humankind's perennial conditions, personal and social; but we understand it by means of the specific historical situation through which it comes. We do not know it until we experience it in our own situation. This is the substance of the next lecture.

The Bible's preoccupation with happenings and their consequences is perhaps the reason why we do not have more explicit theology in the Bible and why the theology that is in the Bible is difficult to harmonize. The writers were for the most part unaware of each other. They fulfilled the obligations of their call according to the beliefs that developed out of their experiences. Each one felt little need to organize the beliefs into a system. Even in the Old Testament where we have some books with composite authors and probably a redactor who edited manuscripts, the theology was not always made to be consistent; and writers of later books did not feel constrained to develop the line of thought already started. In the New Testament the Gospels are a good illustration. They tell the story of Jesus from different perspectives, and the writers do not bother to remove information from the account that creates a conflict with another account. Again, we find that our clue to a solution of most of these problems lies in a careful comparison of the four Gospel stories of Jesus and a study of the situation in the church--including *what the writer said*: literary style, intended audience and the specific conditions to be met in the place where the Gospel story would be read. Again, the letters of Paul are highly specific, even to the calling of names of persons who are involved in events and descriptions of problems that pertain to the churches to which he addressed the letters. Indeed they are letters, written from jail or in a distant city, and resemble more the cares and concern of a coach for his team in competition than literature designed to be translated into a thousand tongues. They became scripture and are translated into a thousand tongues because they are clear about God's activity in the specific conditions of Paul's day.

Particular Becomes Peculiar

To become the particular medium of God's revelation makes God's people peculiar. The charge to Israel was: "For you are a people holy to the Lord your God, and the Lord has chosen you to be a people for his own possession. . . ." (Deut. 14:2; 26:18; see also 1 Pet. 2:9) They were not chosen because they were peculiar, but because chosen, they were to be peculiar. God changes what God touches. Turned around from humanity's side, we would say that the uniqueness of the Hebrew was the belief that God could be known in their history, and their history is their witness to this belief. After the development of critical studies of the Bible and under the tutelage of a secular theory of evolution, many biblical scholars compared the history of Israel with the religions of the countries in which the Hebrews lived. These scholars showed how the Hebrews constructed a system of religion, and their solidarity as a people was explained on the grounds that they had a "genius for religion" just as the Greeks had a genius for abstract thought. Moses' Ten Commandments, for example, are compared with similar codes of other countries in the same period of time. Today, however, many Old Testament scholars are asking the question differently and are getting a different answer. They are not asking, were the Hebrews like other people of their times, but at what points were they dissimilar? A fair answer to that question shows the radical peculiarity of the Hebrews. For example, in lands where the Hebrews lived, idols were numerous and considered potent, but Hebrew leaders constantly warned against idol worship (Is. 2:18-22).

Peculiarity Becomes Portable

We do not deny that the Hebrews were deeply conditioned by the countries in which they lived and by the codes of conduct in vogue at that time. In the New Testament we likewise acknowledge the cultural age in which the word of God came. Slavery, for example, was accepted as a social institution. Yet to admit this is but to underscore again the paradoxical elements in revelation. Revelation must be pertinent to have any force, it must be applicable to a situation to have any meaning. This is God's accommodation to our creaturehood. But God's activity and guidance of a person in a situation is the peculiar element in revelation that is portable. Faith is a quality of life that looks at situations with an expectation of finding God's word of guidance. In the great "faith" passages of Hebrews where the story of Israel is retold we have an account of the highly specific conditions facing Israel in different historical periods. There is no propositional truth expressed in Hebrews 11 except the major contention that through faith all of these specific conditions were met. These conditions ranged all the way from Abel's problem of offering an acceptable sacrifice to God to the destruction of the walls of Jericho. Let us not assume that "faith is the answer" and thus sentimentalize revelation. Faith is not the answer to anything. Christian faith is a quality of life that creates problems and tensions and raises more questions than it can answer. It might be more accurate from a biblical point of view to say "expectation of God's guidance in an understandable word" than to say faith, if by faith we mean a conspiracy of happenings to make our life more pleasant. The person of biblical faith is a person in tension with the prevailing situation.

Situation as Media of Spiritual Reality

If the foregoing paragraphs are true, then only in the reality of the situation is God known, in the completeness of "thought, word, deed" or perhaps "deed, word, thought." It is extremely important to note that the Scriptures show the receiver of revelation utilizing the human situation to convey God's message. This fact should be enough in itself to alert us to the profound significance inherent in human situations serving in a dual capacity as the media through which we know God and the media through which we communicate our knowledge of God to others.

From the Old Testament prophets we can see most clearly the rational word in revelation, the spiritual reality found in human situation, and the utilization of the human situation to convey spiritual truth. The prophets used object lessons, which are acted-out parables. Parables have an unusual ability to convey spiritual truth and we shall examine this particular method in more detail later.

The Word Made Flesh

Since God chose to communicate to people through human event, a messiah became inevitable. Old Testament expectation of a messiah is but the logical deduction of the Hebrews who had experienced God's guidance in their affairs. Why should they not expect God to go all the way and send a divine person to redeem Israel? If they misunderstood the messiah when he came, they misunderstood in the right direction; for they expected a political leader. They were correct in the earthiness of Christ but unprepared for the messiah to be a judge as well as a redeemer.

The exact nature of Christ's incarnation is not the burden of these paragraphs; let us rather note that incarnation was the natural and inevitable continuation of the mode of biblically-described revelation. In Jesus Christ we have the word made flesh dwelling among us, giving us the completeness of God's wisdom for humankind in "thought, word, deed." In order to be the Christ of glory God had to be Jesus of Palestine in the reign of Tiberius Caesar.

Again, as the incarnation was historical, so the incarnated One used the human situation to communicate God's will. We often use the term "drama of redemption" to describe God's message in Christ. This is an unusually apt phrase, if we will but remember that it is real life with dramatic dimensions, not just a simple acting out of parts assigned by God wherein the players are not really free to be themselves. Jesus was the Christ because of what he did in Palestine. The story of his life cannot be told without the account of what he said, his compassion for the poor, his healing of the sick, his courage to condemn the greed and false humility of some religious leaders, his demonstration of God's forgiveness of enemies, his ability even as he hung on the cross to say "Father, forgive them; for they know not what they do" (Lk. 23:34). The greatness, nobility, brilliance of speech and humility of Jesus were enough to make him long remembered; but these qualities have all been approximated at one time or another by others. It was not until the resurrection that the disciples realized that Jesus had conquered death. Adoration now became worship. Discipleship, which had consisted of following and learning from a great leader, now became apostleship expressed in an urgency to discharge Christ's mission.

The New Testament Community of Faith

Down to this point we have been following the line of thought that the vehicle of biblical revelation is an historical event which produced conditions to which a person responded. The person in his or her situation became the active agent of God's word in Jesus Christ. We have been trying to answer the question, "What do we learn about the communication of faith from the biblical record?" If we could stop here, our task of communicating the Christian faith would be relatively easy, at least as far as our mental image of this task is concerned. However, to do so would fail to do justice to the situational aspect of the Gospel, and it would not honor our knowledge of the way the church in New Testament times received the good news from God. We must now turn the whole matter around and ask, "What do we learn about the communication of faith from the way the New Testament church received and used God's self-revelation?" When we ask the question in this fashion, we will recall that the books of the New Testament were written a considerable time after the death and resurrection of Jesus. Pentecost came before Peter preached with spiritual power; and Paul's experience of God on the Damascus road preceded by half a century the book of Acts that describes the event. The New Testament is the literature of a community of faith, reflecting not only its members' perception of Jesus as the Christ but their interpretation of the meaning of that event and their use of the faith that was communicated to them. The time span covers at least three generations--a hundred years--after Christ. We have therefore two major considerations: first, the changing conditions within the community of faith and the implications thereof for understanding the Gospel; and second, the specific way the New Testament church went about the communication of the Christian faith. Both of these are of course interrelated; we will examine each of these points separately and remember that the whole is greater than, and in some ways different from, the sum of the parts.

Conditions Affect Interpretation

We must put ourselves in the position of the New Testament church in order to understand the way that they received, interpreted, and used the revelation of God they found in Jesus Christ. We often get a false notion in this matter by the order in which the books are bound in the Bible. We obtain first an idea of the person and life of Christ from reading the Gospels; and then on reading Acts, we develop a conception of the growing church which, in the pastoral epistles composed toward the end of the New Testament, begins to develop practical problems of administration, the training of ministers and church finance.

Actually, we have three general waves of literature in the New Testament. The first, chronologically, and the nearest to the resurrection event are the letters of Paul which show a living church at work and prayer. This living community of faith is small but aggressive, poor, often confused about God's will and made up of people who continue to sin while claiming the grace and forgiveness of God. This is the period from about 48 A.D. to 68 A.D. The church is found in these letters to be already institutionalized: there are orders of preachers, teachers and evangelists. The sacraments are administered according to a tradition already established and a rudimentary church polity is in operation.

The second wave of writings gives us the synoptic Gospels and Acts, a period from about 70 to 90 A.D. This material comes at a time when the first generation of believers, the apostles and those who knew the apostles, were dying and there was a need for a written account of the life of Christ and the history of the beginning of the Church. If the Church was to live, it had to have a record of the life that created and sustained it. Luke opens his Gospel with a statement that although many others had written about "the things which have been accomplished among us," he finds it important to give an "orderly account" of what eyewitnesses of the life of Jesus and ministers have reported.

The third wave of writing, coming after 90 A.D., consists of John's Gospel, the pastoral letters, and Revelation. These books reflect different conditions. The Gospel of John is less a biography than it is an interpretation of Christ's life with biographical data used to develop the theme of salvation. The pastoral epistles, as the general title suggests, relate to the general church problems which are now more pronounced. Apparently, at first, these matters were handled provisionally with the eschatological assumption that Jesus would return soon. In the pastoral epistles a settled order is assumed and a need to regularize institutional procedures recognized. A reading of the book of James, for example, not only brings out the social class distinction that is commonplace; but also the tone of evangelistic urgency is gone and has been replaced by devotional faith that provides a regulatory norm of Christian conduct.

My purpose in reviewing these familiar facts is not just to make an obvious point that the changing general conditions of the New Testament community over a hundred-year period were the ground of different types of literature. It is to say that the only material we have about Christ and his church has come to us this way and we must work backwards through these changing conditions to really understand Jesus. Conditions, in other words, were at the same time both a contributing reason for the written accounts and in some measure a factor in the interpretation we have recorded in biblical records. We see this even more clearly when we look at the specific books written within the same wave of literature.

For example, when we compare the material given by Matthew as a part of the Sermon on the Mount (Matt. 5:3-12) with Luke's compilation (Lk. 6:20-23), we find that Luke says "Blessed are you poor," whereas Matthew's account reads "Blessed are the poor in spirit." This is but one of many places where Luke gives special attention to the poor. He is also particularly interested in the outcast, the widow, and the universality of the Gospel (Lk. 15). The best explanation is that the living community of faith that nurtured this gospel in Jerusalem was very poor. Matthew's Gospel may have been prepared for pedagogical purposes, some scholars suggesting that it is a textbook for catechumen classes. It certainly reflects an effort to promote continuity with the Old Testament and to exhibit the full range of Jesus' teachings.

We must leave to the specialist a detailed study of this problem. It is valuable to us as interpreters of the word of God and as an important consideration in our study of the situational aspect of spiritual truth. Let us then assume that we follow a sound rule when we seek to understand the conditions of the community of faith in which the literature of the New Testament was developed.

There is, however, a second aspect of the communication of faith in the New Testament that may have more immediate bearing on our contemporary problem: namely, the way the New Testament church uses the revelation of God to communicate faith. At once we must say again what we said earlier--that persons of faith in their "thought, word, deed" were the most powerful communicators of faith. The New Testament church was always calling and recalling its members to their holy vocation as in the words of Paul who said in the letter to the Romans, "I appeal to you therefore, brethren, by the mercies of God, to present your bodies as a living sacrifice, holy and acceptable to God, which is your spiritual worship" (Rom. 12:1).

1. Approach to the nonbeliever. The "living sacrifice" was a personal challenge and it was accomplished by believers in the light of the circumstances of their personal life. However, when the New Testament Christians began a self-conscious effort to communicate their faith to others, they made a sharp distinction between the confessed believer and the nonbeliever.. The method of communication and utilization of material were unique to this task. At the opening of this lecture we quoted Luke's Gospel to the effect that neither wisdom nor

prudence was a prelude to understanding the gospel. If we examine Acts, which contains the church's record of its beginning and some reports of early sermons, we see the sharpness with which the Christians both separated themselves from, and preached to, the nonbelievers. Professor Dodd, in analyzing these sermons, shows how the speaker would usually begin with some contemporary mighty work. The ambiguity about revelation is noted here, for the auditors had knowledge of the event even though they did not see in it a message from God. The preacher then shows the relation between this event and the life, death, and resurrection of Jesus. For a Jewish audience of nonbelievers the speaker would then call to mind the history of God's people to show the common elements between their beliefs and those of the new Messianic society. The message ended with a condemnation of sinners who rejected Jesus as the Lord and Christ.

In the literature of the church there is a good deal of denunciation of the nonbeliever done in the context of dire warning. In Luke's Gospel (ch. 20) we find Jesus talking in the temple when the chief priests and scribes come in with the elders. These national religious leaders ask Jesus to show his credentials. Jesus had to answer the question of the authority by which he taught. He then told the parable of the vineyard which was a judgment against Israel for rejecting the son. The story is followed by the words, "The very stone which the builders rejected has become the head of the corner" (Lk. 20:17). Matthew's Gospel contains much bitterness against Jewish nonbelievers, culminating in the seven woes of denunciation (ch. 23). Peter's great sermon after Pentecost concluded with these words, "Let all the house of Israel therefore know assuredly that God has made him both Lord and Christ, this Jesus whom you crucified" (Acts 2:36). Peter's sermon is typical in that it leads to a decision, it is designed to precipitate guilt. It is intended to show people their desperate condition before God so that they will cry out, "What shall we do?" Peter's answer was, "Repent, and be baptized every one of you in the name of Jesus Christ for the remission of your sins; and you shall receive the gift of the Holy Spirit" (Acts 2:38). The whole method of communication to nonbelievers was aimed at repentance and acceptance of Jesus as "Lord and Christ"; and this approach did not change with sermons recorded as preached primarily to nonbelieving Gentiles. The introductions changed because the Gentile did not have an adequate pre-understanding of religious signs nor a heritage of the law and the prophets. Paul in Athens had to accommodate himself to the condition of the Greeks by his famous introduction whereby he started with the altar to the unknown god and quoted Greek poetry, then moved on to the standard testimony of what God had done in Christ. Although this is adjustment to the audience, this is in the nature of adaptation. The major consideration in the evangelistic witness was conviction of sin and acceptance of Jesus as "Lord and Christ."

Evangelism by its very nature cannot gloss over the condition of the nonbeliever or it has no message. The message is designed for the mature person--one who can be stricken by their condition and respond with faith. It is at this point that we see the difference between evangelistic and educational procedures. The goal is the same, the message is the same. The difference is in the condition of the audience. In evangelistic efforts there is urgency and judgment with an expected change of life. In educational processes there is explanation and guidance for establishment "in Christ" (2 Cor. 1:21).

2. Approach to the believer. The New Testament is the literature of the church. Even the reports of sermons to nonbelievers are realistically seen as testimony to God rather than the preacher's effort to be a successful evangelist. These sermons are recorded not only for their intrinsic value but also because they, too, had a message to the believer. After all, the believer came from unbelief or was in close association with those who were nonbelievers. By the repetition of these sermons the basis of the Christian faith was kept sharp and clear even for believers. Nevertheless, the church itself used the revelation of God in Christ in certain ways with believers. First, they were forced into a principle of gradation based not on a static norm such as age or educational attainment but rather on degree of faith-knowledge. Second, they observed the principle of growth in grace and knowledge (2 Pet. 3:18).

Gradation of material was based on the degree of faith-knowledge a person had. We do not know the bases on which the preachers and teachers made their judgments. Apparently no written tests were used; rather, a judgment was made on the basis of experience. We would say today it was a clinical judgment of the type a doctor makes after years of experience. But there is no question about the judgment being made and the lessons to be learned suited to the degree of faith-knowledge a person had. The chief enemies of faith were considered to be sin, the Jews' need of a sign, the wisdom of the philosophers or the secular spirit of the world. Paul places the blame for his need to grade his work on the sins of the believers. To the Corinthians he said he had fed them with milk, not yet with meat; because of their carnal concerns, they were still babes in Christ (1 Cor. 3:1-2).

To measure capacity for doctrine according to the degree of one's sinful nature is a startling idea and one that would be all but impossible to put into practice on an organized basis. About the only way we could follow this pattern would be on a local church basis where there were regular face-to-face interpersonal relations. Aside from the maturity and faith-knowledge of the teacher as personal characteristics, the person would have to possess a kind of judgment akin to that of the clinician in order to adjust the level of doctrine on this basis. We now grade doctrine on almost every conceivable objective ground; age, educational attainment, informational-knowledge and maturity (used in the sense of one's capacity for handling responsibility). These objective methods reflect the church's serious misconception of faith-knowledge and our inordinate trust in informational-knowledge. These statements, of course, imply that the response to revelation is obedience to God's guidance which requires a good deal more than a person's intellectual assent. This problem will be discussed in more detail in the next lecture; at this point we simply recognize that there is a need for gradation based on human conditions other than objective measurement.

In the second wave of New Testament writing we find the same distinction being made between those who are able to understand and those who are insecure or uncertain in their commitment. For example, the material in the synoptic gospels is cast in the form of the degree of faith a person has in the messianic mission of Jesus. Faith or lack of faith in Jesus Christ is the dominant note, with a strong plea to the readers to remain faithful and to disassociate themselves from the claims of the world. To some extent this represents the problems of the second generation Christian and the growing problems within the church of maintaining an authentic conception of the person and ministry of Jesus. The disciples' feeble faith is shown as causing them to misunderstand Jesus' actions and words. The miracle of the feeding of the thousands is recorded as being misunderstood by the disciples. Later when Jesus told them to "Take heed and beware of the leaven of the Pharisees and Sadducees," the disciples thought they were being scolded because they forgot bread again, whereupon Jesus replied, "O men of little faith." He then proceeded to explain again the meaning of both the miracle of the loaves and the need for spiritual bread (Matt. 16:6-12; see also Mk.

6:52). Many parables had to be explained twice, according to the synoptic gospels. In Matthew (16:13-23) while at Caesarea Philippi Jesus is acknowledged as the Christ; it is recorded that Peter, the person to whom the revelation came, rebuked Jesus for saying that he would have to go to Jerusalem to be killed. Jesus at once attributed this statement to Satan in Peter. Later Jesus said that Peter would be sifted as wheat by Satan but that he would pray "that your faith may not fail" (Lk. 22:32). The synoptics show the disciples as confused and full of unbelief at the events of the crucifixion and resurrection, a state of affairs not remedied until Pentecost.

Growth in Christ

The gradation of doctrine according to faith-knowledge implies the concept of growth in grace, and the New Testament explicitly refers to growth. Regardless of where persons are in their stage of faith-knowledge they are expected to grow, develop and increasingly exercise their talents. This is growth in grace and knowledge of our Lord and Savior Jesus Christ (2 Pet. 3:18) and is different from the usual conception of growth found in educational literature since the development of John Dewey's philosophy. There, growth as growth is a virtue, a process that must continue. There it is linked to intellectual processes whereby the mind forms and reforms explanations of the world on an experimental basis, always striving, never completely arriving. Anyone who has observed children over a period of time can readily appreciate the interest they have in the world about them and their almost incessant "Why?" concerning the nature of the world. Moreover, the child's ability to improve skills, absorb knowledge and develop reason is so pronounced that one can easily see why this process of growth can become at once the rationale and goal of education.

But the biblical conception of growth is different in that the goal is faith-knowledge of Jesus Christ, not autonomous individuality. Furthermore, the growth expected is in certain faith-virtues which are themselves expressed in interpersonal relations, not in increasing units of measure or accomplishment. Indeed, accomplishment, the development of a personal record of achievement that becomes ever greater and more honorific (so precious to the middle and upper classes) negates the real Christian virtues. Christians cannot be proud of their humility!

Probably the normative statement of growth is in Eph. 4:7-16 where the writer indicates that all Christians have a gift of grace and that persons finds their roles according to these gifts--as prophet, pastor, teacher, etc. " . . . to equip the saints for the work of ministry, for building up the body of Christ. . . ." In this way all members of the church seek to develop the spiritual life of others. The principle is also stated in the negative saying that Christians are not to be children (immature) so that they are tossed about by any doctrine. "Rather, speaking the truth in love, we are to grow up in every way into him who is the head, into Christ. . . ."

This conception of growth in grace means a ministry of the laity in the sense that each person has a responsibility to the other. The significance of the injunction is profound in that it is the basis of our call for leadership within the church as well as an exhortation for laypeople to assume a responsibility for others. Growth always begins at the point of one's present circumstance of age, education, personal capacity and opportunity. Growth in Christ is experienced as one gives oneself to the task of helping others become Christian. In this sense, then, being a Christian educator is not optional but essential to one's own spiritual development.

Lecture 4
Response to Revelation: Obedience

We have been examining the biblical mode of revelation to see if there is a method in God's self-disclosure. My primary assumption is that the method God has used is in itself compatible with the message of faith and that, if any of our efforts to communicate the faith are to be blessed by God, they must follow this same pattern. We have implied that method is not independent of message and we have also recalled that the method itself tells us something of the nature of God.

We have been only descriptive. We have said the revelation comes to a person-in-a-situation. We have emphasized the eventful character of revelation, thus pointing out its paradoxical nature: the directness of God's communication for a specific human situation gives it compelling force that disrupts and redirects people and nations, yet the concreteness of revelation for a particular time and place creates a need for interpretation by later generations, a need that opens the gate to private speculations. We must now consider the content of revelation and indicate humanity's response to it when the revelation comes and our response today to the written record of original revelation.

Content of Revelation

The description should continue: revelation comes to a person-in-a-situation about God's will for God's people. The content of revelation is God's will. This involves the receiver of revelation, the one who discerns the voice and words of God for the situation in which one finds oneself. We have pointed out in lecture 1 that this is essentially a mystical experience, involving both the deepest strengths of motivation and the highest intellectual activity. It is real in the sense that it faces the receiver and is communicated in language one can clearly understand. It is personal in the sense that one cannot escape a decision and the consequences of being involved in a serious struggle. It is illuminating in the sense that the receiver now knows what the issues are and what must be done about them.

Describing the experience is interesting but not necessarily helpful. What is the content of this mystical experience? It is not the essence of God. Nowhere in the Bible does the receiver of revelation claim to understand the essential being of God. All we know of God is the way God acts, the way God has worked through human agents in our history. From these acts of God we infer God's essence, we suggest a description of God's character or God's attributes. What we know of God's self is very indirect. This holds true in the Old Testament and is proven by the incarnation in the New Testament. Thus, knowledge of God--knowledge that would predict how God will behave--is not possible; for God is free to act as God desires.

There are several anthropomorphic sections in Exodus where the writer gives us profound theological observations. Moses is shown in chapter 3 as having a great revelatory experience while keeping the flock of Jethro, his father-in-law. God's call for human leadership of the Hebrews comes in a recital of God's previous guidance of the Hebrews and a charge to Moses to go to Pharaoh and demand the release of the Hebrews. Moses demurs and then asks for the "name" of God so he will have authority for the task. God is recorded as saying "I am who I am" (Exod. 3:14). This name of God appears as an enigma unless we see the startling truth of revelation here. The name means God acts, is present, will be. The Hebrew language does not give us the verb tense but only the verb. The tense must be inferred from the context. The nearest word we can use to describe God is the verb "to be" in all of its forms. God is active, God is the predicate, God expresses what is said of the subject, humankind. Such a discussion, although protecting the freedom and majesty of God, is not satisfactory if left at this point. It protects God's holiness at the expense of God's concern for humanity. But as we read the record in Exodus, we discover that God is also the God of highly specific directions to Moses; and the rest of the book then proceeds to enumerate in great detail God's guidance of God's people through Moses so that they may journey toward the Promised Land.

Later Moses struggles with the person of God, asking for sight of God. God confesses fondness for Moses and counters by saying God would recount God's goodness and what God had done but God's person could not be shown. God would show God's mercy on whom God would have mercy, but God's person God would not reveal. To the insistent Moses God finally consents to walk by and let Moses see "my back" (Exod. 33:16-23). All that we ever see of God's person is God's work. In the New Testament the person of God is even more clearly protected as John states in his prologue "No one has ever seen God; the only Son, who is in the bosom of the Father, he has made him known" (Jn. 1:18; see also 1 Jn. 4:12).

If the essence of God or the person of God is not revealed, what then is the content of revelation? As already stated, it is the will of God. The biblical receivers of revelation have a commission or a mission, and they are no longer the makers of their schedule or masters of their lives. One no longer thinks of one's life as something one builds and shapes to fit one's inclinations, needs and pleasures. One now finds oneself in tension with one's surroundings because one perceives God's purpose for God's people. We have said the revelation is objective to the receiver in that it stands over against the receiver; now we add that it is objective in that the will of God is for God's people and through God's people to the world.

If revelation gave us a definition of God or an object to worship, then faith would take a major turn toward sentimentalism and ineffectiveness. Sentimentalism is enjoyment without obligation. Enjoyment can come in worship or in the recognition and response one finds in organized church life. Faith becomes sentimental if it is considered another element to enrich life, to help the individual understand the world, or to reinforce one's fluttering and uncertain ego amid conflicting pressures. These important elements of faith are by-products, not the main product, of revelation. Revelation tells what God wants a person to be and do; perhaps it is not too strong to say revelation is what God wants a person to do and thereby become. The biblical accounts are full of people who had marching orders for journeys they felt they were unprepared to make, yet in the making of the journey they found themselves strengthened. The patriarchal stories of Genesis are told in this fashion; but we must not forget that the New Testament church remembered the life of Paul and Peter in the same way. In fact, the entire list of disciples is presented in the New Testament as a group of fearful and uncertain men all during the ministry of Jesus and beyond the crucifixion scene. For our purpose here let us state that the content of revelation is objective in the sense that God is separate and different from humankind and that what God reveals is more like a plan of action than an idea. It is objective also in the sense that the content is for God's people: those who receive it receive it not for themselves but for God's people.

The individual is the agent. There is no generalized "human" as such in the Bible or elsewhere. A person is always of a time, nation and culture. Individuals are formed in their relations to the social forces which shape them, and they can live only in relation to those same social forces. In the Bible humans are the agents of God for God's people. The revelation is to Abraham for the people, to Moses for the creation of a nation, to the prophets for the instruction of a nation, to Paul for the church, and so on. Our modern method of categorizing segments of corporate life for analysis is comparatively unknown in biblical record. In the biblical record God is Lord of all of life and the writers move with ease and speed from the individual to the group or nation, for God's will was for all. The individual was the agent but the scene of activity was among the people of God.

Moreover, the word of the Lord is to direct the people of God in their mission to the world generally so that the word is objective to the people also. Perhaps this point is as frequently overlooked as the former. In the Old Testament the covenant was not something to enhance the prestige of the Hebrews; rather it was their responsibility to the world. Abraham's commission was to build a nation which would become blessed by God, but the focus of this activity was clear; for the account says "So that you will be a blessing" (Gen. 12:2). Again, toward the end of Abraham's life, God reiterates God's blessing and again follows it with the expected result, "And by your descendants shall all the nations of the earth bless themselves, because you have obeyed my voice" (Gen. 22:18). The long history of the Hebrews illustrates their restiveness at being a channel for God's grace. They sought to be great themselves, to have a kingdom and find strength in political alliances. All of these efforts failed; their kingdom was split and the whole northern half of their nation went into historical oblivion. It was always the remnant that remained faithful to God's guidance that saved them, even in exile. In the New Testament the matter is clearer, for there we have Jesus standing in judgment over the whole history of the Hebrews and offering to usher in the Kingdom of God. Paul, in Romans, chapters 9-11, traces the privileges given to Israel and also her blindness in not accepting the Messiah. The Synoptic Gospels are together in showing Jesus condemning the leaders of Israel for interpreting the covenant and the history of Israel as a blessing in itself, thereby making the Jews a holy people rather than a people for God's holy purpose. Most of the parables and direct exhortations that are contained in the last week of Jesus' life, according to the Synoptics, are teachings leveled against the leaders of Israel for misunderstanding the role of Israel in the world. Although the parable of the vineyard is not the only material of this type, it is recorded by all three Synoptic Gospels; and the meaning is clear both as to the parable itself and also as to the context in which the parable is placed--as a warning to the Pharisees and other leaders of Israel. The stone which the builders rejected is now to become the headstone of the corner (Mk. 12:1-12; see also Matt. 21:33-46 and Lk. 20:9-19).

The content of revelation is not sentimental, that is, not for personal gratification or growth, nor is it intended to make God's people a refuge from the world. The content of revelation is God's will for God's people. As indicated earlier, this means that biblical truth is seldom stated in terms of propositions that represent a timeless and unchanging body of knowledge. Passages that seem to contradict this statement would be the Ten Commandments. Yet we observe two ways in which even the Ten Commandments are conditional. First, they appear at a time when the social problem of the nation is the basis of justice. Without some principles of judgment and justice, no people can exist as a social organization. Second, within the commandments the rule is interpreted in terms of conditions that obtained in that day. The commandment, "You shall not covet. . . ." is followed by a list of things that represent the objects of envy. Few of us today have to worry about wanting our neighbor's donkey, although the problem of envy is an ever-present temptation. When we look at the Psalms, study Isaiah, or read the narratives of Israelite history, we are impressed with the Hebrews' desire to do God's will, their rejoicing in signs of blessing when they had, in part, obeyed God's will, their dismay when they did not have a clear word from the Lord, and a lingering hope of a Messiah who would make clear and straight the highway of God (Isa. 40:3).

Then the Chosen One came; we find his whole life remembered as obedience to God's will. The only childhood incident shows him pondering God's work. His opening sermon declared that Isaiah's program would be actualized in his life (See Lk. 4:16-20 and Mt. 11:2-6.). Matthew's account of Jesus' life has him setting his face steadfastly to go to Jerusalem because only there could he sacrifice his life in order to achieve his vocation (Mt. 16:21). The Garden of Gethsemane scene climaxes the inner struggle Jesus had experienced all through life as he in agony of spirit faced the cross. This is a great temptation scene at the end of his career, comparable to the three temptations at the beginning of his ministry. When Jesus started his ministry, the temptations had to do with the methods he would use in building and proclaiming the Kingdom of God. The accounts show that Jesus rejected all of the usual spectacular humanistic or political methods in favor of teaching, preaching and healing (Matt. 4:23). Now, facing the cross, he must face the temptation of the method of perpetuating his ministry. Would it be better skillfully to avoid a showdown with religious and governmental authorities in order to stay with his disciples and better train them in the affairs of God? Would his dying leave the disciples so distraught and dispirited, so fearful and ineffective, that his mission would fail? Should he just postpone the clash until he was more sure of his disciples? ". . . nevertheless, not as I will, but as thou wilt" (Matt. 26:39).

Conditions

If the focus of revelation is God's will for God's people, then another way of stating the matter would be to say the end result is Christian ethics. The evidence for this statement is overwhelming. In the Old Testament we have moral and ethical teachings on almost every page. Many events are recounted just to illustrate the moral learned from the episode. Sometimes the biblical material reads this point backwards in order to show that the disasters of an individual, David, for example, or the nation can be traced back to a breach of the moral code. In all phases of the literature of the New Testament church we have a steady and insistent demand that God's people live a holy life; very detailed instructions are given. The very form of Paul's letters shows the concern of ethical living. Even in his letters where the most abstract and profound theology is set forth, he usually concludes the letter with several chapters of exhortation for living according to the demands and example of Christ.

The Gospels, especially Matthew and Luke, present us with an ethical demand on the part of Jesus that is so severe that it has been interpreted in many ways to soften the teachings. Some scholars say Jesus' ethic was an "interim ethic" for the short time that Jesus thought remained until the close of the age. Others say it was an illustration of what the Kingdom of God would be like someday. In either case we are counseled not to assume that the vigorous ethical demands of Jesus are to be taken as a rule of life. There is, however, still another view--that the ethical demands of the Gospel as reported in the Synoptic Gospels are a true expression of God's will without any concession to human sin. This view follows the general pattern that revelation results in ethics; just as Jesus is the revelation of God, so his life and utterances are inescapably both a testimony to the true righteousness of God and, simultaneously, the judgment on humanity's relative ethics. Just as in Jesus we have in human form as much of God as is possible, so in Jesus' ethics we have in human form as much of God's will as is possible. In this sense, then, we have a glimpse of the nature of eternal ethics.

Professor John Knox, presenting the point of view just mentioned, goes further to say:

> We often misunderstand Jesus because we are constantly doing our best to avoid recognition of this fact. The righteousness of God is so far beyond our capacity to achieve that in our pride we seek to forget it. We try to deceive ourselves into thinking that we owe no more than we can pay. God's righteousness requires that we deny ourselves; that we commit ourselves unreservedly, passionately, joyously to the good of others; that we be utterly true, simple, charitable and pure, not only in deed and word but also in the secret thoughts of our hearts. But finding that we are unable or unwilling to pay the price of such righteousness, we set up standards of our

> own. Instead of an impossible self-denial we set up a practicable self-restraint; instead of active self-sacrificial good we set up a reasonable disinterestness and are content if we hold self-love or national or class self-interest within moderate bounds; instead of an impossible purity, charity, and honesty of heart we set up a decent morality. And finding such standards practicable, we try to persuade ourselves that they represent not only all that we need to ask of ourselves or that others have a right to ask of us, but also all that God demands of us.[1]

The communication of the content of revelation presents some serious problems. The most serious is the one just cited, the process of toning down the righteousness of God in order to live more comfortably with our desires. We shall examine this matter more closely in the next section of this course. Here let us look at the usual processes of communication and observe that they, too, often function as a way of avoiding the righteousness of God.

The process of communication often followed by Christian churches is to read the biblical material and then to state it in historical terms as understood and interpreted by the reader. Then the church leader will generalize this into a principle, transport the principle to the present, apply it to a common problem and exhort the auditors to live up to the principle. The content of revelation thus becomes information of a moral nature, and the motive for the spiritual life becomes an avoidance of guilt for not doing what is denied, or a feeling of pride for doing what is approved. When this happens, the crucial turn is taken to make Christianity into a religion, usually a religion that simply deifies the commonly accepted moral code of the community. This state of affairs exists because we misunderstand both the process and product of revelation.

The process of revelation demands that believers find the meaning of God in their situation, which means the peculiar and particular way life faces them in areas in which they must make decisions. For this essentially private task everyone is his/her own priest. He/she has the witness of the Bible and the affirmation of the church that through faith, he/she can find the direction his/her decisions should follow. The church leader or teacher instead of transmitting a formula or solution must in fact not do more than suggest possible solutions with the strong affirmation that God's will can be found and followed. The affirmations are about the character of God and the possibility that each person can know the reality of God.

The product of revelation is action. The resulting human action in specific situations gives it compelling power even when read thousands of years later. The product is not confined to the original situation because each situation partakes of perennial human conditions. Perhaps a formula such as this would help: to the extent that human conditions are the same, to that extent the product of revelation is transportable. For example, human sin is a perennial human condition that pervades all personal and social relations. Biblical revelation freely shows God's judgment on sinners and on sin in society. Moreover, Christ the Savior is as necessary for sinners today as he was in Palestine two thousand years ago. But even here we do not transport a principle, we seek to lead others to the Christ who is also contemporary and from this contemporary Christ we learn for ourselves anew the moral demands of the Gospel. Only in this way can ethical living be a product of the new being in Christ. Perhaps we can turn our formula around and say that the extent to which a person follows general moral principles shows the extent to which he is seeking to avoid the living Christ. This does not mean that every Christian will become a law unto themself, nor will it mean that each generation will establish an ethical norm substantively different from the biblical revelation. Christ is the same yesterday, today and forever; but God's will must be learned and actualized in each generation.

In terms of the substance of revelation we would say that the Bible is to be viewed as a laboratory manual. The Bible is an account of what people have done under various conditions in relation to God with an account both of the conditions and the result. We generalize about the nature of God from what we read. The generalizations help us form an understanding of what God would have us be and do in our situation; but, if we stop here, we have a sterile religion, a series of demands and threats of punishment the following of which makes us embittered. This is what Paul called "the law." As long as we are under law, we cannot know the Gospel. The law can, however, as in Paul's case, be the schoolmaster that leads us to Christ. We must not stop with the generalization about God's will as it has been revealed to others; but in the structure of meaning supplied by them we must find God for ourselves. Or, to state the matter differently and perhaps more satisfactorily, past revelation should be the object of our contemplation, not to prove or disprove it; but such contemplation will enable us to see the power and direction of God in order that our minds may be shaped by the experiences others have had and that our hearts may be filled with expectation of God's possibilities for us.

Obedience

Since God's revelation is a plan of action and a quality of life, the response is obedience. This characteristic of biblical faith makes it unique among world religions. The primary obligation is not worship, prayers, personal religious exercises, nor philanthropy; yet all of these things follow when one submits oneself to the spirit of God and in humble contrition realizes sincerely one's own inadequacy due to one's own sin and one's own possibilities in Christ. We might detail the meaning of obedience with the following three points:

1. A response, not a virtue. The response of obedience is not a virtue. Just as we have misunderstood the Gospel by generalizing it into morals, so we have continued the misunderstanding when we suggest that being a Christian is a virtue. When we do this, we automatically seek to develop virtue; we thereby move the whole matter of Christian faith into the realm of human effort and make it the subject of our pride. The only authentic attitude we can have toward a virtue is pride. "God, I thank thee that I am not like other men. . . ." (Luke 18:11) becomes the inevitable prayer of virtue. There are, of course, Christian virtues; however, these are developed not as ends in themselves but as by-products of a relationship with God. Too often we take the parable of the talents (Luke 19:12-26) and use it to teach the need for persons to exploit their own gifts. Actually, the whole parable is cast into the form of a nobleman-servant relation; the money, which was increased by skillful investments, was still the nobleman's money while the reward for service was more responsibility for the servant. The reward of being a prophet is the opportunity of being righteous (Matt. 10:4-41).

A response is by definition a result of stimulation, a reaction to an action. It involves the total person: thought, word, deed. The person responds to God's revelation through the agency of the Bible, a church or an individual. A response is specific. Each stimulation brings a new, but not necessarily different, response. This is why persons of faith increasingly seek the means of grace--prayer, worship, sacrament--because they want and need new stimulation from the divine source of life. Indeed, the stimulation and response leaves a residue of trust, a catalogue of activities completed, of battles won, of temptations overcome, of persons helped; but this is a history and not an honor roll. It is more accurate to say that a person of faith has a history, rather than a stylized nature; and the history itself is not for glory but is a reminder of God's guidance and protection. The Apostle Paul on several occasions gave an account of his difficulties and personal struggle, both to reinforce his own faith and as an illustration to his readers of God's possibilities with humanity (2 Cor. 11:21-12:13). If we want to make a judgment about the quality of a person's faith, we would need to assay its history. God judges on the basis of obedience rather than on the basis of achievement, or what the New Testament often refers to as the "outward" man. Paul states it in this fashion:

> We destroy arguments and every proud obstacle to the knowledge of God, and take every thought captive to obey Christ, being ready to punish every disobedience, when your obedience is complete. Look at what is before your eyes. If any one is confident that he is Christ's let him remind himself that as he is Christ's, so are we. (2 Cor. 10:5-7a).

2. A commitment, not an ideal. Obedience is a commitment to Jesus Christ and not an ideal. We would prefer that Christianity be an idea or an ideal. Then we could think about God and decide whether we believed the idea adequate or inadequate, personal or abstract, near or far, beneficial or demanding, and so on. We come into this error quiet naturally because we are schooled in rational procedures, in cause and effect relations. This is scientific thinking which has been applied so beneficially to the natural world about us. If that mental process has been so successful and measurable with the natural world, why should it not apply to God? The reason is that God is not an object like other objects in the world. The Bible assumes the existence of God's ability to transcend the natural world and penetrate our minds. According to biblical understanding of God, God is not in the world; God created the world. Biblical humanity does not stand in neutral reasoning about God and then shift into gear according to one's decision. Biblical humanity is either believer or nonbeliever. One may deal with the most abstract ideas about God, but one does so in terms of one's prime commitment to God; Job, after his horrible personal miseries and his searching

searching questions about evil could say, "Behold, he will slay me; I have not hope; yet I will defend my ways to his face. . . ." (Job 13:15). The classical definition of theology is "faith seeking understanding"--and note that faith has priority.

The formulation used by many churches as the irreducible minimum of belief for a basis of membership is the phrase "Jesus Christ is Lord and Savior." He is Lord first and then he becomes Savior. Paul used the phrase: "Jesus is Lord and Christ." He cannot become our savior until we allow him to become Lord; for Lord means we are in submission to his will, we are willing to renounce our dependence on the world. Until that happens, we cannot experience Jesus as the Christ. In Jesus as Lord we have the one who exercises judgment and guidance and this experience is prior to Jesus as Savior wherein we find reconciliation and grace. How different this is from much teaching that is labeled Christian today! Often the contemporary church leader presents Jesus only as Savior, as divine, yet ever willing and eager to save. This is not an incorrect presentation of God; but it is incomplete, and if left incomplete, it gives a dangerously false picture of God. Jesus as Savior, or as Savior and only incidentally as Lord, produces sentimental faith, cheap grace, ineffective knowledge because it is subjective, inward, and is used primarily as an antidote to a person's guilt. It turns the whole process of faith inward, domesticates it within the problem context of the individual, and thereby reduces to a minimum a person's concern for and interest in the world of events about them. When Jesus is domesticated within us only as Savior, we then begin to judge Jesus on the basis of how well he handles our tensions, our physical diseases and our fortunes. Although many biblical illustrations could be cited, perhaps the most familiar one is the Apostle Paul who, in a frank autobiographical statement, describes how he sought the Lord thrice to have a disease cured. He did not have his prayer answered according to his desire but rather was given grace to live with his disease. This is the authentic biblical relation to God; it is a commitment to Jesus as Lord and Savior, so that our will is first placed in submission to Christ's will and then our life and destiny is organized and expressed around that dominant centrality--Christ.

3. A life, not an achievement. The response of obedience is a life, not a deed or series of actions. All along we have been saying that the result of revelation is Christian ethical action, but by that we mean that there are overt, socially-oriented deeds which flow from one's faith-

knowledge of God. Actually, one way of escaping the demands of a God-directed life is to submerge oneself into a feverish round of activity that has the approval of the church. Doing the work of the church, one will feel, is surely a proof to others and reassurance to oneself that God is being served. So we are again confronted with a strange ambiguity. We must see the need of our obedience resulting in action, yet the action by itself cannot be a measure of obedience. One of the biblical figures of speech is the injunction that the believer is to be an epistle, ". . . known and read by all" (2 Cor. 3:2).

To be a "living letter" is a rather telling metaphor. Paul is addressing himself specifically to the matter of how the Corinthians are to know that they have an authentic word from God. He makes his case not on an authority that is conveyed by those in authority but by the words that are written in their hearts by the spirit of Christ. Their life was to be both a response to God and a proof that God had been with them. More fundamental than any activity was the Christ in their heart who gave meaning and direction to their whole existence and coming death.

Perhaps nowhere in the ordinary life of the church do we need this simple but difficult word of interpretation more than in our educational activities. Church leaders, desperate for voluntary teachers and youth group leaders, often appeal to prospective helpers with a motivation based on the virtue of church activity. The logic advanced is that since the church is "for" God, her activities are Godly and a special value is inherent in giving one's time and ability in church-sponsored projects. This should be, and may be, true, but by no means is it always true. In fact, if prospective leaders accept an assignment on the basis of the "good" that they are going to do, it is rather clear that they are serving to develop institutional and organizational health; their orientation is basically secular--secular in that they are interpreting the church as a producer of "good character," an essential ingredient for the stability of social order. The church, rather than being the fellowship of the redeemed and the seekers after God's will, becomes the temple in which the culturally defined "good" is worshipped and served.

If this point is stated too bluntly, then recall how often church leaders in seeking volunteers to staff the church's activity will use, often unconsciously, various ways to appeal to the prospect's feeling of guilt. They will say, "The church needs you" or "Please don't let the church down" or "This won't take much time and you owe it to the church." Stated thus, prospects feel that they should comply with the request and they probably do feel better about their religion. By doing church-approved things, their guilt is assuaged; yet they have not had to face the demands of the living Christ who wants their hearts and then their service, rather than their service in place of their affection.

In the broader scene we often observe that denominations and administrative subdivisions thereof formulate an educational program and then say overtly or covertly through the administrative personnel that this program is Christian education. With denominational blessing and vigorous administrative support the program becomes the goal of church activity. The same process of motivation is used--a feeling of guilt is generated if churches do not accept the "program" or, contrariwise, they feel that by following the program they will achieve spiritual success. When any educational program, prepared and packaged at a distance in time and space, is followed as a goal, then church activity has superseded growth in grace as the goal of the Christian faith. A packaged and prepared educational program may be useful, even indispensable, but only if it is considered as resource material to help people to develop their spiritual life.

Notes

1 John Knox, *Jesus, Lord and Christ* (New York: Harper, 1958) 110. Used by permission of the publisher.

Lecture 5
Residue of Revelation: Faith-Knowledge

Christian knowledge stands as a way station between faith and practice. Unfortunately, it is often unexamined, and for that reason we lose our way in trying to help others develop their spiritual life. This is due to a fundamental antipathy between humans and God. Humans would rather not face the demands of obedience, yet one wants to appear righteous; one can achieve this by making Christian knowledge something manageable, something that justifies oneself and at the same time appears to serve God. Incidentally, this mechanism of using a theory of religious knowledge to avoid the real demands of faith is not peculiar to Christianity but is common in other religions. Let us take two examples to show how misconceptions of knowledge reveal a fundamental misunderstanding of faith and how in each case a mechanism is at work to derail one's relationship to God.

First consider those who use faith as primarily cognitive, that is, composed of information, concepts and reason. Although those who hold this view may participate in the full round of Church activity, they approach faith cognitively and expect to settle matters of faith by the same process. They want concepts clarified, information logically arranged, and theology to be systematically developed. Since faith to them is primarily intellectual, they tend to believe that only methods that are verbal and rational are appropriate, such as lectures, discussions, sermons, or historical and linguistic studies. Jesus met a number of people who held this view, perhaps the most familiar is reported by Luke concerning a lawyer (Luke 10:25-37). The lawyer asked point blank, "What shall I do to inherit eternal life?" and Jesus replied by requesting a summary of the law. The lawyer immediately summed it correctly by saying it is love to God and neighbor as self. Jesus concurred in the lawyer's position but added, "Do this, and you will live." This reply should have ended the encounter. The lawyer had the correct cognitive position: Jesus had said that if he would make his answer operative in life, it would be complete knowledge. At this point the mechanism of avoidance comes in, for the lawyer "desiring to justify himself" said, "And who is my neighbor?" Love to God he had already intellectualized and could handle with his mind; now his problem was to clarify a concept--neighbor--so that too could be intellectualized and controlled. His approach was cognitive, that is, religion is a mental activity that helps one justify oneself; that is why he had to get clearly in mind the boundary of neighborly responsibility. Once that boundary was established, he could depend on his mind to control his obligations. But Jesus did not allow the lawyer to escape into his mind, for the story of the good Samaritan was so vivid and compelling in simplicity that the lawyer saw at once that only the Samaritan showed mercy on the one who fell among thieves. The problem was not the definition of neighbor but the practice of mercy. In the context of the story we can say that mercy is equal to love. Jesus was helping the lawyer understand that knowledge of love is both cognitive and relational; indeed, it is not one without the other. Until he could learn the meaning of love he could not understand God. Thus the lawyer's whole life was in disarray. His mechanism of avoidance kept him from God and, therefore, from knowing that he could live in relation to God only by God's grace. We do not know what happened to the lawyer. If he learned the meaning of love, he then stopped trying to justify himself, seeing that it is impossible; and he threw himself on the mercy of God. If he did this, he then had faith-knowledge of God; if not, he would continue to make cognitive statements, perhaps becoming even more accurate in his recitation of religious information.

Second, consider those who believe that faith is primarily precept. Whether they articulate their views or not, they believe the substance of faith is conduct which is expressed either in a style of worship or a certain code of behavior or both. Christian knowledge is equal to a code of behavior; therefore, they look with favor on methods of communication that condition people effectively to a form of worship or behavior pattern that conforms to the code. This is usually accomplished by beginning the training--training is a good word here--early in the child's life or by various disciplines, including the use of force or the withholding of affection. Jesus met this kind of person also.

Perhaps Matthew's Gospel gives more clear-cut illustrations because it is in part oriented against the formalism of the Pharisees. After the Sermon on the Mount Matthew records a group of healing miracles, and then in chapter 9 we find Jesus forgiving the sin of the palsied man. At once the scribes said he blasphemed. A few verses later on Jesus, eating with publicans and sinners, was challenged because he had broken the Pharisees' code of behavior. They believed that in order to maintain one's purity one must keep oneself separate from sinners. Jesus' answer to them turned again on the substance of faith, for he said, "Go and learn what this means, 'I desire mercy, and not sacrifice. . . .'" (Matt. 9:13). After the disciples were selected and had begun their ministry, Jesus on the Sabbath day gathered food for them (chapter 12). At once he was challenged for breaking the Sabbath laws; after answering the Pharisees Jesus again summarizes the problem by saying, "And if you had known what this means, 'I desire mercy, and not sacrifice,' you would not have condemned the guiltless" (Matt. 12:7). A few verses later on Jesus deliberately healed a man's hand in their synagogue. This was too much for the Pharisees. Matthew then records (verse 14) that the Pharisees held a council as to how they might kill him. As the conflict sharpened, the Jerusalem Pharisees delivered a formal charge: "Why do your disciples transgress the tradition of the elders? For they do not wash their hands when they eat" (Matt. 15:2). After making all necessary allowances for the anti-pharisaïcal character of Matthew, including the bitter condemnation of them in chapter 23, we still have clearly before us the picture of the type of person who sees the substance of faith in a code. Since we do not have many of the specific behavior patterns of the Pharisees, we are fooled into thinking we may not have their propensity for avoiding obedience by dodging behind a code. However, if one tries to change some specific behavior pattern of contemporary Christians--say in relation to other races or faiths--one will discover that the reaction is often as sharp and as drastic as that taken by the Pharisees against Jesus.

Note that we have termed the two notions, Christian knowledge as concept or precept, inadequate. It is important to say "inadequate" because they are not false unless they become normative. Faith, as we shall see, has a cognitive feature; and certainly we shall expect faith to be expressed in codes of behavior that regulate our interpersonal relations. Jesus did not condemn the intellectualism of the lawyer nor the Pharisees' zeal to lead a good life; rather, he showed them mercy was a prior condition, sentiment, or disposition. Indeed, Matthew set the matter in perspective by saying of the Pharisees that they were meticulously careful of their tithing but "have neglected the weightier matters of the law, justice and mercy and faith; these you ought to have done, without neglecting the others" (Matt. 23:23).

Christian Experience

The two examples we have used to show inadequate conceptions of Christian knowledge had each been corrected by Jesus to inculcate first the love of God and then other facets of Christian knowledge. To make the Christian affirmation clear we would say that the love of God is demonstrated in Jesus Christ. The nature of love is to create, heal, guide and protect. God sent God's Son by the impulse of love to redeem humankind and to restore fellowship with God, to provide guidance for God's way of life, and to protect God's own from the effects of evil. So to know God we know Jesus Christ. This knowing is experiential, that is, it partakes of our whole being and leaves as a residue not information but affirmation of trust. The natural ejaculation of the Christian is " . . . I know whom I have believed, and I am sure that he is able to guard until that Day what has been entrusted to me" (2 Tim. 1:12).

This affirmation of trust is not the sentimental pietism which grasps at the Gospel in order to secure reassurance of guidance and a guarantee against the unknown beyond the portal of death. This affirmation of trust is stated in the Matthew passage above (Matt. 23:23) as judgment and mercy.

The person who knows Christ first experiences the judgment of God; and then he/she understands and clings to the mercy of God in Christ because through judgment he/she knows he/she has no claim on God's favor. Thus we must learn that Jesus is Lord and then Christ.

The first statement we can make about Christian knowledge is that it is highly personal: in the nature of a commitment, following the uncertain path that leads one to decide one thing rather than another, to open oneself in one direction and close oneself in another. Perhaps it would be clearer to say the first and most fundamental statement we can make about Christian knowledge is that it is certainty of our relationship to God--certainty not in the sense that life becomes clear and agony of soul subsides. This is what piety seeks. No, it is certainty of one's relationship to God so that one feels that the areas of life over which one has control and influence will be subject to God's will and that growth in grace and knowledge will proceed as Christ becomes more manifest in one's life. One, in fact, starts a new journey under new management toward a new destiny. All one can say here is the "I believe." Jesus Christ then becomes the object of our desire for grace and knowledge; and he becomes intertwined with our experience and thought so that we like the Apostle Paul begin a Christ-orientation expressed by Paul by the phrase "in Christ." Christian knowledge in the usual sense of declaratory statements results from our particular experiences with Christ as we face situations, make decisions and live out our destiny. This declaratory knowledge is the result of one's experience with Christ and is therefore subsidiary or derived; as such it is held and explained more tentatively than the basic affirmation that Jesus Christ is Lord and Savior. The Christian experience should, for clarity, be labeled "faith-knowledge."

Faith-Knowledge

Faith-knowledge, as John Calvin so well described at the beginning of his *Institutes*, begins with self-knowledge.[1] Calvin used the term wisdom to describe the understanding one comes to have of oneself in relation to God. Until one knows oneself as "fallen" creature (prone to sin, arrogant, with one's meager knowledge of the world grasping for political or social power over others, boastful in minor achievements and evasive of one's brother's need), one has no need of God. Such a "natural" human may be religious, even a church member, but he/she does not have faith-knowledge of God because he/she feels no need of God. Such religion as he/she has is used to calm his/her restlessness occasioned by guilt or to buttress anxiety occasioned by threats of loss of power or by fear of death.

How then do we achieve faith-knowledge? This is accomplished by seeing first the true nature of our plight before God, by learning that only through God's mercy can we ever hope to be received in God's favor, by finding out that only in service to God's will can we ever fulfill our true destiny. Therefore, we can say that our feeling of guilt and our consciousness of sin are the first signs of God's grace, the first indications that within ourselves we do not have salvation or a dependable future. So, in God's judgment we experience God's grace. Until we are ready for judgment, we cannot experience mercy. Until we know mercy, as Jesus indicated to those who regarded religion as primarily concept or precept, we cannot know God. Moreover this relationship is to God. We can never see our sin and our need when comparing ourselves to others. Paul called this "hardness of the heart" (Eph. 4:18); more specifically to the Corinthians (2 Cor. 10:12) he said when men compare themselves among themselves they are "not wise," that is, will never achieve true knowledge of God. It is only when we take a long sober realistic look deep within that we see our limitations of power, wisdom and virtue.

True, self-knowledge leads to faith-knowledge which is first, repentance; second, forgiveness; third, obedience. The experience of repentance is a self-shattering experience that causes one to open oneself to the leading of God's spirit. The whole matter is a therapy for one's past, a freeing of oneself from the bondage of one's sin, and the opening to a new future for which one begins to rebuild one's life. Such an experience within oneself is not the same despair of life that is currently proposed by existentialist thinkers. They, too, see through humanity's innate self-righteousness, humanity's inordinate posture of pride that leads to all manner of tragic situations--all the way from incompatibility between adults to war and tyranny. Although keen in their analysis, they usually conclude that life has no exit, is absurd, or that suicide is heroic. Their picture of life is powerful and has gripped the mind of postwar humanity because it is deadly accurate; they see beneath the facade of individual and society.

Pious Christians are revolted by the nihilism and vulgarity of many existentialist thinkers, but this is because piety seeks to repress the very elements in life that the existentialist sees so clearly. Faith, on the contrary, comes to grips with the power structure of society, the lusts of the flesh, arrogance of the pride-puffed mind or the prudential justice of a society that serves only the immediate demands of those in authority. One reason the Bible does not lose its urgency and appeal is that it describes persons of faith battling in concrete situations against these forces that come out of our sinful condition, a warfare in which everyone is engaged today. Although the Christian and the existentialist see and understand the depth of human misery, the existentialist who has no God can see only the "nothingness" of life or its absurdity because he/she makes his/her view of humanity a general principle that concludes the story of humankind. The Christian's self-knowledge produces sorrow; but it leads to repentance and in this way sorrow is a prelude to, or a part of, faith--the beginning of a new being in Christ.

The works of Friedrich Dürrenmatt are an illustration of the current existentialist's profound understanding of the human self. In *The Visit* he shows humanity's selfishness and greed overcoming the thin facade of civilization and decency. The story has many important facets that should not be overlooked; but, in short, it tells of a rich woman's return to her native village which is poverty-stricken. Since she has given handsome gifts to other villages, the citizens of Gullen expect her to be lavish in her gift to them. It soon develops that she does offer them a magnificent sum, half for the village and half to be divided per capita, when one of their popular and lovable citizens Anton is dead. It is shown that she had an affair with this man, Anton, years ago, and as a result was driven out of town. Now she is back for revenge. Scandalized at first, the village rallies to Anton, but slowly the processes of greed infect the village. Without wishing Anton harm they buy on credit. Now every villager has a legacy in waiting. Then their minds begin to reason as follows: "Well, Anton did wrong and we believe in justice. . . ." May we add that in the end Anton is legally executed? One can hardly find a clearer exposition of personal and corporate sin than is found in *The Visit*. There is, however, no savior.

In his detective stories such as *The Judge and his Hangman* or *The Pledge* we find Dürrenmatt exploring evil and the senselessness of justice. Here one sees clearly portrayed the self-righteousness of officialdom. In these cases the bureaucratic police, almost uninterested in justice and truth as they operate to stay in office, fill out the stereotyped roles expected of them. But there is a justice in the old detective who operates alone and without official favor as he endlessly and intelligently pursues the evil one. At the end of the two stories there is an ironic twist of plot wherein the detective is right in his hunches and methods but by quirk of circumstances unable to know he was right or having to punish the evil one for something he did not do. Here helter-skelter senseless justice is accepted as normal because the writer seems to have no sense of divine judgment. However, the writer shows with penetrating skill the corruption that is deep within humans and the forces of fate that shape their life.

Nature of Faith-Knowledge

The beginning of faith-knowledge, we have said, is a self-knowledge, but a self-knowledge, as Paul expresses it (2 Cor. 7:10) that is sorrow "For godly grief produces a repentance that leads to salvation and brings no regret, but worldly grief produces death." If the beginning of faith-knowledge is in the need of the self, then we might infer that faith-knowledge is more like the knowledge we have of ourselves than it is analogous to any other kind of human knowledge. Perhaps the following six statements will help to describe the nature of faith-knowledge as it arises in and has its validity in the self.

1. Faith knowledge is personal. We know ourselves as unique, a combination of facts as to age, sex, color, etc. functioning within our range of ambitions, skills, desires and fears. Regardless of what we learn or experience from others, we are uniquely our own and what we accept from others we interpret and use to suit our sentiments. So with faith-knowledge we receive guidance from parents and mentors, ideas from literature and information from history including biblical material; but what we accept is peculiarly our own. This we believe and defend. Faith-knowledge is characterized by inner determination because it is part of ourselves, both as an interpretation of the meaning of our life and as the giving of our life to that meaning.

2. Faith-knowledge is real, but also ambiguous. Our knowledge of ourself is real in the sense that it is the vehicle of our consciousness, yet we are far from understanding ourselves, our motivations and our actions. We love ourselves, yet we often rage against ourselves in self-depreciation. Our emotions cause us to act or speak before our

conscious thoughts can control them. We cannot always explain our conduct to ourselves. Even when we know why we dislike a person, we continue to dislike them. We have come slowly into self-consciousness after we are born, and we will probably lose self-consciousness before we die. So consciousness of God's grace in Jesus Christ comes after we are aware of the whole world of human affairs; indeed, we cannot know God until we are aware of our human finitude. Faith-knowledge when it comes is so real it transforms our lives and charges us with new purposes, yet we are plagued with old doubts. It seems that the new awareness of God's presence brings peace and a sword, confidence and a new dependence. Some problems are solved and new problems are defined. Old fears vanish, but apprehension of being acceptable to God emerges. We become more certain of our personal equipment for life's struggle and less clear as to some of the places we must fight the good fight.

3. Faith-knowledge transcends the self. One of the chief characteristics of self-knowledge is our ability to transcend--to stand outside ourselves, so to speak, and judge our own actions. Indeed, many hours, both awake and asleep--especially asleep--are spent judging, evaluating and shaping our lives. This results in self-praise, justification or blame, regardless of decision. We are painfully aware of this uniquely human trait. Faith-knowledge likewise has the facility to stand apart from itself and offer commendation, reproof, or correction. Perhaps it would be more accurate to say that faith-knowledge brings into a person's life a new orientation for conscience so that one now has a more complicated inner life than ever before. Faith-knowledge causes one to reevaluate the contents of one's conscience and slowly to replace it with a new or at least different set of values. This sounds very easy. Actually, it is so painful that most Christians shrink from the hard, arduous self-transformation that is needed by letting some agency outside the self, the church or a minister, become the guardian and the spokesperson for the Christ of judgment.

4. Faith-knowledge is subject to human distortion. Our self is prone to protect itself by rationalizing its actions as right actions. It tries to develop a good reputation for itself in every situation. But what we dislike and criticize in others we often practice secretly. Stubbornness in others is, in us, firmness and clarity of conviction. We know these things about ourselves in our sober and reflective moments. Moreover, we are not in complete control of ourselves. Anger breaks out at

inappropriate moments, or by a slip of the tongue we reveal what we are trying to conceal. Even the non-Christian understands the pathetic cry of Paul, "For I do not do the good I want, but the evil I do not want is what I do. . . . (Rom. 7:19) Faith-knowledge is never clear or powerful enough to eliminate human distortions. We therefore find our faith-knowledge in God corroded with the acid of selfish pride. The most virile form of pride is spiritual pride; all through the Bible we have God's sharp word of judgment against those who boast of their spiritual attainments. The self's apathy toward God is such that it will seek to change knowledge of God into something cognitive or moral as previously indicated, in order to allow the self to slip into the comfortable situation of appearing to be religious yet continuing its regular mode of life. Even the best faith-knowledge one has is corrupted with one's sin and bound to one's culture; and it is for these reasons one person must be careful not to interpret knowledge of God as normative for another. One must, however, testify to what God has done in and through one's self, but this is a different matter from making one's knowledge of God normative for others.

5. Faith-knowledge is attained in relationship to others. The self is developed and understood within relationships with others. A person does not attain self-knowledge notionally. A very important reason why so much of our self-knowledge is ambivalent and nonrational is because we obtained it through others. We formed our image of ourselves through parents, friends, relatives and playmates. Parents and others who were close to us through infancy and childhood left their life in ours by the way they treated us. Much of our self-image has been introjected by others. Several explanations are offered which may partially explain this phenomenon. One is that while young we are without experience, without a basis of making judgments, so we would really have to accept what adults offer since there is no viable alternate. Also, we love our parents as well as fear them; and in our dependence we identify our well-being with theirs, accepting and incorporating their view of us as true. Perhaps the more philosophical analysis is true, that one knows oneself only in company with others, because only with another person does one find resistance--that is, another will; and one must adjust to that person. Without a world of people one would not distinguish oneself from nature. Whatever the reasons, we come to ourselves in relations as persons and our self-image is built out of this activity. Faith-knowledge surely comes from other people and the written experience of people in

the past. We have no other means of transmitting the affirmations of God's love, nor any other means by which we can see the result of God's guidance. Again a paradox: obtaining the preconditions of faith-knowledge relationally explains its power, for it is conducted by powerfully human emotions of love and guidance, from mature active adults to inexperienced receptive children. This also explains its possible corruption from one generation to another. Once the preconditions of faith-knowledge are present and Christ becomes the subject of faith and service, then the Christian continues in the faith relationally to Christ. In a real sense incarnation is God's own authentication of a communication of faith through a person. The Protestant has insisted that one's faith is in Christ and only in relation to him do we find redemption and spiritual health.

6. Faith-knowledge involves the whole person. Today, it is a truism to regard persons in their wholeness. Psychosomatic medicine has found many close, if not inseparable, relations between one's body with its diseases and one's mental and emotional condition. Even when a person has a purely physical problem, such as a broken leg, we must remember that it is always a certain person's broken leg and never a "broken leg case." We subdivide the person's physical, mental, emotional and spiritual areas for analysis; the divisions are becoming less meaningful. The word "self" is used in this lecture to mean a person's wholeness within the conscious being. This is the way we view ourselves even if we do not understand the inner relation of parts of our being. If I feel "good," I feel "good" all over and express it in words, smile, gesture, lilt of voice, spontaneity of spirit, etc. Faith-knowledge likewise involves the whole being. If knowledge of God involves only the mind or moral practices, it is a mechanism of avoidance and does not represent faith. The whole person is sorry for sin and the whole person responds to forgiveness. In this the ancient Hebrews, lacking modern medical knowledge or vocabulary, identified feeling with the parts of the body, for they knew the heart was sensitive to fear and joy, the stomach to disgust and challenge, and so on. They often used these inner organs to express the wholeness that existed in a person's body. There is no abstract human or human whose parts are abstracted from their being. The only human we ever know is of a certain race, color, age, sex and living within certain describable conditions. Although we abstract ideas about humans from their condition, we must remember that these

abstractions are never real unless they have their residence within a person.

Areas of Growth in Faith-Knowledge

Growth in faith-knowledge is growth of the self in relation to God and by reason of the activity of God's spirit. This may be detailed more explicitly in the following areas of one's life.

First, the self moves to expand the areas in which Christ is Lord. We do not become more humble; that is impossible. We do, however, begin to see that our finitude and modesty must extend to our minds, our myriad interpersonal relations, or possessions, etc. In fact, the struggle to conquer pride will never be successful, perhaps should not be successful, but we will become wiser in our own conceit. After all, there is pride lurking behind the passage "If your enemy is hungry, give him bread to eat; and if he is thirsty, give him water to drink; for you will heap coals of fire on his head, and the Lord will reward you" (Prov. 25:21-22. See also Rom. 12:20). Pride is so close or so much a part of self-identity that we cannot destroy pride without destroying the citadel of self-determination and strength. But pride's energy can, under the tutelage of God's spirit, be shifted from self-enhancement to glory in the service of God's reign. Another example is in interpersonal relations. We are instructed by our Lord to forgive; and in Christ's prayer offered to the disciples as a model we pray "forgive us our debts as we forgive. . . ." This conditional aspect of forgiveness is shocking to those who want an easy religion. It was to the disciples; they asked, "How often shall my brother sin against me, and I forgive him? As many as seven times?" Jesus' answer was "Seventy times seven." That is, forgiveness was not an act that could be completed, but an attitude that was to be expressed over and over again (Matt. 18:21-35). There is absolutely no doubt about Jesus' teaching on forgiveness, for he followed the reply to Peter with the parable of the unforgiving servant who was severely punished for not forgiving. Also, the only recorded comment Jesus made about the model prayer is recorded in Matthew 6:14-15 as a promise that, if we forgive, God will forgive and as a threat that, if we do not forgive, God will not forgive. As long as there is life, there is unexplored or unconquered territory in the soul, subject to growth or new response to the Lordship of Christ.

Second, the self becomes more attuned to the leading of God's spirit. Just as there is a personal antipathy to God, so there is social resistance to God. We are not at this point concerned about the source of this social pressure to avoid God's claim. Perhaps it comes from the collective individual resistance to God, or it may be that organized society creates conditions such as law for justice, force for control or defense, and obedience to authority to insure safety that generates a style of life inimical to the kingdom of God. Regardless of cause, there is an enormous social pressure to conform to the existing state, not only in political theory but in social practice. Moreover, the close-knit group within society (be it the family, community or subcultural unit) presents, maintains and often enforces a code of conduct that is given absolute authority. One comes into conscious selfhood in some constellation of social forces and these constitute normalcy for oneself. By these norms a person is judged as to emotional balance, integrity, skill, intelligence--yes, even sanity. Needless to say, no human society comes very close to the New Testament description of the Kingdom of God, although some societies that provide personal freedom, protection of diverse social philosophies, processes for orderly change in government, liberty of conscience, approach the ideal more than restrictive tyrannical societies. The individual, starting Christian life at whatever age, begins with an inventory of attitudes, reaction patterns and modes of conduct that are all subject to correction or revision by the Holy Spirit. Here is the second area where one must grow in grace and knowledge, and the task is so formidable and the inventory of socially given patterns so stubborn that people are sometimes counselled by the church that this is not an area where change must be made. This bit of advice would have shocked the Apostle Paul but, of course, would have delighted the silversmiths of Ephesus (Acts 19:24-29) or the Judaizers--those who insisted that a person must be ceremonially a Jew first, before one could become a Christian--at the council of Jerusalem (Acts 15).

Result of Growth in Faith-Knowledge

The result of growth in faith-knowledge is trust in God. One gains more confidence in one's own worth as a person and more of a sense of responsibility for the human situation in which one finds oneself. Out of the experiences of one's life one finds meaning and significance, a glory that flows from a "well done, good and faithful servant" rather than a series of achievements of which one is the master.

Such a result of growth in faith-knowledge is extremely difficult to see, much less to pursue. All of our training is against it. We have come of age while science and the scientific method of thinking have dominated the whole social order; also, they have given us so many gifts of healing, production, pleasure, and have so reduced toil, pain and fear of famine that we can hardly conceive of any other kind of knowledge. Moreover, society, responding to industrialization and urbanization, has increasingly felt the forces of life under rational control. This does not mean that war will cease or social conflict will diminish, but it does mean that we increasingly give ourselves to a rational scheme of social control through economic controls, retirement plans, social security, life insurance, etc. Thus, there is compounded in our struggle with physical and social life an inevitable reliance on information and reason. Bathed in such an environment, we instantly assume that knowledge of God is likewise something we can accumulate, manipulate, and use for prediction and control in the same way we use other data. This assumption must be examined explicitly to show the radical difference between faith-knowledge and knowledge of the world.

First, faith-knowledge cannot be stockpiled. We can accumulate a stockpile of religious encyclopedias, concordances, all matter of information about God; this can be collated, processed through business machinery, or taught to parents. But this is not true of faith-knowledge. There is growth in faith-knowledge as pointed out, but it is not a pyramiding of knowledge--it is a living of God's will in concrete situations. The result is not a pile of knowledge that becomes more refined but a history of what happened after the Holy Spirit came upon the apostles and led them.

Second, faith-knowledge cannot be transferred. Information and reason can be taught in all the standard ways. Just as knowledge of history can be transferred and interpreted, so the history of the Church can be transmitted and the receiver can demonstrate by test or recitation that one knows the chain of events. But faith-knowledge must be an active, conscious work of the receiver so that one is in one's own life actualizing the Christ and not simply accepting what someone else declares Christ to be. Inability to transfer faith-knowledge to another does not mean that I do not communicate faith. I can be an agent for testifying what God has done in, for, and with my life and I can yearn that others have this experience. I may use my particular life situation as illustrative material but not as the substance of faith. For me the struggle may be to forgive a brother in circumstances that are unique to me; in someone else the object of forgiveness may be an unfaithful business associate.

Third, faith-knowledge cannot be easily verified. Certainly we cannot equate faith-knowledge with overt signs such as church membership or public espousal of Christian projects or morality. The New Testament warns over and over again against such easy methods of determining a person's faith. On the other hand, we cannot say that some verification is impossible; for there is an outworking of the spirit so that we can observe the changes and growth that take place within one who yields one's life to Christ and seeks to find and follow God's will. Perhaps verification of the growth of faith-knowledge is best discerned by a sensitive and mature observer who, like the physician, knows from experience what to seek and how to judge, yet holding all judgments tentative because growth in grace can continue.

Fourth, faith-knowledge is not closely correlated with cognitive capacity or training. There is, of course, a basic minimum mental ability needed to function as a human being, but beyond that we cannot say that innate capacity or formal educational training correlates closely with faith-knowledge. An illiterate person can be a Christian; so can a highly trained intellectual.

Relation of Cognition to Faith-Knowledge

Jesus, when asked to point out the greatest commandment said, "You shall love the Lord your God with all your heart, and with all your soul, and with all your mind" (Matt. 22:37). Moreover, Jesus used reason to reinterpret the law and the sharpest type of critical thinking to oppose the Pharisees. The whole person, we have said, must respond. The growth in grace proceeds laterally into all parts of the person. Earlier, we also said reason does not lead us to God, nor does the development of one's cognitive apparatus automatically have a direct bearing on the quality of one's faith. These essentially negative statements are to clear the air of gross reliance on reason or informational knowledge for the spiritual life.

Mind is a general term for a person's intellectual processes. For analytical purposes these might be divided into two general areas: *cognition*, which includes reason, knowing, perceiving, and *orexis* which includes feeling, striving and wishing. The latter is usually thought of as the area of the mind most concerned with the moral and religious life. This division is artificial and must not be thought of as a clear-cut boundary or section. Rather, the mind in its total functioning displays features distinct enough to label; and we are at this time seeking to determine the role of cognition in faith-knowledge, in understanding and communicating the Christian Gospel.

First, cognition helps us understand the Christian faith. This is done by purifying and clarifying faith-knowledge. To say that cognition purifies faith does not mean that it produces faith or that faith itself is improved by thinking. Rather, to purify means to remove impurities, corruption, or unnecessary elements. If we say that cognition improves faith itself, we would establish mind over revelation, humans in control of God. Perhaps it would be better not to make these distinctions, but they seem necessary in the present human situation because reason in the western world has come to have a power and glory all of its own. Perhaps it would be better to say that cognition is a part of faith, serving the ends of faith and is itself in need of redemption; or, we could say that cognition is a continuous part of growth in faith-knowledge, for it instructs faith and is itself tutored by the faith of the believer.

Faith-knowledge, we have said, starts with self-knowledge and continues in an intimate relationship to the self. This is what gives faith-knowledge both its converting and recreating power and also its ambiguity. One has only to think of oneself as a person to remember how mixed one's motives are, how easily one is fooled. Here our cognition helps us remove some of the impurities of our faith. For example, we know enough about mental illness to be able in some degree to analyze the motives of persons who claim the leading of God in activities that deliberately hurt the body. In times past we often ascribed saintliness to such behavior; now we assume such behavior to be psychopathic and the symptom of a sick mind. Again, we know enough about the rise of each of our major social classes to be able rather clearly to point out the way social and economic position have tempered and shaped major Christian beliefs and how in the name of Christianity we have fought for social changes that were primarily for our economic well-being.

Cognition also clarifies faith. To clarify faith is to help understand the relationship of faith to the other areas of life, including other mental activity. The definition of theology as "faith seeking understanding" is an illustration of this point. Understanding is the result of a communication system within the self by which we are able to hold on to our perception of reality in order to expand our awareness. Awareness of something means we interact with something, interpret it in our scheme of things, and adjust ourselves to a new reality. The cognitive processes have a reality of their own. They can theorize about life, project hypothetical situations and infer new truth from well-established truth. This inner mental reality questions and gropes after explanations. Education has sometimes been termed an expansion of our awareness. Christian growth might be called an expansion of our awareness of the meaning of God in our lives.

Perhaps the most common use of cognition to clarify faith is the utilization of history and the accumulation of thought from other generations. We are thus able to avoid the mistakes of the past, or at least to warn ourselves of dangers that may be present in a proposal. For example, there seems to be a recurrent mode of interpreting Christian faith as a community apart from the world. These idealistic communities take hold for a while and then slip into disharmony and failure. Lacking any clear biblical direction in the matter, we are able from our history to see the difficulties of such communities and their inability to endure as a witness to faith.

Secondly, cognition helps us communicate the Christian faith. This is done in three ways. *First*, our determination of the meaning of God's revelation. Until we have had a working knowledge of the Bible and Christian history, we cannot adequately communicate it. This is not a factual knowledge, it is an interpretive knowledge. To interpret we must use the best of our reason. There is a close affinity between language and intelligence and we are expected to use the best of our minds to understand God's revelation. This involves a knowledge of language, geography, literary criticism and theology. *Second*, an adaptation of God's revelation for our day. Just as critical intelligence is necessary to interpret revelation, so also it is necessary to adapt biblical material. Our responsibility to children and immature adults requires that we say in clear and effective ways what we believe to be God's will for us in our day. This requires a penetrating insight into the forces and conditions that make up our situation and our community. The Gospel is simple to declare but complex to live in the rapidly changing conditions of industrial society. Since we have been insisting that one learns through the reality one faces, we are obliged to strain our minds to understand God's work for our contemporary life. *Finally*, by using the path of reason we can prepare the conditions for faith. As agents of God's love we cannot create faith but we can prepare a person's mind to understand it when it comes. Protestants have normally placed too much reliance on reason to communicate faith. Too much of that effort was to make faith reasonable, something that every cultured person should have, along with a formal education. Such efforts not only give a false interpretation of Christianity, but also they inoculate people with a false mental image of religion so that real faith becomes difficult to acquire. The cognitive apparatus should be thought of as a path into a person's inner being and as an instrument to prepare the soil for the seed of God's word.

Declaratory Knowledge

Faith-knowledge, although starting with the self and growing in various parts of the self, is not self-contained. One of its major characteristics is its impulse to share. "God so loved the world that He gave His only begotten son. . . ." is a description of the constraint of love. Love must give, share, create, yield and protect; it is a dynamic, outgoing quality of life. Or to state it negatively as the New Testament does: "He who does not love does not know God; for God is love" (1 Jn. 4:8).

Persons with faith-knowledge cannot contain their concern for others. One is prompted by inner longing for others to know the love of God in Christ and the effort to share it will take many forms, always with a declaration of one's own faith-knowledge. In the New Testament the word commonly used for declaratory knowledge was "witness" as in Acts 1:8, 22, where the Apostles were commissioned witnesses to the resurrection. They could not help but testify what God had done in Christ and they experienced Christ in the spirit after the resurrection. Much of the material and many of the sermons recorded in the Acts of the Apostles are of this type. The sermons often review the history of the Hebrew people and show how God's grace and guidance culminated in Christ. (Peter's first sermon, Acts 2:14-36; Stephen's address, Acts 7:2-53; Paul at Antioch, Acts 13:16-41). Also the inner changes brought about by the spirit of Christ became declarations such as Peter's slow but complete change in his prejudice against Gentiles (Acts 10) so that he finally declared publicly, "Truly I perceive that God shows no partiality. . . ." (Acts 10:34)

Declaratory knowledge is testimony to what God has done and what God means in human life, and as such is the substance of faith-knowledge. What we really know by our faith-experience we declare and seek to make important and decisive in the lives of other people who do not know the Gospel. To another person this substance of faith may be only information, but to the believer it is a tangible expression of one's knowledge of God. The emotional drive behind declaratory knowledge is a mark of its origin deep within the reality of self; concern to share it is an indication of its genuineness. It is at this point that we again note the common source of energy for both education and evangelism in the Church. There can be no more authentic mark of growth in Christian faith than a desire to give of grace as one has oneself been given to know the grace of our Lord Jesus Christ.

Notes

1 John Calvin, *Institutes of the Christian Religion*, ed. John T. McNeill (London: S.C.M. Press, 1960) 1.1.1-2.

7

Why I Believe in Christ

The topic assigned by the student committee for this lenten discussion is worded "Why I Believe in Christ." There is a deliberate shrewdness about the selection of the word "why" which requires that I make my comments from within my own personal experience. This discussion is not intended to be on what I ought to believe or could believe or a comparison of various beliefs about the person and work of Christ. Rather, it is expected to be in the form of a personal affirmation of faith.

The second significant word in the topic is the preposition "in"--why I believe *in* Christ. I can change my belief *about* Christ, and indeed I have gone through several stages of belief about Christ; but throughout them all I continue to believe *in* Christ. Perhaps that is why the Apostles' Creed has such universal acceptance among Christians. It affirms belief in God, in Christ, and in the Holy Spirit without trying to solve the problem of the Trinity. In the same way I can give my reasons for believing in Christ without having to develop a logical schema for harmonizing my beliefs.

Source of Belief

The simplest and most accurate answer to the question "why I believe in Christ" is to say I believe because my parents did; and they in turn were nurtured and stimulated in their belief by active participation in the church. Normal religious practices were followed in my home. I can't remember when I started going to church because it was something our family always did.

This talk was prepared at the request of students at Union Theological Seminary, New York, for a Lenten discussion on this topic, March 20, 1963.

Although I am tempted to go into a nostalgic review of my childhood memories regarding the church and the beliefs I acquired, I shall not do so because it would have no value for you. I can't refrain from saying that my religious educational experiences violated many of the cherished views of some educators--I memorized hymns, I memorized the catechism, and I attended church with my parents, knowing that my mother had a small supply of graham crackers which she would give me about the time the sermon started. Some psychologists would say that this experience is what motivated my interest in preaching! Seriously, the church and the beliefs of the church were a normal and natural part of my childhood. I could qualify as an exhibit of the oft-quoted dictum of Horace Bushnell that children should grow up as Christians and not know themselves otherwise.

A second reason why I believe is because of the minister of the church in which I grew up. This minister presented to me a virile, active figure who combined in his person both an interest in ideas as expressed in his sermons and also an interest in persons that made him the unofficial pastor of the city. Again, it would net you little to hear me reminisce about my childhood, so I shall budget my comments to one story. It was said in the congregation that our minister, prior to coming to our church had waged a campaign against a gambling syndicate and that the manse in which he lived was riddled with bullets on more than one occasion. Thus, I grew up with the idea that the Christian faith was supposed to make some difference in a person's life and that this difference was related to the common life of the community.

Although boyhood experiences are not adequate for me today, I must affirm that there is a significance in childhood experiences that we must not overlook. When you become ministers, you will be directly concerned with the natural processes by which the Christian faith is transmitted from one generation to another generation. In the religious concern of parents, the quality of church life, and the personality of the minister, you will find the principal human methods for creating conditions in which faith in Christ can normally grow. Religious faith, to be contagious and convincing, must be incarnate in a person; and so the persons close to a child--parents, adults in the church, and the minister--will be the primary reasons why a person grows up to believe in Christ.

Substance of Faith

Sometime in one's life a person must take command of oneself and one's beliefs if one is to develop an authentic understanding of religion. Individuals must doubt what has been communicated through those who shaped their lives in order to make it their own. Unexamined religious beliefs inevitably tend to be "oughts" standing over against us as commands which not only restrict personality growth but also form a mentality that prohibits adaptation to new human situations which arise. If I am to have a meaningful faith, I must maintain a constant conversation within myself. I start with the "given" of my childhood, but I must reinterpret that "given" with the product of my mind's reflection. My mind is not just a logical stimulus-response machine; it is sensitive to stimulation of all kinds, capable of forming generalizations about contemporary life, and able to relate observations of human life today to conditions of a previous date. The one thing that makes this possible is human history. We know that human history is different from nature. When we read history, we are able to identify ourselves with the characters and conditions of the past; and thus we are not only instructed but also we see ourselves as actors and actresses in a stream of history. Moreover, my mind reacts to emotions of fear, loneliness, sacrificial love, hope and ideals. This whole mental apparatus must be in conversation with my childhood inventory of religious fact and faith. Therefore, today I cannot stop with the "why." I must include the "what:" for each responds to and interacts with the other.

What then is the current state of my internal conversation between the childhood "given" and the questions my mind now poses in relation to Christ?

First, I believe we can know enough about Jesus' historical existence to get a dependable mental image of what he was like. Here I find myself in a strange dilemma. I am not a Bible scholar, least of all one versed in the technical knowledge necessary to form and defend a position about the adequacy of the New Testament record. Yet, I am a believer who needs to know; and I must form some firm generalizations by which to live while the scholars are attempting to settle their differences about the gospel records. I must solve this dilemma, at least provisionally, in order to keep my faith; and I do this by reading the gospel accounts of Jesus. Granted that a considerable amount of interpretation is necessary, I am still able to form a mental image of what

Jesus was like. If I could not form such an image, then I would be unable to maintain my faith. For that reason history is important to me. I cannot form a mental image of another person without knowing about the times in which that person lived, the conditions struggled with and against, the words said in relation to the problems, etc. It is for this reason that I am interested in the new quest for the historical Jesus. We must remind ourselves that the primitive church had the entire corpus of Paul's writings before the gospels were written; but they saw the need for the history of Jesus in addition to the kerygmatic theology of Paul.

I think they needed the gospels for the same reason I need them: in order to have an image of Jesus that is portable through time. Only by seeing Jesus in action in history can we get a dependable image of him. The very process of the gospel writers who took the oral traditions and teachings and put them into a historical setting showed sound judgment; in this way they could show how the Christ of faith handled himself and they could preserve for us an image of Christ we can understand. I see the gospels as an affirmation of the early church that we must have both the kerygma and the didache. Any theology built exclusively on the kerygma--as if Jesus' historical existence has no bearing on belief--has little appeal to me. If I really thought Jesus did not exist, I would probably maintain my intellectual interest in religion--to me it is the most fascinating area of life--but I would lose any energy I now have to discipline my life according to the concerns which I find in Jesus of Nazareth.

Second, the person of Jesus that comes to me from the Bible is one that brings judgment and mercy to me and to my world. This judgment is absolute in terms of my human condition as a sinner. Judgment is not new. We have had many insightful people who have affirmed humanity's inhumanity, and today some of our existentialist writers expose an extremely pessimistic view of humans and their greed. But in Jesus I find one who brings a peculiar kind of judgment. He faces the human dilemma realistically, but he also shows a God who is concerned about my plight as a sinner; thus we have in Jesus God's mercy simultaneously with the words of condemnation. So, in Jesus I find one who illuminates and also alleviates my human condition.

Third, the person of Jesus demonstrates what obedience to God means. I believe that Jesus' search for and obedience to the will of God is the key to his life, the cause of his death, and the clue to a theory of salvation. In Jesus' life of obedience I see the watershed between religion and faith in God. I see religion, including Christianity when it is dogmatized or moralized, as people's attempt to justify themselves and to placate their consciences. Contrariwise, I see faith as an endless yearning after God's will that is actualized in concrete problems which face us individually and socially. Thus, the idea of obedience is, to me, the practice of faith. This is why true faith leads out into new ventures whether it be Abraham breaking away from the pagan religions of his day or the apostle Paul breaking out of Judaism.

Jesus' obedience reached its climax in the Garden of Gethsemane. I understand this event in Jesus' life as a second temptation episode. In the first temptation he was tempted as to the way he would bring in his kingdom. In the Garden of Gathsemane he was tempted as to his vocation. I can see the possibilities of many ideas running through his mind as he knelt in the Garden of Gethsemane. Should he evade the rising antagonism of his enemies in order to be with his disciples a bit longer? They needed him and his cause was dependent upon them. Should he trim his message against the established religious leaders in order to have time to cultivate his disciples' personal faith? His disciples certainly needed a more profound understanding of faith in God. Yet Jesus rejected all of these and other ideas, saying, ". . . nevertheless not my will, but thine, be done"(Luke 22:42). This leads me to believe that in the life of Jesus there is a clue to a theory of salvation. We think of salvation in terms of life after death, but too much concern about life after death can come from an egotistical motivation or from a fear of death. Traditionally, theology has answered the question "What must I do to be saved?" by telling Christians what they must believe. I think the question may be answered by saying we must seek to do the will of God and we will find our salvation in our obedience.

Fourth, in the person of Christ, I find an authority for decision-making. Jesus' life of radical obedience had, in that obedience, a method of evaluating the legacy of Israel's past. Jesus' obedience was not a blind obedience to the past but a critical analysis of the past in the light of the situation in which he found himself. The scribes collated passages of Scripture from the past and tried to harmonize them into a logical system. Jesus, on the contrary, interpreted the sayings of the past in a new frame of meaning. Divorce was approved by Moses and the law, but Jesus interpreted the divorce law within a new frame of meaning when he said God intended a husband and wife to become a new entity, one flesh, and any other interpretation was for expediency (Mark 10:2-9). Or again, Jesus cut through the legalism of the scribes in their requirements for tithing and said that justice, mercy, and truth were more important (Matt. 23:23-24). Jesus did not accept formal authority nor did he bind himself to traditions: he brought a keen critical intelligence to bear on the legacy of the past and interpreted it in a new way. The new way was not a new *law*: it was a reconstruction of the ethical demand so that it had a self-evident claim on the hearer to act in accordance with God's will.

Jesus' obedience is radical because he believed that persons can know within themselves what God's will is. A person is to apply critical intelligence to the legacy of the past, and in that process the person will know inwardly what God wants. Therefore, obedience is not acquiescing to a command from the outside but is a result of an inner brooding on the nature of God that supplies energy and conviction as it formulates action. Not only do I see this process going on in Jesus, but also in Jesus I see the result of his method. Solving ethical problems becomes somewhat like solving our high school algebra problems: we have a few problems worked out with answers in the textbooks to show us how we are to proceed, and then we are expected to solve the others with that method.

Fifth, I see in Jesus an affirmation of the nearness and concern of God. If it were not for Jesus, I would be inclined to accept John Wisdom's parable of the garden as a true statement of reality. The garden, as you will recall, was visited by two men and each came away with a different view. One man, looking around, saw some traces of a gardener and some previous efforts to develop plants. The other man could see no traces of a gardener and assumed there was none.[1] Without Jesus, I would be inclined to say that the evidence for a God who is concerned about humanity is weak and indecisive. Indeed Dietrich Bonhoeffer may not have put it too strongly when he said the modern world has outgrown its need for religion. But in Jesus I see one whose reference was to God and who demonstrated that God can be an ever-present reality--a reality that can in some measure be actualized by those willing to commit themselves to the God Jesus trusted.

Somewhere I read a statement which sums up the matter for me in these words: "Jesus was all that a man can be, and all that God ought to be."

Notes

1 John Wisdom, *Philosophy and Psycho-Analysis* (Oxford: Blackwell, 1964) 154-155.

8

The Quiet Revolution

A quiet revolution has been going on in America since the second World War. The Negro, now numbering close to twenty million citizens, has determined to achieve the stature and dignity of first class citizenship.

Called on to fight for freedom in the second World War, Negroes realized that if they were expected to defend democracy and die for the American way of life, they should also enjoy the rights of Americans. Moreover, they saw that in other parts of the world black people were treated with respect--thus pointing out more sharply that they were victims of irrational prejudice at home.

The Negro's determination to be treated on a par with other Americans was first realized when the armed forces abandoned all segregated troops and as a matter of policy handled all military personnel alike regardless of color.

After the war, Negro veterans were filled with a new determination to see that their children would not have to endure the social humiliation, poor schools, and common-labor type jobs that had been their lot before the war.

Then in rapid order the breaks came. In 1950 the Supreme Court ruled that state universities were required to admit qualified Negroes; and in 1954 the Supreme Court ruled that public schools could no longer be segregated. Meanwhile, Negroes holding good jobs wanted to move out of the ghettos, the areas in which they had been forced to live, and obtain housing in the suburbs or in communities where their children could have better schools and a more stimulating and interesting environment.

This speech was given on radio station WRVR, New York City, March 21, 1963.

In the north the Negro's basic obstacle in achieving personal dignity and freedom was not the law--for the state laws were on the Negro's side. The problem was with housing. The Negro, Puerto Rican, or other non-white persons who wanted to share the green grass, the open spaces, clean air, and good schools of the suburbs found their way blocked. Although the state legislatures in New York and New Jersey, for example, passed strong antidiscrimination laws in employment practices and housing, the Negroes found that there were countless ways for white people to keep them out of certain areas of a city or to prevent their moving into certain villages in the suburbs. Even today the state cannot force the private owner of a home to sell to a non-white person. Since the suburbs consist predominantly of privately-owned houses, the Negro was effectively blocked from buying a home where desired.

The problem was clearly a matter that lay on the doorstep of the white person's conscience; and, when this became apparent, there spontaneously grew up in many local communities Fair Housing Committees to help Negroes and other non-white people buy a home or rent an apartment wherever they desired. *The New York Times* in an article published December 5, 1961, stated that more than thirty Fair Housing Committees had sprung up in Westchester and Fairfield Counties in Connecticut, on Long Island, and Bergen County in northern New Jersey.

The work of these Fair Housing Committees differs from place to place according to local conditions; but they all have the same goal--to help a person of any race buy a home or rent an apartment in areas that previously have been restricted to white people.

On the surface this seems to be an easy assignment. It is actually one of the most difficult problems in human relations. We must remember that middle-class white persons have most of their money tied up in their houses. When a non-white person moves into the neighborhood, it is immediately feared that real estate values will plunge and life savings will go down the drain. It has been proven over and over again that Negroes moving into a community do not necessarily drive down real estate values, but the white persons' fear is so great that they often go into a panic. If it happens that a Negro family moves into a white neighborhood and a lot of people put their houses on the market simultaneously, then, of course, the prices go down. But if the neighborhood can have a cooling-off period to get adjusted to the new situation, then panic selling can be avoided and prices will remain stable.

There are many communities in the metropolitan New York area where Negroes have moved into what had been previously an all-white neighborhood; after the initial shock had passed, life settled down to the same routine as before, with real estate prices remaining exactly where they were. So a Fair Housing Committee not only attempts to find housing for non-white families, it also stands ready to prevent panic selling in a neighborhood into which non-white families have moved.

But the problems of fair housing are more complicated than just occasionally finding a house for a non-white family or helping a neighborhood to accept a family of a different race in their community. In many places the problem stems from the reluctance of a real estate agent to show houses to Negroes, so that the normal business methods of buying a house are not available. Here we must interpret the difficult position in which the real estate agents find themselves. Real estate agents do not set the moral standard of the community; and if the people in the community are absolutely against selling to Negroes, the agent is helpless to make a change. In fact, real estate agents may be quite right in saying that, if one attempts to sell to Negroes, white people will boycott them and they may be forced out of business. However, real estate agents can help to make housing available to any American if they are supported by the people in the community. Also, real estate agents function as counselors to sellers, advising them on price and on other matters. The real estate agent could in many cases point out the desirability of selling to a Negro if the family was of the type that would fit into the neighborhood.

Occasionally, an unscrupulous real estate agent will take advantage of the situation when a Negro moves into a previously all-white community. Since the community is jolted by this new situation and some of the neighbors may put their houses on the market as an act of panic, the agent may encourage this fear in order to get more houses to sell. This practice is known as "blockbusting." It is illegal and unethical. Fair Housing Committees are alert to any blockbusting practices and are ready to gather evidence against the broker who attempts to panic people into selling their houses.

Why do white people have such fear of neighborhood integration? We have already mentioned the white persons' fear of a downgrading of their real estate and a constant fear that they will lose their investment. But we must press the question further. Why do white people have the fear in the first place? Is it not because many white people have an irrational prejudice against Negroes, based largely on their experience with Negroes who were uneducated, unskilled, and held common-labor type jobs? But the quiet revolution has changed all that. Today we have a class of Negroes who are educated, responsible citizens, capable of any job for which they have been trained. These people want the good things in life; and these good things, especially good schools for their children, can be had only if they can move into communities where these services and qualities have been developed. They have the law on their side. They have morality on their side, for practically every national religious group has approved an official statement to the effect that any barrier in housing that is established by race is morally wrong.

So the problem comes back to the conscience of the white person of good will in the community. If you are such a person, you need not wait until some nasty situation occurs. There are things you can do right now to help make a common sense, practical adjustment more quickly to bring about integrated housing.

First, you can read your newspapers carefully to see if there is a Fair Housing Committee in your community. If so, join the effort to eliminate discrimination in housing.

Second, if no Fair Housing Committee exists, start one. Find a half dozen persons, people like yourself who are convinced that the transition from segregated housing to integrated housing can proceed in an orderly and intelligent manner without the dangers of blockbusting or outbursts of ugly feeling. Meet and discuss the problems in your community and stand ready to help make an orderly transition.

Third, talk to real estate agents you may know about the problem and assure them that you are for responsible action to make housing available without prejudice.

Fourth, talk to your friends in the community to get the issue out in the open where it can be discussed in a calm and creative way before an event takes place that catches your community off balance. Remember, the problem of discrimination in housing is caused by prejudice; and this root cause can be treated only when interested people make it their business to create a new climate of opinion. So far, the revolution has been relatively quiet and we can keep it that way if we will help Americans regardless of color to live where they desire.

9

Innovations for Church Education

The Committee planning this program suggested that we think about our church education situation today in relation to currents of thought and movements in our society that are carrying us into the future.

This is an unusual assignment. It calls us to a task that Protestants have tended to ignore. The history of Protestant educational policies for the past century and a half is more an account of stumbling into patterns of action than it is a self-conscious planning of strategy in the light of the developments in our society and in our beliefs.

Perhaps we could afford this haphazard groping in the past because our country had a Protestant ethos. The atmosphere was laden with the Protestant ideas of life which were expressed in our laws, in politics, in foreign policy and in our business procedures. Our society was shaped by the way Protestants defined and solved social problems. The Protestant ethos is still present and active and, in some places, decisive; but as a whole our nation is no longer dominated by Protestant thought. Today a variety of thought patterns grapple with social problems. All of the religious communities find themselves struggling to discover their distinctive attitudes and relate them to a bewildering array of problems. Today we have a radical religious pluralism in which Protestant denominations, Roman Catholic Churches, Eastern Orthodox Churches, Jewish Synagogues, various religious sects and a large number of citizens who claim no religious affiliation live together; and there is no evidence to suggest that this general situation will change during the rest of the 20th century.

This address was delivered on the occasion of the publication of the Cooperative Curriculum Project, *The Church's Educational Ministry: A Curriculum Plan*, November 15, 1965 at the National Council of Churches, New York City.

Radical Pluralism

This radical pluralism is the one overriding condition which alters our total outlook for the future. It is difficult to date social movements because they have a variety of causes and they proceed slowly. Robert T. Handy has traced the history of the shift from Protestant pluralism of the 19th century to radical pluralism of our day; he believes that the shift can be identified as well under way in the 1920s and 1930s.[1] For convenience, we might say that World War II was the event which speeded up social changes already in motion so that by mid-century we became aware of our new situation. This new situation was revealed, though not created, by the election of a Roman Catholic president in 1960. The political control of many of our major cities had, long before 1960, already passed out of Protestant hands. If one limits one's observations to the media of mass communication, one sees reflected faithfully the radical pluralism that now characterizes our culture; this type of pluralism creates a public attitude that religion is private or that it is discussed only in terms of a broad consensus on issues of public morals.

I have borrowed Handy's term "radical pluralism" to distinguish our present situation from the Protestant pluralism which characterized this country during the period when our national documents were written, and when our Church-State relationship in education was developed. For example, in the last quarter of the 18th century it is estimated that only one percent of the population was Roman Catholic and perhaps one twentieth of one percent was Jewish; the rest of our citizens were Protestants or had no religious affiliation at all. In many colonies, churches were established and supported by the State. When the first amendment to our Constitution was put into operation in 1791, it freed the States from favoring any organized religion; but the idea of eliminating religion from its role in the State was not considered and probably not thought of. In his second farewell address(1796) George Washington stated the common understanding of the role of religion in relation to the State in these words: "Of all the dispositions and habits which lead to political prosperity, religion and morality are indispensable supports. . . . And let us with caution indulge the supposition that morality can be maintained without religion . . . reason and experience both forbid us to expect that national morality can prevail in exclusion of religious principle."

Although disestablishment of religion became the official national policy in 1791, religion continued to be taught in the common schools until Horace Mann in the 1830's suggested eliminating all sectarian religious instruction from them. By 1850 we had developed a tax-supported common school movement separate from the churches.

This pattern was developed as a result of Protestant pluralism. Horace Mann wanted to teach a general Christian morality in the schools and leave sectarian teaching to the churches. The Sunday school during this period had a semi-autonomous position in relationship both to the State and the churches. In some places, especially on the frontier, the Sunday school functioned as a common school, but mainly it served the special interests of the churches which desired an agency for evangelism and instruction completely under their control when the churches' formal connection with public education was discontinued. The first amendment removed the power of the State from the support of organized religious bodies. However, the people believed that what the State was not to do officially they were to do voluntarily, and so they proceeded to evangelize the new nation and to permeate its culture with Protestant thinking. In the atmosphere of religious fervor which dominated the 19th century the omission of formal religious instruction from the common school in order that one sectarian view of Protestantism not be given an unfair advantage seemed to be a sensible proposal.

Today, in the last half of the 20th century, we discover that Protestant pluralism is gone and it has been replaced by radical pluralism which creates an official neutrality in religious affairs. This neutrality is nowhere better seen than in the recent Supreme Court cases that have separated religion from our public schools. Today religion cannot be taught in the schools if sponsored by a religious group. Prayers, including the Lord's Prayer, may not be used and Bible readings have been declared unconstitutional. Although there have been no Supreme Court cases on the religious content of Commencement exercises or on the singing of Christmas carols, these practices represent the last remnant of the old Protestant order and are rapidly disappearing from our public schools.

What should we Protestants do in this period of radical pluralism? The old strategy of a Sunday church school plus a youth group and other part-time agencies run by volunteers was fashioned to meet conditions that do not now obtain. The Sunday school and other agencies of the church are the only educational organizations we control and we must not weaken them until we have something better. Over a hundred years ago church people saw the weakness of the Sunday school; but within a Protestant pluralism and ethos that agency became the churches' educational program. Our question is, what can we do today to develop a strategy to meet the conditions we face?

We cannot much longer follow a strategy based on a Protestant ethos: a public school system that generally reenforces a religious outlook and one hour of sectarian teaching a week in a church school. To vent our displeasure at the Supreme Court for tearing down our Protestant playhouse is silly; the Supreme Court has reflected the times, and we Protestants must start a serious and prolonged consideration of what we must do to meet the needs of our day.

A strategy for the future which takes radical pluralism seriously will have to develop a structure of religious education that is coordinated with general education and a program of adult education that is capable of renewing the life of the church in the world.

Objective Teaching of Religion

Let us first look at the possibility of the objective teaching of religion in the public schools. The Supreme Court in 1963 ruled unconstitutional the use of prayers or the reading of the Bible in public schools. Justice Clark, writing for the Court in the Abington School District Case, said, "Nothing we have said here indicates that such study of the Bible or of religion, when presented objectively as a part of a secular program of education, may not be effected, consistent with the First Amendment." Thus, the curricula in history, literature and the arts could include the rich heritage of religion in order to inform the students of the past and to enrich their awareness of the role of religion in contemporary life. Professor P. H. Phenix of Teachers College is now studying this proposition on the assumption that the objective teaching of religion need not be a bland neutrality but that it can be instruction in which religious commitment is a part of the objectivity. We must remind ourselves that this type of instruction in religion has been going on in state universities for a long time. According to Hubert Noble, Executive Director of the Department of Higher Education of the National Council of Churches, an increasing number of state colleges are offering religion as an academic subject and are even expanding their offerings into the graduate department. We must also recall that there has never been a Supreme

Court case which called into question the practice of state universities offering courses in religion. Some informed observers such as Walter Wagoner of the Fund for Theological Education believe that the universities should take over the teaching of religion and that future ministers should receive basic training there rather than in seminaries. I cite these observers because, if they are right, then radical pluralism is already being defined by our higher education institutions. Religion as an area of instruction is capable of being taught by professors who are committed to a point of view, just as a sociologist may be committed to a particular school of thought in sociology. Various professional points of view are the expected condition in any department of a large secular university.

If this meaning of radical pluralism becomes the accepted one--then why could it not move down to the high school? Higher education influences the quality and scope of high school subjects. Why should the teaching of religion not migrate down to the elementary school? Moreover, since the movement is downward from higher education, teacher training will take place in universities apart from any direct church control. It follows that curricula for religious courses in general education will be written by academically qualified persons apart from church auspices.

Such a development is already underway. Professor Phenix's publication, when it appears next year, will speed up the experimentation and the movement. This is not the place to attempt an evaluation of this movement except to say that Protestants must decide whether they want to take this route. The objective teaching of religion in general education is an answer of the educational community to the problem of radical pluralism; if successful, it will do much of the work now being done by parochial and Sunday church schools. If the church should decide that this were a good route to travel, then the church would be free to invest its time, leadership and money in different forms of ministry; it could modify its educational work to complement that which is done in the public schools.

Dual Enrollment

The second possibility is contained in Public Law 89-10 of the 89th Congress. "Elementary and Secondary Education Act in 1965" is a new approach to educational strategy in the United States because it assumes the validity of organized religion's interest in general education and it assumes the reality of radical religious pluralism, neither of which had been assumed in public education since the formation of our public educational policy. If this act is held constitutional, it will mark a new era in the relation of church and state in education.

Although we who are concerned for quality education for all citizens will want to follow all of the provisions in this Act with close attention, there are provisions that we must examine immediately with utmost care because they open up a new range of educational possibilities for Protestants. The first proposal has to do with dual enrollment as a possibility in title I of the Act (Section 205) and in title III (Section 303). In title III, having to do with library resources, textbooks and other instructional materials, it is stated these are to be made available to private as well as public schools and that the supplementary educational centers which are intended to provide a vast array of services to all children will include those who are enrolled in private and public schools (Section 303, b, [3]).

Dual enrollment is a plan whereby a student is enrolled in a private or religiously-sponsored school for part of the day for courses in religion and perhaps courses in English and social subjects; and then attends a public school for the rest of the day for technical courses, physical education, foreign language and sciences. Although there have been some experiences with dual enrollment in Pittsburgh, Hartford and a few other places, the plan was not given serious consideration as a national policy until the 1950's. Although dual enrollment is obviously designed to accommodate the Roman Catholic Church, with its vast commitment to parochial schools, it would be a serious mistake to think this proposal does not apply to Protestants. Since we do not have a parochial school system and because our strategy related to the Sunday school and other volunteer agencies has probably served its day, we are in an enviable position: we can move into this new opportunity without an inventory of buildings or mental presuppositions as to exactly what we must do.

The United States Office of Education has made a detailed study of nine communities which have had experience with dual enrollment. The problems are many. With the problems also come advantages for public education. The Education Act of 1965, by placing the disbursement of the funds in the hands of the public officials, has given public educators an opportunity to enrich and upgrade the education of all students as never before.

The opportunity for Protestants is enormous. Not only can we experiment with new structures, but also we can control the religious education aspects of any religious education center we set up, thus letting religion be expressed in worship and commitment as well as in instruction. Probably the first question many would raise about any large scale development of dual enrollment would be the expense. Much of the expense for instructional materials and some services would be met by public funds, so the major expenses would be buildings and teachers' salaries. I would argue that the value of the program alone requires that we pay whatever it costs even if we have to cut down on other aspects of the normal Protestant parish program. I think that need not be the case. We have plenty of money to support such a program. However, dual enrollment may actually cost no more than we are now spending in the average Protestant parish for education. The crucial factor is the cost of buildings. In using a classroom five hours per day, five days per week, it is possible for one dual-time classroom to do the work five or six Sunday school classrooms could do. This has been carefully worked out by Stanley J. Hallett of the Division of Home Missions, National Council of Churches, for a new community in Columbia, Maryland. Dr. Hallett has shown that if funds tied up in unused Sunday school classrooms were invested, there would be almost enough money to endow the professional staff of teachers needed for a dual enrollment program.

Probably the second question that would come to mind in relation to dual enrollment would be the possible divisive nature of dual enrollment if we had a Catholic center, a Jewish center and several Protestant religious education centers. But the religious education centers could actually add to ecumenicity. It would be possible by a proper scheduling of courses for several religious groups to use a common center during the course of a school day. Religious education centers coordinated with, but physically separated from, public schools might open up not only religious instruction but also the possibilities of an educational ministry. We in religious education have tended to be programmatic and to think we have done our task when we have provided an agency for teaching, a curriculum, or a teacher-training program. In the future we must do more; we must think of education as a ministry and to do this properly we must form an alliance with the field of pastoral counseling.

Allow me a moment to explain the reason for our present lack of communication between religious education and counseling. All through the 1920s and early 30s the religious education departments in our seminaries were the gateway of the social sciences (especially psychology) into the seminary curriculum and into the churches by means of curriculum and leadership training courses. Then in the mid-1930's came the challenge of "realistic theology" and religious educators went on the defensive, attempting to work out a reconciliation with newer forms of theology and Bible study. For over a quarter of the century religious educators have been on a quest for a viable theology which would harmonize the various disciplines that make up the field of religious education.

While religious educators during the past quarter of the century have been trying to reconstruct their field, depth psychology has been developed as a field and is represented in our seminaries by our professors of pastoral counseling and by the clinical training movement. Indeed, in recent years the general movement has pushed beyond the confines of the church, beyond the regular chaplaincy functions in hospitals and prisons, and is now in close interaction with the medical profession in a number of academies. Within the past years this movement has given birth to a new phenomenon: the ordained Protestant clergymen, clinically trained, doing full-time professional counseling in an office apart from any direct church connection. The newly formed American Association of Pastoral Counselors in 1964 listed 164 such centers and indicated that there are many others.

I want to propose that there be a coordination of the concerns of the religious educator and the pastoral counselor in the dual enrollment religious education centers for the guidance of students and as a ministry to their families. At the present time, pastoral counseling services are used chiefly when a person is too sick to function properly or is in a crisis situation. However, counseling in crisis situations is almost always too little and too late. We must develop ways to create conditions for mental health and to spot the early stages of mental and emotional disorders before they become acute. This important function of pastoral counseling cannot be done within our present church school structure. However, if we develop religious education centers coordinated with public schools, then we could staff these centers with religious educators and with leaders experienced in pastoral counseling. Together, these professionals could serve the child and family in a structure that would make religious instruction and guidance possible.

Let's assume for a moment that religious education centers for dual enrollment are declared unconstitutional or that Protestants refuse to develop them. In that case, I still argue that religious education and pastoral counseling must be coordinated in order that our work in the future be in the form of an educational ministry rather than of a program. Let's take the high school adolescents, for example. Teenagers come of age under difficult circumstances because the society around them is confused and is changing rapidly. The educational situation has become fiercely competitive. Teenagers about the age of 15 or 16 must be rather clear as to whether their vocations will lead them to college or not, and, if to college, what type of college they want to attend. This is asking a lot of a young person. Where can one go for guidance? Although one's parents can help in some ways, they are too emotionally involved to be of significant help. Our best high schools in our wealthy communities may have one fairly well-trained guidance counselor for every thousand students; it is no wonder that these high school counselors play the game safe and stick close to a student's performance on standardized tests when they have their five minute interview with each student. If high school guidance people ever tried to take the students seriously as persons, the whole program would collapse; for the schools would have to employ a large corps of guidance counselors in every school. Perhaps the school is correct in limiting its involvement with the student to the mind.

It is my contention that it is natural for the church to be interested in the whole person: the church is freer than any other institution in the community to minister to teenagers and their parents. There is no reason why we should not bring religious educators and pastoral counselors together and develop an educational ministry to teenagers. This ministry might start with the teenagers' study program by helping them do well the one thing they must do as teenagers, namely, be learners. This ministry would stay close to the teenagers' vocational plans, supplying and interpreting tests but primarily offering them persons to whom they could relate and with whom they could talk as they make the decisions that shape their entire future. This ministry would develop group meetings which would probe the ethical and moral problems teenagers face. However it is conceived, it would be to teenagers a ministry rather than a program to which they must belong. We can develop such an educational ministry quite apart from any provisions of the Educational Act of 1965; but we cannot do so unless we can move away from our program-curriculum mentality and can begin to train professional leaders who have the ability to function as ministers in the field of education.

Protestant Ecumenism

Let's get back to the provisions of the Educational Act of 1965. This act seems not only to endorse dual enrollment but also it offers a fresh reappraisal of educational responsibility. American education has always prided itself on local control. The Education Act of 1965 affirms local control but in a far-reaching way never before legalized. Title III of the act on "Supplementary Educational Centers" requires (in Section 304 [a]) that local educational authorities must set up a committee representing the "cultural and educational resources" of the community to plan, establish and carry out the program locally. Representatives from non-profit private schools are required to be on such a committee.

To show our Protestant dilemma, let me ask, "Will local school boards request a representative from a Protestant Sunday school?" I doubt it! For the first time in our history we have a structure established by law to coordinate to some degree our various local educational efforts. I believe that back of this law is the assumption of radical pluralism, namely that religious and private schools have an interest in education which is to be recognized and stabilized.

If this be true, then we Protestants have our work cut out for us. We will have to make a tremendous shift in attitude about education which will shake our most cherished prejudices. First, we will have to see that radical pluralism allows for religious schools partly supported by the State. Our long struggle against the Roman Catholic Church's desire for public funds and public recognition in education is over. That struggle was partly the result of Protestant and Catholic theological differences; but from the Protestant side it was an effort that made sense only while we had a Protestant ethos and during the period when we could consider the public school our silent ally. Now we must join hands with all religious groups and face, in common, the problem of religious education in relation to public education.

Secondly, we will have to see that radical pluralism means a new kind of Protestant cooperation. We cannot have a religious education center for every denomination. We must coordinate our efforts and do a kind of long-range planning we have never done before. The record of Protestant cooperation in education is excellent; in fact, it is one of the bright spots in our past and our present. Protestant denominations have had a close coordination in the formation of Sunday school curricula for over a century and a half. The International Council of Religious Education and its successor, the Division of Christian education of the National Council of Churches, have given unparalleled demonstrations of cooperation among denominations for the past half-century. We must build on this remarkable foundation of national cooperation the *local* cooperation necessary to meet the needs of our new day. To be specific, will Protestants in the community be able to get together and name a person who can represent their interests on these proposed educational committees? Will Protestants be able to give up some denominational pride, even some denominational characteristics, in order to cooperate in preparing curriculum materials for religious education centers coordinated with public schools? Will we be able to curtail congregational investment in educational plants in order that the Protestants of the community put up one educational building adequate for each school district? This is where we are to be tested and here is where we must construct our future.

Adult Education

I said at the beginning that we had two major problems. The first was a new structure for religious education in our day of radical pluralism and the second was an adult education plan which would help us reform the church in this generation. Let us now look at this second problem briefly.

Adult education is still the quiet backwater of the church rather than the dynamic, bubbling center of the spring. Today, a third of a century after we repudiated liberal theology, we still follow the *tactics* of liberalism in education: attention is focused on children and youth on the assumption that, when they grew into adulthood, their fine religious training will bless the church and community. We must come to our senses and see that society has a way of molding--educating, if you will--the rising generation which cancels out much of our religious education. Religious education will never be more than a holding operation if we concentrate our attention on children. We must turn the tactics around and focus our attention on adults if we want to form and reform the church. But where is there a denomination today that spends a tenth of its educational resources on adults? Do not denominations still spend years on a new curriculum for children and then, as an afterthought, put out something for adults?

I know the problems of adult education are many and difficult to solve, but we can no longer ignore the needs of our time. On the one hand, we are getting more and more young adults who have taken first class courses in religion in our universities and who want and need an educational venture which will help them work out the meaning of faith. On the other hand, we have large groups of adults in our churches who still think that the individualistic piety which formerly characterized our Protestant ethos is satisfactory for all personal, social and political problems today. These two groups don't mix easily, but this condition should be the definition of our problem, not the reason to abandon it as unsolvable.

Our commitment to adult education should be entirely on religious grounds. Our biblical heritage shows us that each historical era in the Old Testament is a reinterpretation of the past and that the New Testament is a textbook on how the adults of the early church worked through their Jewish tradition in the light of God's revelation in Christ in the conditions they faced. This biblical paradigm should always be before us even though it presents us with a challenge we fear to accept.

Langdon Gilkey, professor of Theology at the University of Chicago, is in close touch with the "death of God" theologians and the methods of philosophical analysis; yet, he does not find the solution to the church's problems here or in any other new theology. Rather, in his book *How the Church Can Minister to the World Without Losing Itself* he says, ". . . the Church in its practical existence can only be saved by religious education."[2] His idea of religious education is a vigorous multichannelled program of adult education which will prepare adults to reprocess the past in terms of contemporary life. He is correct: there is no other way. We must focus our attention on adult education.

Although I am sobered by all the problems with adult education I find that the fundamental issue is whether or not we see the church as being dependent on an educated, articulate, adult population. If we do, then we can begin to struggle with the problems.

Let me make two practical suggestions which may help establish the central importance of adult education and improve its quality. Adults live in a fast-moving world in which much of the material to which they react is presented visually. Editorial comment, background information, and discussion on TV and in magazines is related to events as they happen in the world. When these adults come to the church, they have printed materials which were prepared a year or two earlier. Unless the teacher is unusually skilled, the relation of the Christian faith to the real world is usually absent.

I would propose that several denominations set up a closed-circuit TV system on which they could broadcast drama, interviews, discussions and lectures so the material would be more relevant to events which suggested the program. I am not talking about a mass TV program to the unchurched but an instructional program to stimulate and guide adult groups in local congregations. Such a move would not and must not eliminate local leaders or discussion; it would use only methods which are already available so that fast-moving ideas and events can give point to our biblical and theological study.

One more practical suggestion. Protestant churches have to think through their relation to the community in this new era of radical pluralism. We can no longer protest here and there and occasionally join in a cleanup campaign on the assumption that when the crisis is over the Protestant ethos will close in and all will be well. In a day of radical pluralism we must redefine our relation to the community. We must abandon the notion that we are kept tax-exempt by the community because we improve people's morals and therefore, in Washington's terms, create the conditions for "political prosperity." Rather, we must see the community as the place where we work institutionally as well as individually. As an institution, the church should approach problems through the structure of society, such as welfare, health and recreation, as well as law. This calls for a level of knowledge and skill we do not now have. To move this suggestion along, I would propose that the churches of a community take five to ten percent of their budget, pool the money, set up an agency to study and make plans to solve various community problems, including racial relations and civil rights. The work of such an agency should be channelled both to city hall and to the churches, for these data would be part of the curriculum for adult Christian education.

Moreover, as the churches budget funds to relate themselves significantly to the community, so they must budget leadership. We must abandon the notion that we are in competition with the community for leaders. We must share leadership with the community, using the church as a training center for those values which express our faith in God.

Notes

1 The term "radical pluralism," used by Robert T. Handy in lectures and converstaions, is given a historical setting in *A Christian America* (New York: Oxford UP, 1971) 184-225.

2 Langdon Gilkey, *How the Church Can Minister to the World Without Losing Itself* (New York: Harper, 1964) 98.

10

The Relation of Seminary Training to Congregational Education

My assignment is to "consider the work of the professor of Christian education as it is related to the educational processes that occur in the local congregation." My instructions also state that I may "approach the assignment either in terms of what the relationship is or in terms of what it ought to be." I elect to approach the subject in terms of what it ought to be.

What is the subject? I assume that it is "the work of the professor of Christian education" and that "work" is restricted in this assignment to that area which relates seminary training to the education carried on by a local congregation. When stated this way, I believe it is proper to say that the topic can best be examined by first identifying the educational situation of the local congregation and then--by deduction, inference and a bit of imagination--suggesting what the work of the seminary professor ought to be in training educators for the local church.

The Congregation as an Interpretive Association

First, let's look at the congregation as a voluntary association of people who are primarily interpreting and communicating the most important things in life to each other and to their children. I have tried to make the case in my book *Where Faith Begins* that the socialization process instructs the child in a world view which sets a perceptive system, teaches a moral code that results in an internal guilt-and-shame producing conscience, and forms a self-image that is the basis of one's notion of God and one's relation to other persons.[1] This socialization process is transcultural and transhistorical. It is, in short, a description

---

Prepared for the Graduate Professors of Christian Education, meeting in Dallas, Texas, February 11-12, 1968.

of a natural human phenomenon that takes place in tribe, clan or close association of people in home, neighborhood or community.

For Christians, I see the congregation as a place where the faith is interpreted and transmitted by this socialization process. It is interpreted through the interactional process between adults in the life and worship of a congregation and through the families. James Gustafson has stated the matter generally in these words:

> If one can restore the significance of the word 'practical' to the highest status it has in the Kantian use of the 'practical reason,' one can say that the voluntary character of the church is of practical importance. It is the human organization of life through which a Christian moral community can come into existence, and from which influence and action move into the world.[2]

It is from such a voluntary association of Christians that "influence and action (can) move into the world." But there will be no movement into the world unless the congregation sees movement into the world as a proper expression of its faith. That is why I have insisted that the interpretive function of the congregation as expressed in sermon, study and discussion groups is essential, if not prior, to engagement with the world. Such interpretation means an understanding of the past, particularly of the Bible, and a critical appraisal of the present and future in the light of the past. In other language, the congregation is a "value-factory"--a place where old values are refurbished and made operative and new values are designed and manufactured. I think no one seriously questions the role of the congregation as a place where values are repaired, but there is profound skepticism about the ability of the congregation to design and manufacture new or improved values. I share this skepticism; yet, I believe that it is possible to make some modest progress in the direction of developing values for our contemporary life. Progress will be made only as we are able to bring our critical intelligence to bear on the problems of contemporary life. I see education in the church as a way to initiate and maintain the interpretive process which is essential to a value-factory that also turns out a new or improved set of values.

So much for a position statement about education in the congregation. Let us now look at the congregation as an association that has educational potential for developing a well-rounded citizen, that is, for bridging the gap between the school and subject matter-oriented experience of the child and the full-orbed realities of life. In order to do this briefly, let me use the stunning article entitled "Education and Community" by Fred N. Newmann and Donald W. Oliver which recently appeared in the *Harvard Educational Review.*[3] These students of public education see two major images of modern American society in active competition.

The Great Society image is of a large industrialized, urbanized, specialized, technically competent nation that is pushing back the boundaries of ignorance and attempting to use all of humanity's skill and knowledge to make all freer to develop themselves and to enlarge their future. The profound optimism that underlies this image of the future is linked with a strategy which offers services directly to the individual. National programs of financial aid, medical aid, homes for the aged, and so on, are designed to meet specific individual needs. Likewise, the Great Society approach is deeply involved in education. More federal money has been spent on education during the present administration than ever before because new ways have been found to bypass or persuade state educational authorities to spend money in local school systems and to "de-fuse" the church-state issue so that federal funds could be shared by private schools. However, the really big issue that is developing (which also illustrates the mentality of the Great Society approach to education) is the rapidly forming alliance between big business and education, now properly referred to as the education industry.

Big business has discovered the educational market and the prospects of federal government spending. Francis Keppel, who left the office of U.S. Commissioner of Education to become head of General Learning Corporation (founded by General Electric, Time and Silver Burdett Company) says the figure of three hundred dollars per child as average expenditure for education in the mid-1950's will become six hundred dollars per child in the mid-1970's; and the one billion dollars that the government is now putting into education per year will grow.[4] George Haller of General Electric has said, "The potential future market in educational systems is a very attractive one. Unlike the market for refrigerators and radios, it seems to have no conceivable saturation point."[5]

Since 1964 eight large learning corporations have been formed by the giants of American textbook, magazine and electronic companies. Their ability to lobby for gigantic federal grants to finance the educational machinery they are manufacturing is almost beyond belief. From all of this activity two things have a bearing on church education.

First, the educational hardware these giant corporations are planning is designed for the individual. The promise is that children can now educate themselves at their own rate and the teacher is to become more of a manager of instructional materials than an instructor. Granted that in this early phase of educational technology exaggerated claims will be made, whatever success this massive effort has will be success in individual instructional terms. What kind of personality will pupils tend to develop if they are isolated more and more from others as their minds are stimulated and trained? The school has always accepted some responsibility for social values on which a democracy can maintain itself. Will the school lose interest or find less time for this hard, slow, nonmechanical, social type of instruction?

The second thing that is coming clear is that these merchants of educational hard- and software are going to develop a "systems" approach to education. A systems approach is a development in management circles whereby objectives are clearly defined and then the whole system of leaders, supply and communications needed to obtain that objective are brought under control. There is no doubt of this system's effectiveness in the management of construction projects or the vast enterprise of national defense. But what will it mean in education? No one knows. Francis Keppel and others say it will not disrupt the normal authority of local school boards, but anyone who has seen how powerful the state departments of education and the textbook manufacturers are in setting the content of education cannot help wondering. Certainly we can predict that educational hardware, curriculum and teachers are increasingly going to be systematized, and the content of the subject taught is increasingly going to be the central fact in education. This has developed rapidly since Sputnik went up in 1957 and it will continue strong during the foreseeable future.

Another view is expressed in the *Harvard Educational Review* article--an image in which the human community is the dominant motif. Community in this sense has its 18th and 19th century voluntary association connotation, of course. That does not mean that the psychosocial needs for community have disappeared. Rather, much of the current malaise in our society comes from pressure to force individuals to subordinate a sense of interrelatedness and mutual interdependence to achievement and mobility. Its depersonalization--which leads to a feeling of powerlessness in the face of giant bureaucracies--can be traced to the lack of personal qualities that are supplied by proper experience of community. The article proposes that these critical matters are going to worsen unless we are able to strengthen a sense of community where desirable social values are learned and articulated.

Communicating values could become a reality if we would learn to think of education as taking place in three contexts. The first is the school context where systematic instruction takes place in basic skills. The second is the laboratory-studio-work context, in which the student learns how things are made and human events take place. It was the third setting suggested by Newmann and Oliver that arrested my attention, the community-seminar context. There the writers suggest that there must be reflection on community issues and on "ultimate meanings in human experience." The description of what they envision reads with few exceptions like a manual in adult education from one of our more alert Protestant denominations! They list topics such as the conflict between adults and youth, the family in modern life, racial prejudice, sex education, child-rearing practices, use of leisure, population control, moral implications of advances in biology, and so on. They illustrate the possibility of this community-seminar context with church-sponsored projects.

In the congregation, then, is centered a dynamic educational process of socialization both for its own members and also (if properly managed) as an educational mission to the community. What does this mean for us, for our work in the seminary?

For me it means that religious education must continue to maintain lively connections with all of the disciplines of the seminary because all of them are involved in interpreting the Christian faith. These connections may be no more than personal ones with other professors, but I am inclined to think it should increasingly be an arrangement whereby a professor of Bible, theology or history joins with the religious educator, either in a classroom or a field-work situation to work with the problems of communication.

I also think we must continue our normal work of relating the Christian faith to the social sciences. The intellectual problems in relating the two have not been solved although they are easier in some theological systems than others. However, the type of social science that is involved in social criticism, such as that used by Newmann and Oliver, is readily available to us. Perhaps our problem is that we have depended too much on writers and leaders who have abstracted what they wanted from the social sciences rather than on people who are actively engaged in a study of individuals. Last year for example, I audited the staff conferences of the department of psychiatry at St. Luke's Hospital in New York. Each week a prominent psychiatrist from the hospital (or some other teaching hospital in the metropolitan area) would read a paper on research he was conducting. On several occasions these psychiatrists went out of their way to comment on the importance of the educator in shaping the child's life. One psychiatrist even depreciated his role in the total scheme of things in relation to the role a good educator could play in developing a child's ego. I was struck by all of this because I often deal with students who are apologetic about their educational role. Because they read books that use psychoanalytical theories to explain child development, they assume that the psychiatrist with all of his training is the top dog; but psychiatrists who deal with twisted egos marvel at the role of the educator who trains the healthy ego!

Seminaries differ widely in their faculty makeup and in the kinds of social scientists that are available. However, within our limits I believe we must push on with the conversation among these groups. My covert hope is that one of these days we religious educators will be able to participate in a team effort with university researchers to probe some of the areas of religious development that at the present time remain largely unknown to us. When that day comes, we will be in a better position to help the congregation in its educational mission because we will know more about the role of religion in human development.

The Congregation in an Urban Setting

Thus far I have been talking about congregations in the mainstream of middle-class America. Now we must take a look at the crisis of the church in urban centers and see what that situation demands from the departments of religious education in our seminaries.

There is no need to offer details about a situation that is well-known to all of us. America is already an urban society. The issue that we face is the condition of the urban poor, usually gathered in residential pockets, often of a common racial or ethnic background. There people exist in crowded quarters, denied the most elementary public services of sanitation and police protection. Their hope of participating in the bounty of American economic prosperity or cultural life has failed or disappeared. The American dream of rising to higher social status through self-help is almost unknown. Public education as the standard way to economic self-sufficiency and self-esteem is ineffective. Studies in New York have shown that the longer students stay in the public schools in ghetto areas, the further behind they become in reading and other basic intellectual skills. Such conditions are the breeding place of crime. The *New York Times* of January 29, 1968, revealed that one third of all murder, rape, felonious assault and robbery in New York City is committed in the three major ghetto areas. Some is related to the use of drugs and alcohol, which are used to escape the frustrations of living in the ghetto. The social situation, compounded by a racial caste system, makes the educational ministry of the church in the ghetto seem weak and timid. Indeed, the church itself seems almost an anachronism in the modern inner-city situation.

The Board of Education of the United Presbyterian Church commissioned Edward A. White, Charles Yerkes and Gerald Klever to study for a three year period the nature of the church's educational ministry in an urban setting. Their report, entitled *Education in the City Church* is a brilliant analysis of the total social and religious situation.[6] Their suggestions about education would drastically affect our interpretation of religious education and our methods of training leaders for inner-city situations. I shall summarize a few of their findings before moving on to the way this report could affect our work in the seminary.

The inner-city problem is primarily one of powerlessness, which breeds despair, emotional impotence and helplessness. Lying, cheating and stealing are normal ways of carrying on the battle for the elementary needs of food, shelter and a little bit of spending money. The only way the church can get at this situation is to help "empower" the people of the slums.

A goal of "empowering" people is complicated and has many psychological and social dimensions. But at this point let us restrict ourselves to the way this goal requires a different view of church education and a different view of the church's response to public education. The question is "What can the church do to help these people achieve self-respect and understanding of their world?" rather than the restricted question of how the church can teach its beliefs. These questions are not mutually exclusive, but traditional answers to the latter question often rule out the former question.

The writers of this study see three major changes in church education that will be necessary to empower the poor. The first is a change in administrative structure. No congregation in an inner-city situation has the resources for good education even if it tries to do no more than carry on a traditional program. Therefore, a cluster of churches of various denominations or an area-wide judicatory such as the presbytery will have to be the agency to formulate and administer the educational program. Second, teachers will have to be trained to make learning interesting and exciting, and it is proposed to supplement voluntary teachers with public school teachers who may want to have a "moonlight" job on Saturdays in the church school. But these teachers are not to be trained in the usual way--they are to become first a community of teachers capable of starting their educational work without any preconceived formal curriculum. Third, the report deals with the intent and content of church education. The church must use all of its facilities and leadership to enrich the lives of inner-city people and particularly to offer children tutorial and counseling services. The content of education must connect with life as they have experienced it. This means church education must contain a study of the history of the poor, how to make changes in living conditions and, in Negro areas, a study of the Negro heritage. Church education must bring to the surface and help people overcome the ideology that has been used to keep them powerless, such as the notions of racial superiority or equal opportunity or the fiction that individuals can succeed if they try hard enough. Moreover, the theory of objective tests, particularly IQ tests based on the verbal behavior of middle-class children, has to be explained and discussed. Few of these topics are now treated in a systematic fashion in our church school curricula. Christian education, according to this approach "is a re-education in power."

This report also calls for a different view of the congregation's responsibility for public education in the community. The prevailing form of education in the public school establishment is for the benefit of students who are now participating in and benefitting from American society. But the urban poor, especially the Negroes, are excluded from the rewards of this society and therefore have no incentive to learn or assume responsibility. This situation was pointed out as early as 1944 in Allison Davis' essay on the socialization of the adolescent, but it has come to us with renewed urgency today.[7]

This task of helping the public school to be effective ranges all the way from the multitude of things that should be done to support the school and fight its battles with City Hall to the more specific task of recruiting teachers and supporting them in their work. In some areas the congregation will have not only to carry on a struggle to help the public school be effective, but also it will have to help individual students who have dropped out of the system. In Harlem the Church of the Master is sponsoring a day school for dropouts and has seminary interns actively engaged in finding the teenagers in the community who have been unable to adjust to the public school.

It is difficult to be precise about what all this means for our work in the seminary because our instructional resources are so varied. But let me point out four ways this description of education in the inner-city church may affect the work of the professor of religious education.

(1) The basic problem of education for the urban poor is now squarely before us and there is no possibility of its being easily solved or going back into hiding. It is the new dimension of church education. At the least we will have to include this phenomenon in our courses to cover adequately the field of modern religious education. Although we can continue to make a distinction between education the church sponsors and the responsibility of the congregation in public education as I have done in this paper, we do so because the congregation has a theological rationale for its teachings. But we can no longer avoid our responsibility to help the urban poor achieve the dignity and respect they are due as human beings. One means of achieving this self-regard is through the quality of the education received. Some of us who are in a university setting will be able to do more than interpret Christian education to include the inner-city situation; we may be able to reexamine our degree programs to see if we have made it possible for students to include courses in urban education and sociology.

(2) For the special conditions of education in the inner-city church, religious education as a field of study will need to join forces with the seminary's department of Church and Community or Sociology of Religion in an effort to serve the students going into ghetto ministries. I do not know what the nature of this alliance between religious education and the Church and Community department should be. It could be in the nature of a joint seminar. I am inclined to believe it would be more effective if it were related in some way to a ghetto area containing a cluster of congregations that had some working relationship

to each other and some common understanding of their community goals.

(3) Allied with this suggestion is the proposal that we may need to reappraise the vocations for which we prepare our students. We are all acquainted with the vocational expectation of the standard, self-supporting middle-class congregation. We are not so well prepared to train educational specialists for ghetto work. Think for a moment of the teenage situation. The ghetto adolescent, particularly the Negro, is different in many important ways from the teenager in our average, middle-class church. Although we can sometimes supply field-work opportunities for our students in the ghetto situation, we can seldom provide them with good supervision. It may be that our best contribution to a student who wants to specialize in a teenage ministry would be to factor into his training some field supervision by a nearby school of social work. We must not forget that the learning style of the inner-city child is different from that of the average white, middle-class child, and the adult education situation is drastically different from that of the average Protestant congregation. So, any student who expects to specialize in inner-city work presents us with concrete problems of educational guidance which most of us have not solved very well.

(4) The prospect of training teachers for church education, in the light of this last comment, shakes up a great deal of the standard textbook material about teaching and places in jeopardy any efforts to train teachers in close relationship to a pre-established curriculum. The person who experiences life in the ghetto is so different in value-orientation and social development that nothing less than an extremely skilled and self-confident teacher can be effective. We could, of course, argue that a really good teacher for a child of any socio-economic level is free from artificial curriculum patterns and is capable of developing materials and methods suitable to the occasion. But our problem in the inner-city congregation is compounded by the fact that many of the adults who teach have had little formal education and need a great deal of help. That is one reason why the Presbyterian study recommended a teaching community to develop morale, skills and learning, apart from any pre-established curriculum. I will not attempt to be more specific at this point, for I want to treat the whole matter of teacher-training next and approach it as a general problem rather than restricting it to the inner-city situation.

Improving Professional Training for the Church Educator

All kinds of reforms have been suggested for the congregation's educational work and many promising experiments are going on. It should be a part of our work in the seminary to keep informed about all new developments and to initiate or participate in all efforts to provide a better environment for education than the traditional Sunday school. However, I do not believe that the professor of Christian education should assume administrative responsibility for innovation in church education. Our contribution to such enterprises is our knowledge of the field generally and our specific skill in training the leaders, especially teachers who will work in such enterprises. For that reason I do not plan to discuss in this paper the merits of any particular educational enterprise. Rather, I want to turn our attention to the matter of preparing leaders for the local congregation.

The local congregation needs a variety of professional leaders in religious education, but few churches are able to afford more than one. The director or minister of education is often overburdened with administrative work and is unable to reserve a significant block of time for study or to work directly with the teachers to improve their skills. Although I do not want to discount this condition, I also do not want to hide behind it. In fact, I want to challenge the assumption that the "overworked administrator" is the basic problem with the professional educator in the local congregation.

It is possible to think of the professionally trained educator in the local church as the teacher. This position was inaugurated by John Calvin in Geneva and has a long history of usefulness in Protestantism. Within the last few decades there has been a revival of interest in calling to local churches ministers who have had training to teach and who spend their full time in this activity. It is also possible to conceive of the church educator as a trainer of teachers, rather than a principal who manages the church school. If we took seriously the role of the professional church educator as a teacher or as a trainer of teachers, what would it mean for our work in the seminary?

It would mean many of us would have to reconsider the methods by which we train our church educators. I am not in a position to judge the whole spectrum of graduate training available, but I am fairly well acquainted with the kind of training that is sponsored by many seminaries. Generally, we rely on some form of supervised field education for training in teaching. For the many students who are placed with a skilled and understanding master teacher this is just what they need to develop themselves and their skill. But there are two major problems with the field education program which are becoming more apparent: one is the difficulty, if not impossibility, of finding enough places where there is a skilled and understanding master teacher, and the other is the lack of control we have over the placement situation.

Studies have been made of what happens to apprentice teachers when they do practice teaching in public schools. The evidence is that apprentice teachers learn more about how to adjust to the environment and demands of the school as a public institution than they learn about teaching itself. As a result, some of our leading universities--Stanford University is one illustration--have withdrawn their apprentice teachers from schools and are now training them in controlled situations on the campus of the university. This is not a return to the old laboratory school idea, for the laboratory school was a model as well as an experimental school. The lab school had the responsibility of providing the total education of the child while it served as a place to train teachers. The newer method of teacher-training in controlled situations is often called micro-teaching. In micro-teaching the children are employed to be students completely apart from their normal school situation so that the apprentice teacher may concentrate on the specific skills to be developed.

I would guess our situation is not greatly different from the public school experience. My hunch is based on the observation that our seminary graduates slip into the role of a principal when they get into a local church, rather than into the role of a trainer of teachers because they feel more competent as administrators than as teachers. If this hypothesis is correct, then we should experiment more with methods of teacher-training for church education. This might be done along the lines already indicated by micro-teaching. It could be done by an analysis of episodes of teaching recorded on audio or videotape that students carry out in their field work placement. Another possibility is to make the seminary itself the laboratory situation. Many of us work in the center of a teaching institution which is seldom critically examined, and few of us share the various teaching activities in which we engage. In some seminaries there may be teachers--including religious education professors--who have the ego strength to put their teaching on the block for examination or where the professors may be willing to use advanced students as assistants to perform specific teaching roles in introductory courses, such as lecturing on specific topics, leading small group discussions, tutoring, helping to construct and grade examinations; in these cases the seminary situation itself may become the source of teaching experience in a controlled environment.

Perhaps I should explain my interest in controlled situations. I am working on the assumption that teaching uses a variety of skills that may, in sum, be considered an art, but which in its parts can be taught. This means that the apprentice teacher must have an opportunity to practice these skills under supervision. Thus, the advanced student in religious education who is not very skilled in lecturing could, in the controlled situation in the seminary, have these efforts analyzed and allowances made for any additional training needed. Although the analyses may be possible in the normal field-work situation, the opportunity for practicing skills cannot be managed without forcing the church group to abandon its primary purpose. You may feel that I have overstated the case for developing teaching skills in a controlled setting and have not balanced this presentation with other virtues that are found in the local church placement. Such may be the case. I don't care to argue the point because my real concern is not to depreciate the field-work position but to appreciate the need for better methods for training professional educators in the church to be teachers and teachers of teachers.

Notes

1 C. Ellis Nelson, *Where Faith Begins* (Richmond: John Knox Press, 1967).

2 James M. Gustafson, "The Voluntary Church: A Moral Appraisal." *Voluntary Associations*, ed. D. B. Robertson. (Richmond, John Knox Press, 1966) 321.

3 Fred M. Newmann and Donald W. Oliver, "Education and Community," *Harvard Educational Review* Winter 1967: 61-106.

4 Francis Keppel, "The Business Interest in Education," *Phi Delta Kappan* January 1967: 188.

5 Fred M. Heddinger, "Will Big Business and Big Government Control R and D?" *Phi Delta Kappan* January 1967: 218.

6 Edward A. White, Chalres Yerkes and Gerald L. Klever, *Education in the City Church* (Philadelphia: Board of Christian Education, Presbyterian Church, U.S.A., 1967).

7 Allison Davis, "Socialization and Adolescent Personality," *Adolescence, Forty-third Yearbook*, Part I. (Chicago: National Society for the Study of Education, 1944) chapter 11.

11

Can Protestantism Make it With the "Now" Generation?

Can you remember years ago when some students at Yale University made headlines by swallowing goldfish and thereby starting a craze of similar exploits in other schools? If not, do you remember when groups of college students competed to see how many people could be crowded into a telephone booth? Students have had fun and blown off steam with these and other stunts for a long time--until recently. In fact, since Black students invented the "sit-in," students have not wasted much time clowning around. For the past decade students have dug into a wide variety of social and political issues. They are probably one of the most feared unarmed and unorganized groups in America today.

Was this a passing phase that characterized the youth of the 1960s merely because civil rights and the war in Viet Nam caught their fancy? Is this rising generation indulging in long hair and unconventional ways just to see adults twitch? I don't think so. I believe that the generation under thirty is coming to an awareness of themselves and their world that is significantly different from the world that shaped the minds of adults now aged 40 to 60. Our problem is not the generation gap as such. To discuss it that way leads us either into sentimental pleas that adults try harder to understand teenagers or into false hopes that as soon as these kids get married and settle down, they will become as we did, standard Protestants. The problem is much deeper--it is not a generation gap but a culture gap.

An address given to members of the Division of Christian Education, National Council of Churches, February 14, 1969, Chicago, Illinois.

Ethics

The new generation has developed a different ethical orientation. The older generation was careful about personal morals and indifferent about social problems. The current generation says that what they do as individuals is their own business, as long as it doesn't hurt others, and that what counts ethically is what we do about the poor, weak, or colored people. Starting with the civil rights movement in the early 1960s, this new generation became more aware of inequities and more concerned to right these social wrongs than any youth generation in American history. They expose the materialism and hypocrisy of our society with deadly accuracy. At the Presbyterian Church, U. S. student convention in Atlanta this past Christmas, one student said that the most obscene thing he ever saw was a Diet Pepsi billboard perched high over a terrible black ghetto. We of the older generation would probably not "see" the irony because our perceptive system, built in earlier days, would allow us to see only the sign.

But even more remarkable is the newly developed notion that an individual can select the wars thought worth fighting. Selective pacifism is this generation's retaliation against the war in Viet Nam, and this is all but incomprehensible to the older generation. We need not review the parades, confrontations and strikes that have gone on for the past three years to remember that many of our young people are in jail because they will not go to Viet Nam. Even more disquieting is the small but significant number of officers and nurses in the Armed Forces who have come to believe the Viet Nam war is wrong and who have been court-martialed for disobedience.

Although I doubt that the precedent of the Nuremberg trials has much weight in our law courts, the principle of holding Nazi officers responsible for their action even though they were obeying orders from properly constituted authority is a strong point in the current ethical stance. If persons are against the war in Viet Nam, then in spite of governmental authority they must resist or be held personally responsible as the Nazi officers were in the Nuremberg trial.

Life-space

The meaning of "life-space" is changing the religious outlook of the younger generation. We have known for a long time that the earth is round and turns about the sun; this fact didn't change our religious thinking very much. But in the past ten years we have witnessed one space exploit after another and the facts about our planet and our universe are being absorbed by the younger generation with a meaning that is significantly different from that of the older generation's understanding. Our middle-aged astronauts on Apollo 8 read the Genesis account of creation and we of the same generation felt reassured. But younger people, I think, absorbed the facts, the distance, the cool efficiency of the computers, the courage of the astronauts in venturing outside the earth; above all, they retain the visual image of the earth as seen from the moon.

They are absorbing in the blood stream that nourishes the mind a sense of the earth as a small part of a dynamic, expanding universe; and then with this "mind" they are trying to understand the Christian faith in terms of idioms and symbols coming from an earth-centered universe. Three or four years ago when the "Death of God" controversy was alive, Erik Erikson published *Insight and Responsibility*. Taking note of the controversy, Erikson said that there are times ". . . when a sudden sense of alienation is widespread. Our time shares with Luther's an alienation composed of corresponding elements: *fears* aroused by discoveries and inventions (including weapons) radically expanding and changing the space-time quality of the world image; inner *anxieties* aggravated by the decay of existing institutions which have provided the historical anchor of an elite's identity; and the *dread* of an existential vacuum."[1]

Erikson also observes that when we have a severe identity crisis because of the redefinition of life-space, people have a need to delineate sharply what they are *not* as part of the struggle to understand themselves anew. Some of the ideological static we hear from the rising generation is an effort to tune in on a different conceptual wavelength, and we should stand by in case they get a message.

Self-Image

The "now" generation is also developing a different understanding of the self. It is seen in the widespread use of drugs. I do not refer to the hard-line dope addicts, because they have deep psychological needs. I have in mind the widespread use of pills to induce sleep, to stay awake or to tranquilize. The smoking of marijuana to heighten the joy of a moment must be mentioned in a separate sentence since it is illegal. The present generation's widespread use of drugs shows their concern to control their emotional states for the needs of the day.

Furthermore, recent advances in the biological sciences have opened up control of life itself. *The New York Times* on Sunday, February 2, 1969, reported a case of a woman who had Down's syndrome, or Mongolism, in her family. Dr. Henry L. Nadler, of Northwestern University, analyzed the chromosomes of her unborn baby and told her that the child was a boy and a Mongoloid. She had a therapeutic abortion and then became pregnant three months later. The second analysis showed that the baby would be a normal girl, and so it was. When I was a college student science told us with assurance that one birth out of so many hundred would be a Mongoloid. Today, science makes it possible to anticipate the birth of a Mongoloid, and the difference in these two statements is profound.

So much has been written and said about the revolution in sex ethics due to the easily obtained and effective birth control pill that I need not do more than mention that virginity, so highly prized by the older generation, is now viewed by many young people as a condition, not necessarily a virtue. The editor of *Cosmopolitan* magazine is probably closer to the realities of the present generation when she says, "The issue for the young girl is not whether she will have premarital sexual relations but whether she can cope with the many problems it entails." While the older generation spends its time in agonizing over this new attitude, the present generation is formulating the psychological rationale for a self-image that sees sex in a different way.

This is a complex matter, but it has been summarized in the current *Harvard Educational Review* by Abraham Maslow. Maslow claims that what is happening in psychology is "not an *improvement* of something; it is a real change of direction altogether. It is as if we had been going north, and are now going south instead." In brief he holds that there have been two major comprehensive theories of human nature. The first is that which underlies the behaviorist, experimental theory of psychology which flourishes in universities. These psychologists have never been interested in the higher elements of personality, such as altruism or the search for truth and beauty. The second is the Freudian theory--with many variations--which informs the clinicians and social workers. These psychologists attempt to explain or relate all of a human's activity to experiences in early childhood, omitting the higher needs of humankind, such as the intrinsic needs for goodness, justice or order. Against these, Maslow says, there is a theory now called "third force psychology," that has a different conception of the self. "For the first time in centuries," Maslow says, these psychologists talk of a human "essence." Humans have unique characteristics (many of which are weak in comparison to culturally-imposed morals) which must be discovered and made explicit. This humanistic psychology is aimed at self-discovery; sex is just one of the natural endowments which is to be explored and actualized and which is unrelated to social conventions.[2]

Issues for the Church

By this time many of you will have noted that I have been following a method used by cultural anthropologists in analyzing culture. I have noted that social values, world view, and self-image are significantly different for the generation that came of age during the past ten or fifteen years from that of the generation that came of age before World War II. Therefore, we must see the problem as a clash of cultures. There is the church culture: middle-class, prosperous, and busy operating the levers of power that control our society. Contending for power is an evolving culture, vague and diffuse, made up of many of our church-nurtured young people, that challenges the basic assumptions on which the church-culture operates. We must not get in a position of defending the church-culture against the youth-culture, or vice-versa. Both cultures have emerged as human reactions to social conditions and traditions. The way to move ahead is not to be sidetracked into a debate when we hear the slogan, "Jesus, yes; Church, no," but to examine carefully the issues that form the clash.

The first issue is: Where is authority for religion?

At the time of the Reformation, Protestants rejected the church as the authority and substituted for it the Bible. Actually, the reformers did not leave it there. They knew the Bible was a library of manuscripts, composed over a long historical period, using many literary forms, and difficult to interpret. Both Luther and Calvin proceeded to produce commentaries on almost every book in the Bible; they wrote creeds to summarize Biblical doctrines. From the beginning, the Bible was interpreted; and Calvin instituted the teaching minister as a normal part of the congregational leadership in order that all believers be instructed in the faith. As long as we had a commonly interpreted creed, and an effective church organization, we had an authority that was strong enough to test believers' fitness to partake of communion, or to try them for heresy.

Religious authority is also related to our changing view of history. The reformers saw history as a factual account of the past which could be made more accurate by diligent study. We see history as an interpretation of the past that is as much a commentary on the present as it is a story of the past. In 1967 the United Presbyterian Church adopted a Book of Confessions containing creedal statements dating from about 381 to 1967. In doing so it no longer limited itself to the Westminster Confession of Faith (1647). This action illustrates the modern view that we live in a stream of interpretive episodes; and each creed must be judged in relation to the problems and mentality of the era in which it was written. This process relativizes the past and focuses attention on the present as the place of judgment. In so doing, religious authority, which is associated with past events and thoughts, is weakened.

Along with creedal interpretations of the Bible, Protestants have emphasized individual conscience as the ultimate authority. Conscience, moral theologians have said, is the proof of God, the practical authority for one's life. But today the educated person will not accept conscience as the authority for religious life. Sociologists have presented to several generations of college students data showing conscience to be socially conditioned. Psychologists have several theories about the formation of conscience, all of which deal with the way children were handled by their parents and are unrelated to any conception of God. These studies open up to the student the relation of culture to personality and help them see that conscience has been, and can be, on any side of any issue. Most people, for example, feel guilty about stealing; but some children, trained by their parents to steal, would feel guilty if they did not.

Conscience as an authority worked well when there was a relatively homogeneous Christian ethos in this country, when the family was a rather stable group, and when the church could offer straightforward teachings on the current personal and social problems. The ethos is still here to some extent, but the various media of mass communication, especially TV, throw into dramatic conflict a wide range of standards and opinions about everything. This confuses parent and child alike. The churches face an extraordinarily complex social structure today and cannot speak with assurance about very many things; and when the churches do speak, many Protestants, rather than listening in order to have their conscience formed, will in the name of their own conscience, oppose what thoughtful church leaders are saying. In any case, the younger generation has been exposed to such a wealth of conflicting codes of conduct that they have, in self-defense, begun to formulate their own codes and to develop their own ways of reacting. They are Protestant in that they have made conscience their authority; but it is highly individualized conscience, not greatly influenced by the teachings of the church nor by the traditions of the past.

Authority, I believe, is related to respect; and that is at the heart of our problem. How can the local Protestant church help parents shape the lives of children so that conscience might be properly formed? How can the parish church's educational program be a means of helping children increasingly form rational judgments and become increasingly sensitive to human needs? How can a congregation relate itself to the community so that it serves the area and has the respect of the people served? We must learn to answer these questions if we are going to help the younger generation develop an inner sense of authority for their religious life.

The second issue is: What is the purpose of religion?

Our answer would include statements such as, to know and worship God, to receive guidance in individual and group activity, or to obtain eternal life. In these and other answers theologians often single out two basic human problems that religion solves: guilt feelings and attitudes toward death. The heart of Christian theology is that Jesus Christ died on the cross as a sacrifice for sin and that all who believe in him shall have eternal life. How interested is the rising generation in the orthodox solution to guilt and death?

To a generation stunned with three senseless assassinations of their spokespersons (one of which appears to have been the result of a highly organized effort), to the first generation to see its nation fighting a war live on TV with weekly body counts, to a group that sees American society placing a low value on the lives of the poor and colored, death is a common occurrence. Death is not taken casually, but the young people seem to be hardened to it. This social condition seems to have changed the way death is related to religion, even though as individuals young people are concerned about their own demise. We might speculate that the way a child's ego is formed nowadays in relation to incessant and vivid violence on TV has associated death with struggle and power rather than with religious faith. In any case, death doesn't scare young people into the church.

Understanding the rising generation's lack of guilt is much more difficult. I remember just a few years ago in a high school confirmation class a girl said to me that she saw no point in the pastor's prayers for forgiveness and the class agreed with her. I can't imagine what has happened; but whatever it is, it is manifested in various Western countries. The Dutch Catholic church for example, has abandoned the confessional except on demand, and there is little demand. Perhaps the young people's ethical code referred to earlier (that as long as an individual acts responsibly and does not interfere with the rights of others, one can do as one likes) is connected with the third force psychologists' contention that persons must actualize themselves through experimentation with a wide range of activity; this combination may be producing a personality structure that can manage its own guilt.

Whatever the reason may be for the rising generation's ability to handle death and guilt differently, religion, at least in its institutional form, is uninteresting to them. It could be, of course, that the oft-heard comment that persons want to be religious in their own way is a utilization of the salvation story without the liabilities of association with a church. Articulate young people often see the church as a citadel of middle-class values, a part of the problem with society rather than an institution that can lead or help with the social crises we are facing. Although I think this judgment about the church is superficial and shows an almost total lack of understanding of human institutions, that is a fair summary of what many students are saying.

Perhaps the real problem is that the rising generation, shaped by new forces and ideas, is proposing that the purpose of religion is the humanization of life and that the role of the church is to change society to serve all people. Many Christians would agree, but young people have more than a vague goal in mind. They now have their hands on a strategy of social change that is alarming if not entirely new. The old classical strategy of the church was to convert people and to assume that these changed lives would in their daily work Christianize the social order. This has proved to be a failure because the church did not show the converted persons how to be religious on their job and actually undercut this expectation by saying in effect that what they really needed to do was to convert more people. The outworking of faith was conceived in terms of personal morality; and although this is quite important, it was a narrow ethical platform that did not include all sorts and conditions of persons.

The new generation's strategy for social change is used against social institutions and the church. It started, I guess, when a black woman in Birmingham had all the abuse she could take and refused to relinquish her bus seat to a white man. The bus boycott by the blacks, under the leadership of Martin Luther King, Jr., opened up the possibilities of direct action to change social customs and laws. The strategy was refined by college students in Greensboro, North Carolina, who refused to leave a public lunch counter, and the "sit-in" became common. This strategy reached its perfection in the method known as confrontation, which is based on the proposition that the ends justify the means: any method of getting power is seized, thus forcing the authorities to acquiesce on certain issues or to change the power structure.

The strategy of confrontation is a form of civil war, with all of the dislocations and bitter feelings involved. When we note the way this new generation embarrassed the Democrats in Chicago last summer, toppled several university presidents, and brought about widespread educational reforms in the policies of major universities, we have to put aside our feelings of despair and ask why all of this should happen. The answer seems to be that older systems of making change in society or institutions are too slow and too unresponsive to new conditions. Our processes of communication are so fast and graphic that the younger generation is able to shape up programs of action to meet needs long before social institutions can adjust.

The church is caught in a cruel dilemma. There is little opposition to the purpose of making life more human for everybody, but there is great opposition to giving this purpose a high priority and to the strategy of confrontation. This means that the church must learn ethics from the younger generation, a task that is staggering to behold and one that hits where it hurts.

It was a group of students at Union Theological Seminary three years ago who studied the investment policies of New York banks in South Africa and then forced the ethical issue as to whether a Christian institution should support South Africa's inhuman social system by using these New York banks. As a result, denominations have reinvested their money and the ethical issue has been raised for all to see. It was a student group that put pressure on the Faculty and Board of Trustees of

Union Seminary to sell their Dow Chemical stock and to entrust a new committee with forming guidelines for investing the seminary's endowment funds. Whereas in the past we have been proud of the famous ethics teachers *at* Union, today we must recognize that the students are active in teaching ethics *to* Union as an institution.

Along with the word "involvement," the word "relevant" has emerged as a key concept. The current student generation's interest in social reform has led some people to think this is a resurgence of native American anti-intellectualism. Such is not the case. This generation wants to know; but they want to know about life as they see it, and they see things we older people can't bring into awareness. They want to know why children starve in America today, why 21 people with annual income of over one million dollars can legally escape any income tax, why ghetto children in New York City fall further and further behind the longer they stay in public school, or why the churches continue to spend millions of dollars to build and decorate houses of worship when the elementary human needs in the neighborhood are neglected. These are hard questions. The ordinary academic procedure of making the subject matter of a course an end in itself will not answer these questions. Although our colleges and seminaries have responded slowly, they have moved under intense student pressure toward having problem-centered courses, seminars on cases, or courses in which students make up the questions and invite in the professors and others in the community who may help with the answers.

Can the church respond to the demand for relevance? Top level church leaders and our best educational institutions can change to fit new conditions; but can congregations meet the test of relevancy? How can church leaders help congregations change from their study of Moses as subject matter to Moses as the paradigm of the freedom God wants all people to have today?

The third issue is: What makes a person religious?

The older generation assumes people are religious if they associate with the work and worship of the church, with attendance at public worship being the main criterion. The youth generation has always dropped out of the church in late adolescence and then returned after marriage and the start of a family. So the absence of the current youth generation from the church scene is not abnormal; but there is an uneasy feeling that this generation is not coming back.

Why? Because this generation is suspicious of all institutions and especially of the church. The church to them is too slow, too involved in what they call "Mickey Mouse stuff," too closely connected with conservative centers of power that exploit people, and too concerned about American superiority in a world where the poor nations are getting poorer. We all know there is truth in all these criticisms; yet the church means a lot more than these characterizations indicate. We must not get squared off in a debate about whether the church is what it ought to be. Many young people have found their own answer: they say one can be religious without the church, that one can use one's life in service in many different ways. My own belief is that this notion is theologically impossible and psychologically defective, but there it is. My forecast is that the church is going to have to reorient itself to human needs--but human needs more broadly responded to than merely through social action projects--or it will gradually attract only that segment of the population that is normally tradition-minded.

Linked with the current generation's lack of interest in the church is their effort to find a more satisfactory worship experience. Experiments with all kinds of celebration ranging from dance to spontaneous acting out of impulses are tried. Communion celebration sometimes with Coca-Cola and cookies without benefit of clergy or any prepared form of worship is attempted. Such attempts at worship are easy to criticize and can be predicted to have a brief life expectancy; but we must ask what this outcropping of deviant behavior signifies. My guess is that these efforts at worship are symptomatic of a profound struggle on the part of the young people to find a way to share and enjoy their interpretation of how a person is religious.

Implications for church leaders

These three issues are complicated and no suggestions will resolve them quickly. This youth generation is developing an outlook based on their cultural situation. The proper reaction is not to try to resolve anything but to examine the outlook and see what truth there is in it.

This is difficult to do because most of us suffer from one of the oldest religious diseases, the ark-complex. The ark in King David's day symbolized the power of God; and when the oxen which were carrying the ark stumbled, Uzzah grabbed it so it would not be damaged--in spite of the order that it was not to be touched (see II Samuel 6:6-8). We feel that we have to rush to the defense of the church whenever it is criticized. We should relax and say to ourselves that the institutional aspect of the church is not worth saving and that what is holy and good in the church God will preserve in a form pleasing to Godself.

If we could get rid of the ark-complex, we would be in a position to listen to what is being said by the younger generation and enter into a conversation with them. We should not ask the question, "Can Protestantism make it with the "now" generation?" It betrays our paternalism and our zeal to keep the old forms going. Rather, we should go to the youth, the poor, the black, the oppressed and engage in dialogue about our mutual concerns. In our conversation with the "now" generation we may gain a better understanding of our faults and give a clearer testimony about how Jesus is Lord of the church in changing times.

Notes

1 Erik H. Erikson, *Insight and Responsibility* (New York: W. W. Norton, 1964) 204.

2 Abraham H. Maslow, "Some Educational Implications of the Humanistic Psychologies," *Harvard Educational Review* 38 (1968): 685-696.

12

An Appeal to Professors and Researchers in Religious Education

We work in an exceedingly complex field. Neither religion nor education can be defined exactly and our whole enterprise is concerned about human beings who vary in age, sex, race, socioeconomic levels and interests. Moreover, we live in a time that is self-consciously historical. We're not only aware of all of the elements that make up religious education; we're also conscious that the era in which we live is a historical phase that will change. This radical historicizing of our lives is relatively new and the church has not yet thoroughly absorbed its meaning. Gerhard Ebeling gives us the impact of this new awareness in these words: "Never in the whole history of theology up to modern times was there such a thing as taking a historical view of a theological problem." Ebeling goes on to point out that the Bible--as well as all literature from the past--has to be understood historically and is "not simply timeless truths." This modern way of thinking relativizes the past as well as the present and requires a new sense of responsibility for trying to direct the course of human events.[1] Thus, religious educators are deeply involved in all the ambiguities of modern life--including the direction they think history should take in the future.

These characteristics of our present age are shared by everyone working seriously in the field of religion. What seems to be unique is the way some theologians and biblical scholars are using the social sciences to help them understand and use the present in their work. This is not to say that theologians have just discovered the social sciences. On the contrary, ever since Darwin the intellectual leaders of the church have responded to (and often incorporated into their thought) data about human beings from the biological and social sciences. Rather, what is

---

Presidential address, Association of Professors and Researchers in Religious Education (APRRE), 1973.

unique is use of the method of research and work of the social sciences as well as a more extensive use of the data that emerges from these sources. It is not the purpose of this paper to trace the reasons for these developments. It may be the events of the 1960s (such as the ability of two American presidents to wage a terrible war in Indo-China without a declaration of war, the revelation that we are a racist and sexist society, and the informal but effective rulership of a military-industrial complex over our lives) that require theologians to assume more responsibility for discussing the present human situation in relation to God's activity in the world.

My hunch is that the events of the 1960s were but a trigger that set off a new venture among our church intellectuals that had been developing for a long time. It may be important to recall the enormous development of ideas about human behavior that has emerged in the twentieth century. The century started with the child study movement and almost every facet of child development has been studied since that time. In the 1920s Freudian psychology became more respectable and, augmented with the work of the neo-Freudians, is firmly established among many intellectuals as well as psychotherapists. In the 1930s the work of the cultural anthropologists became well-known and widespread. These movements were integrated for the first time in the late 1930s by a series of studies sponsored by the American Council on Education concerning Negro youth. Allison Davis' book, *Children of Bondage* (1940), is one in that remarkable series of studies. Then in the 1940s the thought of Kurt Lewin became better known, resulting in the development of research and study of human groups--a development which has spread in many directions in the past twenty years. I've probably left out some important developments, such as the influence of philosophical analysis in clarifying the use of religious language; but the purpose of this recital is not to exhaust the range of developments but to help us pause for a moment to see where we are.

A Different Milieu

I want to avoid the dramatic notion that we're entering a new era. Rather, I would suggest the more modest observation that a different milieu is developing in which we religious educators need to find our place and make our distinctive contribution.

It has always been convenient and correct to date the beginning of the modern religious education movement with the formation of the Religious Education Association (R.E.A.). The people who founded the Association were leaders of religious and educational thought, and they occupied the highest positions of trust in our universities and seminaries. The first bulletin of the R.E.A. (August, 1903), "A Call for a Convention," listed ten purposes of the founders. These purposes either called for the use of the social sciences in the teaching of religion or they requested the upgrading of religion as a subject by better teacher preparation and by coordination of religion with other subjects. Reading those ten objectives today reveals how completely the first generation of professors and researchers saw their work as a part of the liberalizing influences which were spreading through the churches and universities.

The special role of religious education professors in the modernization of American Protestantism was the introduction of the social sciences into seminary curricula. The first generation of professors brought psychology and some sociology--or at least social criticism--into the intellectual diet of ministers. Even as late as World War II, there were many fine denominational seminaries that had no curricular source of social science except that supplied by the religious education professors. In many seminaries prior to World War II even pastoral counseling was taught by the religious education professors. After the war, the situation changed almost everywhere. Pastoral counseling and the clinical pastoral education movement developed and flourished and now have places of their own in the seminaries. Sociology of religion is now taught in many schools.

But more important than an identification of professorships is the extent to which the methods of investigation, the "empirical" data and the central focus of the social sciences on humankind has permeated the whole theological enterprise. If one goes into the bookstore of the typical theological seminary today, one will find an exceedingly wide range of materials about persons and society that are required reading for theology, history and Bible courses. Some theologians are saying today that God's purpose in the world is to make life human; some historians are claiming that their discipline helps us to understand the present and to write scenarios for the immediate future; biblical scholars are emphasizing that the hearer of the word is an indispensable part of the hermeneutical circle.

I do not want to imply that religious education professors and researchers brought all of this about. In addition to the social sciences there were movements of thought in philosophy, notably process philosophy, existentialism and phenomenology that have focused attention on the human situation. For example, Martin Heidegger in some places in *Being and Time* seems to be giving a description of the role of cultural values in the formation of persons which would be affirmed by many social scientists who have studied how the self is shaped by society.[2] About the same time, Alfred North Whitehead was writing that God was not a monarch but that God and world were mutually involved.[3] There were also streams of social thought influenced by Karl Marx coming into the Christian west that inspired many of our ethicists to assay the social and economic order in the light of Christian moral values.

It is probably more accurate to say that the first generation of religious educators brought the social sciences into theological education; and since that time, we have participated with an ever-enlarging circle of church intellectuals in an effort to use our knowledge of human life from any source as a part of the interpretation of the Christian tradition. We who are now in the third or fourth generation of religious education professors and researchers need to realize that the milieu in which we work in the future may be significantly different from that of the past. Already on most faculties we find ourselves only some among many who know and use humanistic philosophy and social sciences.

What then do these developments mean for our work? Does it mean that we give up theory and fall back on our age group expertise because few "academic" professors have experience with, or interest in, the ongoing programs of religious education? Or does it mean that we should continue to select some special area of interest within our ever-broadening field and make our contribution to the agency we serve by our special knowledge? Most of us are now following one or both of these alternatives, but I would like to appeal to all professors and researchers of religious education to consider two other alternatives that may be more in harmony with the future.

Neither of the following proposals is completely new because some members of our guild have already made notable contributions in each area. What is needed is a more common understanding of how the changing milieu may make a difference in the way we work and the tasks we undertake in the future.

Theoretical Formulation

The first has to do with theorizing. Ever since religious education became a field of study and research, leaders have explored theories. Whether we start with Horace Bushnell or George Albert Coe and move to Luther Weigle and then through the decades, we would find a formula for writing a theory of religious education. Theorists are either in reaction to a prevailing theology or practice of the church (Horace Bushnell or James Smart) or they are riding the crest of a new, powerful movement (George Albert Coe and the early Luther Weigle) or they have absorbed some area of human knowledge--say psychoanalysis--by which they orient all of religious education (R. S. Lee). Often these theories have had wide influence in the church. George Albert Coe and Luther Weigle had enormous influence in the church during the 1920s-1930s, as shown in curriculum revisions and by the development of leadership training for church teachers sponsored by the International Council of Religious Education.

We still need our theorists; indeed, we need them more than ever. When we read the works of the first generation theorists of religious education, we can't help being struck with a certain simplicity in theology and psychology. Today we have much more knowledge of human behavior to coordinate and that means that we have an even more urgent need for theorists to order our knowledge so that it is understandable as a system and useable in normal religious education work. It is this enormous expansion of knowledge about human beings and the use of much of this data by theologians and biblical scholars that leads me to say that perhaps the work of the religious education theorists should change. This is suggested in part because one person cannot easily integrate all of the data necessary for forming theories today and in part because professors in other fields have moved decisively into areas that were once our private preserves.

My appeal to religious educators who have an interest in theory is to team up with a congenial colleague in theology, Bible or history who has made a pilgrimage into this promised land of the "now." The results of such teamwork will be stronger and more significant for the church than if we continue individually to produce theories.

The Practice of Religious Education

Religious education as a field of study and research has always been characterized by some persons who have kept up a lively dialogue between theory and practice. A brief review of the work of the curriculum committee of the International Council of Religious Education in the 1920s will show that religious education professors were leaders in developing the graded lessons and the "life situational" approach to teaching. Probably all of us can recall the work of two of our most creative and best-known second generation professors--Harrison Elliot and Paul Vieth. Each advanced and enhanced the field of religious education. Elliot did so by his concern for the involvement of the learner in the discussion method. Vieth did so by identifying goals of religious education and making them useful in the teaching-learning enterprise and by development of the audio-visual method. These and other professors improved the practice of religious education at a time when the intellectual environment was unfavorable and at times hostile. They had to struggle with their "academic" colleagues for the integrity of religious education as a field while they were simultaneously inspiring thousands of teachers and local church leaders to improve their ability to translate the Christian message for the modern world.

It is the thesis of this paper that those days of struggle between religious educators and other intellectuals in the church are now past. Today and for the foreseeable future, many intellectuals with various fields of expertise are concerned with the proper utilization of contemporary human life in the hermeneutical process.

Perhaps I should be more explicit. Everyone who interprets the past does so with a set of assumptions. These assumptions include the interpreter's research methods, the kind of data he or she considers to be true, and his or her own belief system. These elements get fused into a pattern or template which makes it possible for the interpreter to observe a wide variety of data and form it into meaningful statements. Henry Pitney Van Dusen, a theologian with eyeglasses ground to the prescription of "American liberalism," was able at the end of a long and fruitful career to see those things in the past and present which supported the fundamental beliefs of that outlook.[4]

Part of the set of assumptions that an interpreter brings to the task is his or her notion of the role of persons in the process of communication. Here the situation becomes more complex. Many theologies with widely differing beliefs include the notion that theory can be applied to practice; that one can deduce from theory what practice ought to be. Thus, unitarians and trinitarians can, and often do, assume that ideas that are rooted in history and developed by reason have priority over the contemporary human situation to which they are applied. It is the priority or preeminence of the role of ideas over the significance of the human situation that is the point, for I assume no one today would claim that ideas just float above history and culture.

Biblical studies represent the area where we are most concerned. The historical-critical method of Bible study at first contributed to a liberalism which was devoted to the use of reason in religion and to the evolutionary hypothesis that progress in spite of ups and downs was toward a better social order. Later, the historical-critical method was used by neo-orthodox theologians to clean up the biblical text and make way for strong affirmation of traditional theology. In neither school of thought was the human situation given the same credence as ideology. Nor was faith and its profound problems given the attention lavished on technical studies of the text. Some biblical scholars label this situation a crisis and are appealing to their fellow scholars to find a new category of interpretation which pays attention to the struggle of human souls.[5]

The proposed category of interpretation is, of course, not new but is a renewed effort to find the source to experience the power of faith in God. The historical-critical method is assumed in relation to the Bible and the use of reason in relation to all human affairs. What is relatively new is the insistence that human life, especially the mind, is formed by social interaction and that the individual's self-conscious effort to understand the strange but powerful forces, hopes, fears, and self-enhancing urges that well up within one's being are essential to the hermeneutical process. Therefore, human life is both the source and the object of systems of meaning (theology) and human life must be kept in dialogue with ideas and information that come from previous generations. This approach to the problem of hermeneutics is itself a theory and many intellectuals spend their time theorizing without any special concern for its actual use.[6] Others--such as Walter Wink and Tom Driver, to mention two professors at Union Theological Seminary--actually follow the logic of their assumptions and use the present situation of persons as data on a par with ideas from the past.[7]

In light of this terse survey I would propose that the religious education guild of scholars return to the vision that informed our predecessors in the 1920s. The program they undertook was to use the social sciences, mainly educational psychology, both to question the Christian faith and to interpret it. Today the methods of analysis of the human situation are much more complex, and the store of knowledge much greater; but the purpose of many contemporary theologians seems to be similar to those of the religious education professors back in the 1920s. I do not mean that we must go back to the 1920s and start over again, although it might do us good to reread the thinkers of that time. Nor do I mean that those people anticipated our era--they did not. Their notion of "life situation" would be too simple and superficial today. It was their daring affirmation that human life as it is lived is a part of the interpretive process that is back in fashion in a new and profound way.

If this analysis is even partly correct, then I believe that we, like our 1920s predecessors, need to give special attention to the teaching of religion. There are, of course, other areas of the practice of religious education--worship, for example--that deserve and require study and research. But I will select classroom teaching because that is the occasion when a religious educator makes a planned and deliberate effort to translate the Christian religion. Moreover, classroom teaching is the place where--statistically speaking--more people are involved in religious education activity than any other formal mode of education. It is also the area where we have very little research data. The United Presbyterian Study in 1966 is one of the few efforts to try to discover what actually went on in the church school classes.[8] I am not aware of studies of the teaching of religion in private or state secondary schools or in college classrooms. We have a lot of curriculum guides, teacher-training manuals and even some studies of the amount of religion learned, but little about what actually goes on in the classroom.[9] Public schools are in about the same position, according to Maxine Greene, a professor of philosophy of education at Teachers College, in a review of a book by Harry S. Broudy. Together they affirm that there is no "scientific theory of teaching" and that the amount of theory that can be applied is "pitifully small."[10]

Also, the rapid development of the movement to make seminary work more self-consciously professional suggests that religion educators focus attention on the function of the minister as teacher. The image of the minister as teacher is clear and powerful, especially in the Reformed tradition. The most visible manifestation of this movement is the development of doctoral degrees in ministry which claim to train persons to a certain definable level of competence in the major functions of ministry. Teaching--along with preaching, healing (counseling) and leadership of the church in the community--is one of the ancient functions of the clergy. If we broaden the conception of classroom teaching to include the teaching of groups of officers and adults, then ministers do considerable teaching even if they do not have regular church school classes. If we're successful in this venture, ministers might become interested enough in teaching to duplicate with their church school teachers the kind of training they themselves have experienced. By selecting teaching as one of the central areas of religious education, we may be able to focus our attention and our research skills in an area of ministerial competence that will give our work a rationale and discipline that it needs.

This appeal does not mean that teaching religion is a simple matter. I need not detail all of the factors that go into the activity--such as a conception of what religion is or various teaching strategies that can be employed. What is important at this point is the possibility of the contemporary human situation and the biographies of individual learners becoming parts of the hermeneutical process. This appeal therefore does not mean we simply begin to search for the best teaching methods of general education and then apply them to religion or that we use more technologies such as videotape in our training methods. All of these things might have their proper place, but I am appealing to religious educators to do both their theoretical explorations and their experiments in training "competent" ministers with their colleagues from other disciplines, and to use their special knowledge of human life from the social sciences as a part of the interpretive process.

If this proposal seems to have merit, how can we explore more decisively the teaching of religion? First, I would suggest that we make this area the general topic of our 1974 meeting. Such a suggestion implies that some professors and researchers will begin to develop projects that can be reported at our next meeting. Moreover, there has been some experimentation in Cambridge, Mass., Chicago, San Francisco, Richmond, and New York that I know about. The persons associated with these enterprises should be invited to write up their experiences. We might commission some of the theorists among our guild to work with their colleagues and compose theories that would provide leads for research as well as stimulation for our developing programs to bring about competence in teaching. Second, we might ask the Executive Committee of the APRRE to appoint a small committee to meet occasionally during the coming year to coordinate whatever work our members develop and to prepare an annotated bibliography of materials which would help us all become better acquainted with the issues and opportunities involved.

There is a special need for our members to be kept up to date on the specific programs that seminaries develop for appraising competence to teach religion. Whether we like it or not, doctoral programs in ministry are developing rapidly and seminaries are announcing training programs based on the notion that professional competence in ministerial functions can be identified, appraised and improved. It would seem to me that the portions of these programs devoted to the development of the minister as teacher should be on some kind of "hot line" to all of our members during the next few years as we struggle to meet the challenge of this new goal of theological education.

Notes

1 Gerhard Ebeling, *Word and Faith* (Philadelphia: Fortress Press, 1963) 364-365.

2 Martin Heidegger, *Being and Time*, trans. John Macquarrie and Edward Robinson (New York: Harper & Row, 1962) 163-168.

3 Alfred North Whitehead, *Process and Reality: An Essay in Cosmology* (New York: Macmillan, 1929) 519-533.

4 Henry P. Van Dusen, *The Vindication of Liberal Theology* (New York: Charles Scribner's Sons, 1963).

5 Brevard Childs, *Biblical Theology in Crisis* (Philadelphia: Westminster Press, 1970).

6 James M. Robinson and John B. Cobb, Jr., eds., *The New Hermeneutic* (New York: Harper & Row, 1964).

7 Walter Wink, *The Bible in Human Transformation* (Philadelphia: Fortress Press, 1973). See also Kent Harold Richards, "Changing Contexts for Biblical Interpretations," *The Christian Century* November 7, 1973: 1100-1101.

8 *United Presbyterian National Educational Survey* (Philadelphia: Board of Christian Education of the United Presbyterian Church, 1966).

9 One illustration from England of the amount and kind of learning that takes place in the classroom is Harold Louke, *Teen-Age Religion* (London: S.C.M. Press, 1961). An appraisal of the effectiveness of Catholic education was done by Joseph H. Fichter, *Parochial School* (Notre Dame: University of Notre Dame Press, 1958). See also, Reginald A. Neuwien, *Catholic Schools in Action* (Notre Dame: The University of Notre Dame Press, 1966).

10 Maxine Greene, rev. of *The Real World of the Public Schools* by Harry S. Broudy, *Harvard Educational Review*, May 1973: 287.

13

Where Have We Been? What Does It Mean?

You will recall that Henry Ford said on one occasion that history was "bunk." By that he meant we could overcome the past by forgetting it and using our time and energy in the present to build the future we wanted. Unfortunately, history is not bunk. The present with which we have to work is made up of the immediate past; and to ignore it is to indulge in romantic thinking and actions--as Henry Ford did on one occasion. You may remember he outfitted a "peace" ship during World War I and sent it to Europe on the assumption that the nations over there would see the error of their ways and stop fighting. They paid no attention to this quixotic gesture.

If we want to be effective and influence individuals in the church, we must come to grips with what has happened in the past thirty or forty years because those events have shaped the mentality of the generations with which we work.

Let us examine briefly what has happened during the last forty years in (1) *theology*, (2) *society* and (3) *church life* and then indicate what these trends mean for us in our work for the next few years.

1940--Early 1960s

Theology

Christian education does not exist by itself. It is a part of the church's life and is therefore affected by the theology of the church. From the 1940s until well into the 1960s, there was a broad theological consensus both in Presbyterian circles and among theologians whom we label neo-orthodox. Although there was disagreement on details in the

---

An address to the Association of Presbyterian Church Educators meeting February 7, 1977 in Louisville, Kentucky.

main neo-orthodoxy insisted that God was revealed in history, especially through the biblical account. If you would like help in defining neo-orthodoxy, I would suggest that you read the *Interpreters Bible* commentary; for those twelve volumes were written in the middle of the period and were generally informed by this theology. In the United Presbyterian Church the Faith and Life Curriculum--and in the Presbyterian Church U.S., the Covenant Life Curriculum--was directly influenced by this theological stance.

We must also remember that during the same period of time we were engaged in a gigantic war experience. The humiliation experienced at Pearl Harbor in 1941 drove us into a long total national war effort. Reinhold Niebuhr and others founded *Christianity and Crisis* as a theological effort to influence America away from isolationism and toward an alliance with other nations struggling against Nazi Germany. The revelations of the demonic nature of Nazi Germany--especially the systematic murder of about six million Jews and others--justified the judgment that World War II was a righteous war.

Society

In the 1950s we lived out the situation of a nation that had won a war. We felt that we were right about the war and that our style of life helped bring victory. The national mood was conservative because victory appeared to bring confirmation of our life and work.

It is hard to recapture the national mood of the 1950s. You must remember that we were content not because we were lazy but because we believed we were right. Enterprising researchers at Purdue University in the middle of the 1950s asked young people to read a set of statements on a typed sheet of paper and then sign if they agreed. A high percentage of the young people refused to sign the statement, thinking it was too radical. The statement was a typewritten copy of the Bill of Rights. But to many young people in the 1950s that was a radical statement which might interfere with their careers. In fact, the National Council of Churches in its Sunday morning TV programs aimed at young people, devoted a number of programs to the problem of conformity and complacency! The church was busy trying to wake up young people to the world around them. Perhaps the whole decade could be summed up in the words of Casey Stengel, the baseball manager, who on one occasion was in the process of winning another world series. He was asked by a reporter what pitcher he would use for the next game. Casey gave the name of his pitcher who had beaten the other team the previous time he pitched; and then he added, "Who argues with success?"

It is hard to recall how self-confident and complacent we were in the 1950s and how orderly our life appeared. The generation that came of age during that period are now 40 to 50 years of age and are now the parents of teenagers who came of age under quite different circumstances. Is there any wonder that there is a conflict in the viewpoint of these generations!

Church Life

During this period the church had a well-defined national program. We had a mission board designed to spread the gospel in the United States and another designed to spread the gospel throughout the world. This was a simple, direct way to organize our work, and the average person knew what the work was about upon just hearing the title of an agency, such as "The Board of Christian Education."

The Board of Christian Education was not only visible--it had an executive who was a leader. If you did not like what was going on you could talk with him or write him a letter. By this process a dialogue was maintained between individuals and judicatories of the church and the agency representing Christian education.

Moreover, the Board had an editor-in-chief who was a theologian and an educational leader for the church. I have only to mention James Smart of the United Presbyterian Church and Rachel Henderlite of the Presbyterian Church, U.S. for you to realize how fortunate we were in those days.

But the important thing was that the church had an agency with excellent leaders who would create and administer a total program of Christian education. The program dealt with leadership training, family education, camping, youth projects, ministry to students and many other things. Under it--and through it all--were curriculum materials.

I do not want to idealize the denominational curriculum we had in the 1950s. Since I was involved as consultant in both denominations and wrote a few small pieces, I know the problems and limitations of the curriculum. I do, however, want to laud the process through which we went to produce the curriculum. The editor would gather the best theologians, educators, and biblical scholars of the church for consultation. The process required that we think through our theology, update it and apply it to new conditions in society. Because the best of our denominational ministers and leaders were involved, it forced us to reconcile some of our differences and find the common beliefs which represented our tradition. A denominational curriculum is the self-image of the church; as such it provides a norm to which we can subscribe or a standard by which we can measure our distance from the common beliefs of the denomination. Moreover, when the curriculum was finished after four to six years of study, work and testing, it was introduced into churches by a program of leadership training, and the whole church was stimulated to think about its theology.

The process of developing a new curriculum also excites other elements in the church which help the denomination shape itself and its beliefs. We must not forget that the *Westminster Study Edition of the Bible* came out of this era, and that commentary helped mold the mind of the United Presbyterian Church. The Presbyterian Church U.S. produced the *Layman's Bible Commentary*, a twenty-five volume work that continues to shape the thinking of teachers in that church.

One more word about this pre-1960 period that we must not forget: the word "growth." The self-confidence of the era was expressed in the popularity of young couples having large families. Everything seemed destined to grow as everything had grown since the forming of our nation. With unlimited natural resources and the promise of nuclear power, the glories of science producing DDT to rid the air of bugs and penicillin to rid the body of germs, we had the feeling there were very few problems we could not solve with science.

Throughout this period the Presbyterian Church expanded. Many of our presbyteries appointed church extension committees which surveyed metropolitan areas for locations for new churches. Some of these committees were so confident that they bought property for new church building before residential subdivisions were established; and in many cases they were right in their judgment.

Early 1960s--1976

Theology

Then somehow in the early 1960s things changed. The neo-orthodox theological consensus began to wane. No general school of thought shoved it aside or took its place. Rather, the whole theological enterprise in the United Presbyterian Church took a different turn. In place of asking what was distinctive, the church seemed to be broadening its appeal and asked how we were like other denominations and how we affirmed the whole Christian tradition. The result was to approve a Book of Confessions and thus historicize the Presbyterian faith. By adding *Confession of 1967* the church gave a special boost to the doctrine of reconciliation in the midst of social and racial conflict. These same tendencies developed in the Presbyterian Church U.S. They, too, prepared a set of confessions to take their places alongside the Westminster Confession of Faith and a new Declaration of Faith was developed to give a contemporary flavor to our church beliefs. Passed by the 1976 General Assembly this package of confessions is now before the presbyteries for approval.

So today, we have a pluralistic theological situation. In addition to our traditional confessions, we now have theology of special interest groups--such as liberation, feminist and black theology. And, of course, we have a resurgence of civil religion and of both pious and intellectual fundamentalism.

Society

We all remember the social situation of the last 15 years but let me recall briefly some of the major events.

President John Kennedy and Martin Luther King, Jr. were assassinated. Suddenly, we had to face the hidden truth that violence was as American as apple pie. Moreover, an examination of our history only confirmed the large role of violence in our being. Although sobered, there seemed to be little we could do to break out of our enslavement to violence. The belief that we were reasonable people was shattered.

Black students under the influence of Martin Luther King, Jr. developed the sit-in. All through the 1960s, civil rights were affirmed and achieved. Sometimes the blacks got just laws, and other times favorable legal decisions; but above all they finally reached the conscience of the nation. Thus, a hundred years after the freeing of the slaves, there was a freeing of the spirit of black people to be persons in their own right. The belief that we were a just people was shaken.

Somehow we got involved in a war in Southeast Asia. We were unwilling to get out or to use enough military power to win. We did not know what the war was for, nor how to stop it. We had enough revolts, riots, and civil disobedience to convince President Johnson that he could not be reelected. These events taught a whole generation of young people that they could not trust political leaders and gave this group of young people an aversion to almost anyone in authority. The belief that we fought only just wars to liberate others lost its persuasive power.

We elected President Nixon, who developed what we now call "the imperial presidency." That is, he set himself up above the laws and customs of our nation. He used the power of his office to shape the nation in the direction of his own ideas without regard for the constitutional rights of individuals. When we learned accidentally of the depth of his betrayal, he resigned rather than face impeachment. Now the adults of our nation feel betrayed; and more recent revelations of the misuse of power by the CIA and FBI have made us wonder if we can trust anybody. The belief that government officials serve the common good was jolted.

Church Life

This jolting of some of our most cherished beliefs during the past 15 years has produced an unusual church situation. We have a split youth generation. Many seek certainty in dogmatic theologies and movements. Others have lost confidence in all institutions and are adrift. But more disturbing is the young adult generation--those who are starting families and vocations. In the past, this group returned to the church as a part of the settling-down process; but they do not seem to be doing so today.

Both Presbyterian denominations are becoming smaller. The membership in the United Presbyterian Church from about 1940 to 1965 showed an almost uninterrupted membership growth. Membership has declined steadily since 1965. The story in the Presbyterian Church U.S. is about the same, except that the decline did not start until about 1970. I have heard people respond to this situation by saying that these declines represented a shaking out of people who were frightened by the Angela Davis episode or other prophetic activities of the General Assembly, and the church is better off without these marginal people. Others have advanced the theory that the Holy Spirit is preparing us for a great revival which will soon take place. Some believe the zero population growth movement is to blame for our declining church membership.

Let's leave the speculation aside and face the fact of morale. The psychology of growth and the confidence it engendered are gone. This is our basic problem. None of us has had any experience with a "stable state" psychology. We equate a lack of growth with failure or we feel guilty and seek reasons for seeming to stand still. A no-growth mentality may be the most difficult problem for us in the immediate future.

The no-growth situation is compounded by inflation. People have less to give. Judicatories and church institutions have to cut back. Our program becomes more and more restricted. Morale suffers and some of our most creative leaders are forced to seek employment elsewhere. Unless the inflation situation is brought under control, we will in a few years see hundreds of churches slip below the financial level at which they can support a minister. Then we will have a new dilemma: a large supply of ordained ministers and a large number of churches without pastors. If this happens, our sense of frustration will deepen.

Our Presbyterian Christian education leaders--facing the break up of the neo-orthodox consensus, the heightened interest in special group theologies and the disastrous results of inflation--joined with other denominations to produce instructional materials. The joint Education Development project was formed and is now fully operational. Given the circumstances, I guess we made the right decision. It saved money because we took the curriculum already in existence in several denominations, updated it, and laid it out so local churches could choose the type they liked. But the denomination did not benefit from the process of thinking through a theology for our day.

I want to conclude these comments about our recent past with this general observation. I believe that at the deeper level of our being there has been a change in theological outlook. This change may be more important for our contemporary situation than inflation or restructuring the denominations. In fact, the changes in belief may explain our no-growth situation. In brief, I am entertaining the notion that since World War II there has been a steady erosion of belief in the attributes of God that underlay the evangelical stance of our denomination. There is some research which might throw light on this deep area of the self. Catholic University has received a very large grant to study the religious education of children and young people. Their first studies are just now coming from the press; and the United States Catholic Council has asked me and a few others to critique these research data. One piece of data from the studies has to do with beliefs of undergraduate men at Williams College. Tests were made in 1948 and concluded in 1974. By the end of that period of time, fewer students believed in God as wise and as an omnipotent creator, in immortality, in the value of the church, or in the usefulness of prayer. Studies made of undergraduate men at Dartmouth College and the University of Michigan from 1952 to 1974 show a similar drift away from traditional beliefs about God.

Well, a few studies do not document a trend, but with the absence of any other data it can be proposed that the heart of our problem is theological. The resurgence of fundamentalism among teenagers and on the college campus is not to my mind a sign of renewal or revival. Rather, these movements with doctrinaire theologies are making progress with people who have grown up in the church or have had a Christian background through their family life.

What Does it Mean?

Let us then turn to the present. What do these things mean to us who do the educational work of the church?

1. We must help people experience and understand the Christian faith. The fundamental problem for ministers and church educators is the inculcation of beliefs. This activity should have first priority--not for the usual reason that we need to understand our faith but because of the confusion about theology. Church people, young and old, yearn for the self-confidence that comes from an understanding of faith. But many of the old ways of expressing faith are inadequate. The effort on the part of both of our denominations to write a new confession is proof of this desire. The fallacy is to think that the new confession will satisfy the desire.

Another way of stating the matter would be--what does it mean for a denomination to have a book of confessions? It means that we have historicized our faith. We have said officially that creedal statements are always formed in relation to the life and thought of the culture in which they are lived. We have affirmed that old creeds have to be interpreted in the light of the conditions that brought them forth--that we must attempt to write new creeds every generation. We have said the denomination must be a manufacturing plant for theological beliefs.

But does the church understand how different from having a confession it is to be constantly working on a confession? I don't think this has become clear to the average church member. But, now that the General Assembly has made this fundamental change in our outlook, the church educator has been given a new and indispensable task of helping people work on the meaning of faith for our day.

The congregation is the focus of this educational activity; believers are gathered in face to face encounter--sharing their hopes, fears, celebrations, griefs, sins and in other ways expressing their faith. The constant interaction of individual believers about their lives as they work and worship together is the place where faith is fostered and given meaning. Faith is something we receive from God through community, the family, friends and congregation, and it is the inward, invisible trust we have in God.

The meaning church people give to faith, beliefs and/or confessions is worked out in the congregation. This outward visible expression of our minds is an effort to comprehend how faith relates to the world around us. That is why confessions are commentaries on culture and why so many, especially Calvinistic confessions, are mainly about ethics.

Our problem is how to work with the natural interaction which goes on in the congregation in such a way that it will be informed and corrected by the Bible and by the thought of previous generations. Preaching and corporate worship are traditional processes for doing this. We educators need to give more attention to how we can be a deliberate part of the process. A simple way would be to study some of the confessions. A more comprehensive way would be to set up a plan whereby a congregation works through its own beliefs and writes them out, debates them, and finally approves them. It would take several years; but such a process could be stimulating and would be in keeping with the way the first generation of Christians helped shape some of the books of the New Testament.

Or, one could start with the church school curriculum that has been prepared elsewhere and shipped to the congregation with the hope that it will be suitable. Is it? Does the theology in the printed curriculum properly express the faith? Should the young people be working through other issues? These and other questions could be transmitted to a representative group of adults along with a proposed curriculum. If adults studied the instructional materials and worked through these questions, they would become more sensitive to theological and educational matters and would simultaneously improve their ability to function as educators in the church and home.

2. We need to be people-centered in our educational work. Christian education has a long tradition of being person-centered because education is an activity aimed at the individual. But church educators have a way of not believing their own rhetoric. It is quite possible that--in the great decades of the 1940s and 1950s when we were self-confident and getting larger every year--we paid too much attention to the program and printed

curriculum materials and not enough to persons. Certainly we gave our time and energy to children, and adults got the "left-overs." That may be one of the reasons why the adult population of our churches was unprepared for the 1960s and for all the social turmoil and changing ethical standards which emerged. Now we are faced with a reversal of emphasis. Many educators are turning attention to adults, especially older adults, because they constitute an increasingly large percent of our congregations. A certain amount of this attention to adults is overdue, but we are now in danger of overlooking the needs of children and young people in our churches and communities.

I would like to insist that we not play favorites with age groups but stick to our religious affirmation that all individuals are important in the eyes of God. The proper understanding of that statement calls us to look around in our community and to inquire about the conditions of children and young people. This could result in a reactivation of the Sunday School as an evangelistic agency to reach persons who have no one caring about their spiritual development. Or, it could result in the utilization of our educational buildings as day care centers.

In this regard I want to say an encouraging word about families. The data about divorce and the breakup of families is disheartening. The emotional conditions in many of the families in our congregations are sad. I do not want to minimize or gloss over these matters. But we Christian educators must not forget to see the family as the place where the individuals are deeply influenced. Earlier I mentioned that the Catholic University had received a large grant to make extensive studies about the religious education of children and youth. They have studied all of the studies for the past half century, and they have sponsored a few studies of their own. The evidence is everywhere and overwhelming that the family is the single most important influence in generating a person's conception of God and his/her devotional life. Babies are still nurtured by adults, and some of our finest educational work can be done by helping those adults be good parents to their children.

3. We must change the conception of growth. Somehow, we Americans have connected growth with goodness and rightness. If an institution or project did not grow, we tended to believe there was something wrong. Now that we are facing the necessity for limiting growth, we must become more precise about the meaning of growth. It is true that a church and its program can be so good it will attract people for the right reasons and it will become larger. It is also true that a

church can remain in a "stable state" and the people may continue to grow "in grace and knowledge of our Lord and Savior Jesus Christ" (2 Peter 3:18).

What does it mean to grow in grace? A few moments of thought about that question will help us see that church members represent one of the greatest evangelistic fields today. Or, if you want me to say it in Christian education lingo, we need to remember that one of our educational goals is wholeness.

Most of us lead segmented lives. We have several sets of ethics, one for the telephone company, one for our church associations and another for dealing with the Internal Revenue Service. Should we not have a single set which demonstrates our belief in God? Growth in grace would tend to bring these parts together in a reasonable harmony.

Most of our people have a devotional life even if it is more evident on Sunday than during the week. But how can we be in the mood of devotion about people who need food? I pose the problem not because I have the solution but to show how much work we must do if we accept the notion that growth is inward as well as outward.

4. We Christian educators must develop our ability to train leaders. It is a waste of time to long for the good old days when we had a Christian education apparatus from the local church to the Assembly. That has been dismantled and will not be reassembled in the foreseeable future. Although the middle judicatories are expected to provide help for local churches, many of them are too overwhelmed with other problems and also with inadequate budgets to be of much assistance. We must accept the fact that Christian educators in a local church must use their own initiative to develop leadership programs in their own churches. Our reference points now are the session and the needs of the congregation, more than the presbytery or synod.

This condition can lead to undesirable results. If followed to its logical conclusion, it would mean a congregational form of government and a loss of our common theological heritage. On the other hand, it could--as I have attempted to point out in this address--force us to work diligently with our congregation so that it would become a good example of Presbyterian theology.

14

Issues for Christian Educators Related to the Development of Conscience

Hamlet in his famous soliloquy said:
To be, or not to be--that is the question;
Whether 'tis nobler in the mind to suffer
The slings and arrows of outrageous fortune,
Or to take arms against a sea of troubles,
And by opposing end them?

Shakespeare answers his question by an analysis of the options: to live and struggle with inevitable human conditions created by oppression, pride, unrequited love, injustice and bureaucracy or to die. To die seems better, except for "the dread of something after death." Since no traveler has ever returned from that undiscovered country, we all decide that we would "rather bear those ills we have . . . than fly to others that we know not of."

Thus conscience does make cowards of us all;
And thus the native hue of resolution
Is sicklied o'er with the pale cast of thought,
And enterprise of great pitch and moment,
With this regard, their currents turn awry
And lose the name of action.
(Hamlet Act III, Scene 1, lines 56-88.)

Human life makes no sense, according to Shakespeare, so the logical solution is death. But we are afraid to die and face the possibility of

---

A paper read to the Association of Professors and Researchers in Religious Education meeting in Toronto, Ontario, Canada, November 23-25, 1979.

judgment; so we resolve to take hold of life and engage in great enterprises. But the life of action is not very satisfactory either, because the thought that our achievements may not help us after death sickens our souls.

Shakespeare uses conscience in this passage to mean our common human condition. Both options--to be or not to be--produce fear, a condition of cowardice which causes us to shrink from life and death. In this sense a person *is* a conscience and our whole life is a moral struggle.

In describing conscience in this broad way Shakespeare did not lose sight of a more precise meaning of the term. In many passages he uses conscience to mean the sense of guilt we feel when we do wrong. Probably nowhere do we have the accusing conscience better described than in a speech of King Richard.

> My conscience hath a thousand several tongues,
> And every tongue brings in a several tale,
> And every tale condemns me for a villain,
> Perjury, perjury, in the high'st degree;
> Murder, stern murder, in the dir'st degree;
> All several sins, all us'd in each degree,
> Throng to the bar, crying all 'Guilty! guilty!'
> (King Richard the Third, Act V, Scene 3, lines 193-199.)

In this passage we have not only the feeling of guilt, but also we have the element of transcendence. King Richard is in despair because he knows he deserves the pain he experiences. He recalls the memory of the persons he has murdered and states that, if they came to his tent during the night, they would have reason for vengeance.

The ability of a person to transcend self and see the general conditions of anxiety in which we live, as well as the results of our hostility to others, is the theme of Donald Miller's book *The Wing-Footed Wanderer* (Nashville: Abingdon Press, 1977).

Miller's Method

Miller's method is meritorious.

He defines conscience as "a dispositional unity of knowing, doing, and feeling wherein a person is joined together with other persons in a community of moral purpose and direction." (Page 15.)

By this definition, Miller is able to show that conscience consists of feelings, ideas and judgments in relation to one's whole self and that these matters are formed by--and expressed in--various human associations to which one belongs. He uses the general ideas of psychoanalysis to show how conscience is formed, the research of Piaget and Kohlberg to show how it develops and changes, the methods of cultural anthropologists to indicate its relativity and a critical examination of human experience to find the transcendence of God which gives conscience strength and proper direction. The result is a book of exceptional merit which must be read several times in order to appreciate the delicate balance of data and originality in forming useful concepts.

Books on conscience are difficult to write because, as Shakespeare indicates, they deal with the whole human enterprise. The problem is always how to account for something as precise and practical as conscience, which comes from something as primitive as existence and as pervasive as culture. Almost every topic related to conscience is relative and full of ambiguity. For example, Miller quotes a famous passage from *Huckleberry Finn*. Huck has Jim, a runaway slave, on his raft when two men come searching for the slave. Huck is stuck between doing what the law requires by turning Jim over to his owners and doing the decent thing in helping Jim gain his freedom. Huck manages to lie about Jim and thus help him to escape, but his conscience bothers him. Huck says that if he had done right, that is, the lawful thing and given Jim up, he would have felt bad. Now that he has done wrong because he lied about Jim's presence on the raft, he feels bad. This is too much for Huck; so he says he will not worry about such things in the future--he will just "always do whatever comes handiest at the time." (Page 71.)

Purpose of this Paper

The purpose of this paper is not to review Miller's book nor to evaluate it. Rather, it is to use the book to identify issues that are important to Christian educators as they consider the way conscience develops and functions. The order of the following issues is not significant, but the way we attempt to resolve them is important in our work as Christian educators.

Issues

1. Can we, through our church programs, help people develop a (positive) conscience that will transform the restrictive, inhibited conscience which was formed in early childhood? (Miller, page 38.)

Miller uses Freud's explanation of the formation of conscience in the small child. This formation comes about through repression of various urges and drives and becomes largely unconscious. The most basic element in this process is the sexual attraction for, and identification with, the parent of the opposite sex. This process is usually completed at age six or seven but it leaves an inventory of emotions which often brings mental and physical distress throughout life. Indeed, psychoanalysis is a way of getting back to those early experiences so a person can face them consciously and learn to live with the consequences.

Miller does not accept a Freudian determinism whereby all of life is a playing-out of the emotions learned in early childhood, but he is concerned that we give them proper attention. If we agree with Miller's position, then we Christian educators have much to think about. For example, should we put more of our resources into early childhood education, including more emphasis on education of parents of small children? Should we close our colleges and put that money into Christian kindergartens? Should we develop church school teacher training courses which are designed to deal with the teacher's emotional makeup on the theory that the teacher is communicating through her/his personality something that is as important as the substance of the lessons? Should we foster research on the relation of a person's early experiences to his/her beliefs about God? A theological question emerges: is revelation of God always in discontinuity with a person's early childhood experiences? A psychological question remains: is the doctrine of forgiveness a treatment for the accusing conscience or can the experience of forgiveness lead a person to a proper regard for others?

2. If the *morals* of childhood (based on fear of punishment) can be replaced or modified by *ethical rules* (based on group ideals and growing personal integrity), how can church education foster such a process?

Miller uses the work of Erik Erikson to establish the notion that a person's ego is shaped by institutions, ideology, parents and other significant adults, and peers--as well as biological factors. The ego, by this analysis, has the possibility of growth, and adults are able to "sponsor" positive development by the ways they relate to children. The process on the part of children is to accept and absorb in a rather conscious way the attitudes, values and styles of life of the adults they like and admire.

The idea of helping children develop their egos has not often been an explicit goal of Christian education. To make this a goal would challenge the whole structure of the church school as a voluntary enterprise. Many parents would be confused if not frightened by a formal statement that ego development was a goal of the Sunday school. Moreover, the time available--one hour per week for about nine months per year, the classroom setting and the use of voluntary teachers was not designed to foster psychological maturation. If we made this attempt with our present church school, would we turn our classes into discussion groups and select leaders who were good models of adult life we wanted rather than people who knew the Bible and theology? Or, would we support church-sponsored day schools in order to surround the child with adult models and a Christian environment? Is there an intergenerational or a congregational model which will pay more attention to the moral development of children and help them form ethical rules for life situations than does our present school model of Christian education?

3. How can the role of reason be increased in the development of conscience when the ability to do logical thinking is not normally acquired until about the age of 12?

Miller's chapter on conscience and reason is a brilliant analysis of the major ethical theories about conscience and a sympathetic review of Lawrence Kohlberg's stages of moral reasoning. Although Miller accepts Kohlberg's thesis of a child going through stages in the ability to do moral reasoning, he enumerates six limitations to this position.

Miller shows how a child progresses in moral reasoning ability in intervals of about two years up to the age of twelve. There are enough differences in the six two-year stages to raise important questions for Christian educators. Should curriculum materials be written according to capacity for moral reasoning at two-year intervals? Our printed curriculum material from denominational houses is seldom closely graded. On the other hand, there are wide discrepancies between individual children in the same age bracket in terms of mental maturation. So we are back again to the problem: can the average voluntary church school teacher be trained to suit ideas and experiences to each child in the classroom? Since the answer is "no" for most congregations, we are left with the frustration of knowing more about how children develop moral reasoning than we can use.

But the more serious matter is the problem of children not having the mental means of logical reasoning and of making judgments which require historical perspective until the age of 12 to 14, when they are already set in their ways, have already absorbed social class values at a deep level and have a world view. These things, of course, will be tested and occasionally modified as the children grow older; but the number of adults who make a significant change from what they have experienced in their first 12 years of life is very small.

4. Since conscience develops naturally in children as they respond to the admonitions and hopes of the people around them, how could we help adults care more about the quality of our common life?

Miller defines conscience as "a dispositional expression of human agency that develops as a mixture of human virtue and weakness within various communities of loyalty." This means that we are inclined to express ourselves in the light of what we have absorbed from the people who raised us and to whom we have a sense of loyalty. Out of this milieu we develop our sense of obligation, intentions, values and ideals. In adolescence and young adulthood we begin to pull things together into a formal formulation of beliefs. Miller recognizes that to describe this developmental process is not enough; we must also have some moral principles in order to obtain an ethical conscience. Miller likes the term "the humanization of conscience" by which he means "a striving for individual integrity within a community of mutual recognition, trust, and purpose." (Pages 142-145.)

If Miller's description of the ways virtues develop is correct, then we have to pay much more attention to the influence of groups of people on the moral development of children. The family and adults in the community have a direct influence on the formation of virtue, but how can the church influence neighborhoods? Or, can the congregation become the kind of distinctive social group to which people will relate with great loyalty? What is necessary to bring about such a fine state of affairs? Are worship, preaching, evangelism, group activity, social action and recreation the means for helping our adults learn how to care for the quality of our common life and, therefore, incubate better ethical structures in our youth?

5. Since culture provides a powerful "ready-made" and often unrivaled explanation of the world, social values and personal beliefs

which are activated in and through conscience, how can humankind change to meet new conditions or how can individuals respond to God's leading?

Miller accepts the evidence that culture shapes persons and persons in turn transmit the culturally-held values and world view. (Chapter 5.) Culturally induced beliefs are inculcated very early in children's lives and become absorbed in the unconscious part of their beings. In many primitive societies these assumptions are unargued and unchallenged and therefore are constants. But even in societies where there is a conflict of values, changes come about slowly because individuals associate their well-being with the values and world view deep within their being.

Emile Durkheim said the content of conscience is social. That is, what we feel good or bad about is socially conditioned. This statement leaves room for individuals to question whatever is the accepted style of life and thought at any given time. But the basic problem is how can people break out of their cultural jail when most often they accept the jail as a normal or even divinely ordained style of life? The more we know about the way culture permeates the core of our being, the less likely is a revelation which questions the "rightness" of our present life situation.

Miller gets his clue for solving this puzzle by going back to the stories of Genesis. There he finds that Abraham by some leap of mind saw justice and goodness as more important goals for society than injustice and anger. This leap of mind is not subject to analysis. It is an unconditioned insight into the nature of life which results in a mental image of how things can be different and more desirable. For Christians, the source of this leap of mind is God who is "continually giving comprehensive signs of the divine presence." (Page 187.) The comprehensible signs are really states of being--such as a person's awareness, perception, intentionality, mutuality and virtue. In these states of one's being, one can understand God's will and thus develop one's conscience in the direction of righteousness.

For American Christian educators this fifth issue is the most baffling. We live in a complex, rapidly changing society. Our cultural values are diverse and confusing. Different competing values come at us through the mass media with seductive power. Moreover, our children are buffeted by diverse styles of life at an age when they cannot sort out one standard from another. Is our society too open? Should we become more clan-like in our churches and communities in order to give our children some stability as they mature--say, up until about middle adolescence? Is there any hope of helping families or clusters of families become so concerned about the moral development of their children that the parents will deliberately form a style of life different from the secular, consumer-oriented neighborhoods in which they live?

The theological questions which form around this issue are rather well-known, so let us deal with only one. (1) Is God "out there"--ready to be apprehended by persons who have the ability to do so because they are aware of God? Miller believes that the biblical record can be read this way. (2) Others believe that God is more assertive, that God breaks through the cultural jail with a "revelation" of what God wants. The human beings who receive the revelation are usually weak and frightened people, unable to get much done without constant coaching and help from God.

The first idea assumes a fairly rational understanding of conscience and makes for a rather smooth development. Given this point of view, society can be slowly but surely changed as we foster the enlightenment of conscience.

The second idea assumes that individuals are resistant to change and will not accept a higher level of ethical standard or engage in a struggle to provide justice for others except under threat, promise, or a combination of these two motivations. From this point of view, society is changed mainly through conflict and the change is maintained only by constant vigilance.

As seen by Shakespeare and many modern psychologists, conscience is a term for the moral aspect of human nature and the conscious decision making aspect of one's self. In this sense the issues of conscience for Christian educators are related to human development and the establishment of ethical standards which make for a just and caring society.

Conscience is also a term for various feelings within the self, such as guilt, duty or satisfaction. These feelings are directly related to the set of experiences and human relationships persons acquire as they grow. The issues for Christian educators in this regard are related to the ways in which life situations can be related to the story of the Bible and the Good News of salvation in Jesus Christ in such a way that believers will seek a God-desired outcome for the way they live.

15

Why is Christian Education at the Center of the Church's Life?

I want to say a special word to those of you who tonight are starting your graduate professional training in Christian Education: you have enrolled in a great school.

Throughout my career as a Christian educator I have been associated with the faculty of this school where many of our finest leaders in Christian education have been located. Everywhere I go in the Presbyterian Church, U.S.--and increasingly in other denominations--I find people who have attended PSCE or who have been influenced by its graduates. The educational opportunities here, at Union Theological Seminary, and at the other higher education institutions in Richmond are tremendous. I hope you will treat these institutions as an explorer treats a new territory. While you are here learn all you can about the church, its beliefs, practices, traditions, and--above all--about its potential for doing God's will in our time and place.

All of us assembled here at the beginning of this academic year have a commitment to the educational work of the church. It may be well for us to pause before we plunge into our year's work to remind ourselves that education is at the center of the church's life. Christian education is not something that came into existence with the founding of the Sunday school in 1780, or with Calvin's academy in 1559, or with the capitulary of Charlemagne in 789 which directed that schools be established in each monastery or bishopric. No, education has been at the center of the church's life since its beginning.

What has changed through the years has been our awareness of how education takes place and the methods which may be employed to

---

An address at the opening convocation of the Presbyterian School of Christian Education, Richmond, Virginia, September 10, 1980.

transmit the faith to the next generation. Much of your time and attention during this year of study and supervised field education will be given to the "how" of education, in order that you may become an effective worker in the church. So, I would like to use this time at the beginning of the year to remind us that what we are doing is something on which the spiritual welfare of the church depends. Let me mention four reasons why Christian education is at the center of the church's life.

Education is a Part of Belief

The first reason why Christian education is at the center of the church's life is that education is a part of belief.

Beliefs are central to our human life. All people about whom we have historical records had beliefs about the origin of the world, the meaning of death, and what was acceptable moral conduct. These beliefs were as much a part of the people as the food they ate. They transmitted their beliefs to their children just as confidently as they did the skills of hunting or cooking.

I am speaking here, of course, of beliefs that are held to be true--not beliefs to which people give lip service because they think they should. Formal statements of belief in a creed may be true; but, if the people voicing the creed are doing so only because they want to appear to be orthodox, then they are pseudobeliefs. Such pseudobeliefs have little educational power.

We see education as a component of belief when we see persons living what they believe. If a group of people believe that they should eat only vegetables, they will do so and will use every opportunity to explain to others the values they find in this diet. Likewise, if a group of Christians really believe that they should tithe, they do so; and they tell their children in many ways and on a hundred occasions that a part of their income should be dedicated to the mission of the church. If you truly believe something, you will communicate that belief by words and by actions. That is what I mean by saying that education is a part of belief.

R. S. Peters, professor of the Philosophy of Education at the University of London, has used this compulsion to communicate what we believe as a basic element of his definition of education. His words are: "Education . . . involves the intentional transmission of what is worthwhile." This definition requires considerable discussion. One must decide what is "worthwhile," and opinions will differ. One will need to identify what "intentional transmission" includes. Will it include conversation and visual art as well as classroom instruction? However these questions are answered, Peters has shown that when we believe something we will inevitably transmit that belief whenever we can.[1]

Probably the finest biblical illustration of Peters' definition is the Shema. This old and well-known passage from Deuteronomy reads as follows:

> Hear, O Israel: The Lord our God is one Lord; and you shall love the Lord your God with all your heart, and with all your soul, and with all your might. And these words which I command you this day shall be upon your heart; and you shall teach them diligently to your children, and shall talk of them when you sit in your house, and when you walk by the way, and when you lie down, and when you rise. And you shall bind them as a sign upon your hand, and they shall be as frontlets between your eyes. And you shall write them on the doorposts of your house and on your gates. (Deuteronomy 6:4-9.)

Perhaps this inexorable connection between belief and education is the reason why Jesus selected the vocation of a teacher for his public ministry. He is identified as a teacher more times than he is by any other title. His friends, enemies and disciples all refer to him as a teacher. Matthew starts his Gospel by giving a careful explanation of the lineage of Jesus, his selection by God and baptism by John, his resistance to temptation and the selection of disciples. After these things have been done, according to Matthew, Jesus starts his public ministry by going about "all Galilee, teaching in their synagogues. . . ." (Matthew 4:23.)

Educators Share Responsibility for the Truth

The second reason why Christian education is at the center of the church's life is that educators are as responsible for the truth as any other vocational group in the church. When we educators are working with children, youth groups, or adult classes, we are the theologians in those situations. The fact that some of the people are immature or ill-informed does not mean that the educator can retail "pop" theology or superficial biblical data. On the contrary, it means that because we are educators we know how to share the truth of our faith with people of varied age, social class or educational background.

Some of you who are just starting a study of Christian education in a graduate professional school may wonder why it is even necessary to mention these matters. There are two reasons.

The first is practical. In some parts of the church there is the idea that theologians and Bible scholars discover truth and educators have the methods to get the truth across to lay people. There is, of course, some point to this statement. Theologians who give full time to a careful examination of ideas about God and who are concerned for the total life of the church are the people on whom we depend to help us think about God and to prevent us from accepting superficial or erroneous notions about our Christian faith. Moreover, educators do know a lot about methods of communication and about the needs and interests of different age levels. But the point is that Christian educators must always realize that they have as much concern for truth as theologians, even though they may not have an encyclopedic knowledge of theology. Educators must say to themselves over and over again: "I am the theologian to this group of people with whom I am working. I must have a sound theology and a thorough, working knowledge of the best biblical scholarship or I will fail in my duty to these people."

The other reason I bring this up involves our recent history. In 1936 Professor C. H. Dodd published a book entitled *The Apostolic Preaching and its Development* in which he made a strong case for the role of proclamation in the New Testament church.[2] The *kerygma* was a statement of what God has done for us in Jesus Christ. At that time Dodd's insistence on the importance of proclamation was a polemic against a liberalism which did not take seriously the testimony of the disciples that Jesus of Nazareth was the Messiah. As such, it was an effort to bring the divinity of Christ into proper harmony with his humanity.

But others picked up the Dodd theme and began to compare the *kerygma* with the *didache*; that is, the teaching of Jesus and the teaching of the disciples. Those who did so usually insisted that the *kerygma* was prior and therefore superior to the *didache*. Fortunately, this comparison of proclamation with teaching has died out. Unfortunately, the idea that teaching is subordinate to proclaiming continues in the minds of some church leaders.

There is just enough of this discussion left in the church to remind us educators that there is only one truth in the Gospel and that various means of communicating it are in order. All have their special place. The Apostle Paul is our best guide in these matters. His characteristic way of spreading the gospel in a new town was to preach in the synagogue or on the street. But, if he stayed any length of time in the same place, the account says that he started teaching. The last section in the Book of Acts is probably a faithful picture of Paul's way of working. Paul was in Rome waiting to be tried. "And he lived there two whole years at his own expense, and welcomed all who came to him, preaching the Kingdom of God and teaching about the Lord Jesus Christ quite openly and unhindered." (Acts 28:30-31.) Paul did not make a difference between *kerygma* and *didache* except that they were two ways to share the gospel.

Paul settled the matter for all of us who work in the church. In his letter to the Ephesians he said there is "one Lord, one faith, one baptism." We are all to serve Jesus Christ according to our gifts--"some should be apostles, some prophets, some evangelists, some pastors and teachers, to equip the saints, for the work of ministry, for building up the body of Christ. . . . " (Ephesians 4:4-14.)

Educators Share Responsibility for the Church

The third reason why Christian education is at the center of the church's life is that educators share responsibility for the whole church. The words just quoted from Ephesians are clear and precise--all vocations in the church have a responsibility to build up the body of Christ. The evangelist does it one way, the prophet another way, and educators their way.

The way educators take responsibility for the church is an important issue on which there is no general agreement. The liberal Christian educators in the first part of this century thought they should give most of their time to children and youth. Their goal was to raise up a generation able to change the church and society. This strategy failed because children tend to grow up and to appropriate the values and religion of their parents and of other adults who are important to them.

About twenty years ago I began to formulate a different strategy. I proposed that we think of the congregation as the educator and of the activity of the congregation as curriculum. This would shift attention to adult education. The adults who were parents would influence their children; and as decision-makers in the congregation they would help shape the spiritual and ethical context in which people would be motivated and formed. This became known as the "socialization" model of Christian education. Others joined the enterprise by working out the implications of this model in terms of worship, instruction and other aspects of congregational life.

This is not the time or place to explain or defend the "socialization" model of Christian education. What bothers me most about the critics of this approach is their lack of concern for the congregation. Often they proceed as if Christianity were a private religion and as if learning were an individual matter. It is my assumption that the Christian religion is a faith which *requires* congregations. We have no illustrations in the New Testament of a person standing alone. The individual is always related to a congregation. The congregation is the place where persons share their faith, hopes, fears and dreams. It is the place in which they find forgiveness and through which they serve the world around them. Perhaps the reason some Christian educators do not want to take responsibility for the congregation is that it is such an inexact entity. The physical aspects of the congregation are exact enough: size, average age of members, budget, location, history and even--to some extent--the congregation's self-understanding of its mission. But beyond these overt facts there are many covert forces in the congregation; class distinction, jealousy between individuals, struggles for leadership, wounded egos looking for revenge, or pious posturing. These covert congregational forces seem to scare some Christian educators enough to cause them to say that we had better stick to the classroom where we can control the educational environment. I understand that position, but I cannot accept it.

There is not a single item in the list of covert congregational forces which would be new to the Apostle Paul. He found all of them plus others in the churches in Corinth, Galatia, Ephesus, Thessalonica and Rome.

What was Paul's response to these human factors in congregational life? Did he say, "I know there are rumors about quarreling in the church at Corinth, but I am not going to bother about such matters because after all I just preach there"? Or, did Paul say that the presence of Gentiles in the church at Rome was of little concern to him because he just wanted to send them a letter to be read in their study session? The answer is "No." Paul assumed that preachers, teachers, evangelists and administrators were all concerned about the spiritual welfare of the congregation and that the work of each vocational group was to "build up the body of Christ."

The most recent book on the theory of Christian education is *Christian Religious Education* by Thomas Groome (San Francisco: Harper and Row, 1980). Here the author gives a description of the "socialization" model of Christian education and cites the writings of most of us who are identified with it. He then criticizes this model as being inadequate because it does not pay attention to society, to needed reformation in the church, nor to the maturation of an individual's faith.[3] It may be that we who have attempted to take the congregation seriously as a means of education have neglected to insist that systematic instruction is a part of the work of the congregation. In my case, I attempted to put the informal life of the congregation in balance with formal instruction when I spoke to the Boards of Education of the two Presbyterian denominations in 1970. In that essay I said: "The general purpose of education is the same as the purpose of the church, but the particular role of education is to foster deliberate efforts to help persons in the church develop a Christian mentality."[4]

You see, I have no quarrel with Groome about the deliberateness of education nor about our attention to individuals. But I still insist that we must do our work within the context of a particular congregation and for the purpose of helping that congregation become more adequate as the body of Christ. If Christian educators want to disassociate themselves from the life and work of the congregation because of the complexities involved, that is their option. But they should not then complain that they are considered second-class citizens or that church leaders pay little attention to them.

Educators Serve Special Needs

The fourth reason why Christian educators are at the center of the church's life is that we serve some special needs of the church. This is the most obvious reason for our vocation, so I shall not enumerate all of the things we do, such as writing curriculum or directing vacation Bible schools. Rather, I would like to say a little bit about a few of the areas involving Christian educators--with the hope that I can interest you in making education the great vocation it deserves to be.

For example, take age-level religious education. Although education has been a part of the Bible from the very beginning, Christian education as a field of study started with the 20th century--in part because the child study movement was strong at that time. Every twenty years or so we have had a somewhat different proposal as to what children of certain ages can learn about religion. The current one is an effort to adapt Lawrence Kohlberg's stages of mental judgment about moral problems to the acquisition of faith. How well this will fare in the market place of ideas I do not know.

It may come as a surprise and maybe a disappointment to learn that we educators have not settled the issue of "ages and stages" of human development. But, to me, that is a good state of affairs! I think human beings are too complicated to be easily categorized. It is more desirable to have several theories than to have one. Several competing theories will cause you to think as you compare one theory with another and with your own experience. This area is so wide open at the present time that I hope some of you will specialize in age-level Christian education and, out of your study, will write good books on Christian education among the age groups that you understand and appreciate.

Teaching is a task which seems, on the surface, to be the same regardless of who does it. Conventional wisdom suggests that perhaps the only differences among teachers are their personalities and the methods they employ. But teaching is a complex activity, part art and part science. Teaching is an activity in which one must use everything one knows. One's idea about age-level ability, the psychosocial situation of the pupils, the beliefs and values of the congregation, educational theory and theological outlook are all involved in teaching. Understanding how all of these elements are related is one of the great challenges about being a teacher in the church. And--for all we know about teaching--there is much more to know. If teaching turns out to be your special interest, you can help all of us by sharing your experience in this field. Every church needs better teachers. There is no limit to the service that can be rendered by those of you who take teaching as your special interest.

I could go on with comments about worship, personal religious living, the importance of adult education, the need for new and better literature for use in the home, the role of recreation, the significance of music and the arts and other areas where educators have special interest. But we do not have time. Let me conclude with a few words about moral development.

Moral development is a field of study started by religious educators in the 1920s. Four--or perhaps five--basic theories have been proposed about the way people develop morally, and all of them have their devotees today. I am not prepared to select one of these theories as superior to the others, although I am fairly sure that the "stage" theory of Lawrence Kohlberg is not very helpful to us in the church. It deals mainly with reason and we in the church are also concerned with faith, hope and love. I am prepared, however, to insist that this is an exceedingly important area for church educators to ponder and that we have much to learn. I hope that some of you will take moral education as your special interest. It is worth ten years of concentrated study and experimentation on your part because the church needs guidance as to how to help our people live the faith we believe.

Welcome

This lecture ends with a welcome. Welcome to the field of Christian education. Welcome to Christian education because it is at the center of the church's life.

Welcome to PSCE, a great school of Christian education where you will have ample opportunity to develop your mind and your skills as an educator.

Notes

1 R. S. Peters, *Ethics and Education* (London: George Allen and Unwin, 1966) 35.

2 C. H. Dodd, *The Apostolic Preaching and its Developments* (London: Harper, 1936).

3 Thomas Groome, *Christian Religious Education* (San Francisco: Harper and Row, 1980) 118-127.

4 C. Ellis Nelson, *Is Church Education Something Particular?* (Richmond, Virginia: Board of Christian Education, Presbyterian Church, U.S., 1970) pamphlet.

16

Formation and Transformation

The Presbyterian Church of Korea is to be commended for selecting Christian Education as a theme for its 100th anniversary. This emphasis shows that the Korean Church is looking into the future, for Christian education is the biblical way to build the future God desires.

In the Old Testament the Shema summarizes theology in this brief verse: "Hear, O Israel: the Lord our God is one Lord; and you shall love the Lord your God with all your heart, with all your soul, and with all your might" (Deut. 6:4-5). Believers are expected to communicate their faith in God by teaching it "diligently" to their children, by talking about their faith in all the ordinary activities of everyday life, and by keeping God's commandments uppermost in their minds during their work and play.

In the New Testament Matthew concludes his gospel with a final appearance of Jesus as he gives his last instructions: "Go therefore and make disciples of all nations, baptizing them in the name of the Father, and of the Son and of the Holy Spirit, *teaching* them to observe all that I have commanded you. . . ." (Matt. 28:19-20. [Italics added.])

These passages illustrate the connection between theology and education. This connection also reflects a natural human situation. Whatever we really believe we pass on to our children, friends and fellow workers. There is something about a belief which urges us to share it with others. And what we believe most dearly we communicate most fervently--even, in extreme circumstances, giving up our lives rather than giving up our beliefs. In this broad sense, then, we can say Christian education is all of our efforts to transmit our faith in God to others. A more narrow definition would read: Christian education is whatever we do *intentionally* to communicate our beliefs to others.

An address prepared for the Centennial Celebration of the Presbyterian Church of Korea. Seoul, Korea. August, 1984.

The leaders of the Korean Presbyterian Church must have had both the broad and narrow definitions in mind when they planned this centennial celebration. If they had wanted to glory in your splendid past century they would have invited historians to recount the early struggles of missionaries and converts to establish the church of Jesus Christ in this land. If they had wanted to be triumphant, they would have invited church leaders from other countries and denominations to examine your rapidly growing, vigorous church which is increasing its influence in this nation, the United States, and many other countries where Korean Christians have gone.

However, rather than looking to the past, your church leaders selected a theme for your 100th birthday party which looks to the future. For Christian education, in the broad sense of living our beliefs, is all that we do to communicate the gospel so that children who are the future and adults who are the present may "grow in the grace and knowledge of our Lord Jesus Christ" (2 Pet. 3:18). Christian education in this wider sense has many agencies through which it works in a variety of ways to communicate the gospel. Other speakers will discuss the opportunities of Christian education in schools and colleges, the relationship of theology, culture and education, the special situation of Christianity in Asia, and other topics of concern to you as you move into your second century. My role in this celebration is to discuss the theology of Christian education as it relates to the life and work of a congregation.

Formation

The congregation's responsibility for Christian education is universally acknowledged. In the western world, especially in the United States, this responsibility has been discharged by sponsoring a school. The theology behind the Sunday school as an agency of Christian education was simple and direct. We have a responsibility to raise our children according to the baptismal vow "in the nurture and admonition of the Lord." Since in America there could be no teaching of religion in public schools because the government was neutral in relation to religion, congregations formed and supported Sunday schools.

The Sunday school as an agency for Christian education worked well in America as long as the surrounding culture was Christian in outlook, as long as ministers were recognized leaders of the community, and as long as the homes from which the children came provided careful guidance to them throughout the day. The Sunday school as an agency does not work well today because this support system has changed. The culture of the West is increasingly secular--that is, concerned with the "here and now," with little serious concern about God's will for the world. Ministers are seldom influential leaders in community affairs anymore. Homes are broken by divorce or are so overwhelmed with duties if both parents work that there is little time or energy left for parents to guide their children. Today, in many American homes guidance of children goes by default to their playmates or to what they see on television.

School-Centered Education Reconsidered

This collapse of the support system which made the Sunday school the major agent of congregational education in the past has caused us to reconsider the way in which a congregation discharges its educational responsibility. This reconsideration may be helpful to Presbyterians in Korea as you plan for the next hundred years.

We now realize that the congregational schools are important but are not completely satisfactory for communicating the Christian faith. They are important because they provide Christian fellowship and because they focus attention on what should be known about Christian beliefs. But they are inadequate if they are expected to be the principal means a congregation uses for Christian education. The reasons are as follows:

First, if the Sunday school is considered the *principal* agency of education, there is a tendency to overemphasize the doctrinal side of our religion. A school tends to deal with the mind and thus to take care of one aspect of our life; but it is not very good in helping us also learn how to love God with our heart, soul and strength. Let us take forgiveness, for example. Our Lord instructed Peter and the other disciples to forgive, not seven times, but "seventy times seven" so that forgiveness would become a distinctive characteristic of Christian life (Matt. 18:21-35). He taught his disciples in the model prayer to include forgiveness and commented at the end that, ". . . if you do not forgive men their trespasses, neither will your Father forgive your trespasses" (Matt. 6:15). To know the parables about forgiveness is essential; but we must also receive forgiveness and give forgiveness before we can truly say that forgiveness is deep within our soul. Thus, knowing *about* forgiveness as well as *experiencing* forgiveness requires a community in which the teachings of our Lord are taken seriously.

Second, if the Sunday school is considered the *principal* agency of a congregation, it focuses attention on children and we begin to think that education is necessary for children but optional for adults. If this happens, then we will make children's needs and interests the center of the educational enterprise. To some extent this is good and right; but, if we go too far in this direction, children will enjoy Sunday school and then will outgrow it because it does not deal with the perennial themes of life such as sin, forgiveness, evil, death, and moral issues which confront us every day. Although childhood is a stage of life that must be taken seriously, it must not be separated from the joys, temptations, pains, or pleasures of the adult world.

There is also the danger that if education is considered primarily for children, education may become highly individualistic. This is so because when we turn our attention to children the most striking fact about them is their growth. We then have a tendency to focus on individuals and think in terms of ways we can help each one realize his or her highest potential. This desire comes from the finest motive and is the proper goal of secular education. But Christian education has a goal beyond individual attainment. That goal is to serve Jesus Christ through his Church; thus, the individual is always subordinated to God's will for the world. So the individual is never the final product of our educational work. The final product of our educational work is to seek and do the will of God in the community in which we live.

Congregation-Centered Education

These comments about congregation-sponsored schools are not negative about schooling or about the deliberate teaching of our religion. Rather, they are designed to show that we must start our deliberations about communicating the Christian faith with the nature of the faith and then design educational processes which will help transmit it without changing its nature.

Christianity is about faith in God as revealed in the Bible and in the life, death and resurrection of Jesus Christ. All people have faith in the sense that they trust other people and have beliefs by which they live. It is the Christian faith in God that makes the quality of faith different from those who trust other gods. How is such faith in God communicated? The answer is not easy because faith is not taught by logical or educational processes. Faith is something we acquire from the people we admire and respect and something we develop in our own life as we relate ourselves to God through the ordinary events of life. In this sense faith is the sum total of who we are and that for which we live.

Biblical Hebrew does not have a noun which can be translated "faith." The word usually translated "trust" or "faith" is the verb *he'-^{e}min*. Its broad meaning is "trusting/believing." Its more precise meaning is "to be certain in one's mind." It is remarkable that the Hebrew word for faith in God is never used for faith in false gods. The word is used in Christian worship as "Amen." We use it to conclude our prayers, for our prayers represent our clearest affirmation of God's glory, our deepest yearning, our finest hopes, our earnest pleading, and our most sincere pledge of allegiance. We address our petitions to God with confidence that some response will come into our consciousness. Prayer is the supreme act of our conscious self. That is why we conclude our prayers: "Amen." We want to declare that we are "certain" about God's rule and God's power to protect and guide our lives. "Amen" to a Christian's prayer is the exact opposite of vague religious faith concerned with human goals here and now. It is likewise correct to say "Amen" to belief statements about God, for in so doing we affirm what we know. The practice must have been well-known in the Corinthian church, for Paul argued that a person who claimed the guidance of the Holy Spirit must speak so others could understand. Then, if there was agreement about what was said, the congregation could say "Amen." (1 Cor. 14:13-19. See also Psalm 106:48.)

When we take seriously faith as the purpose of our educational work, we will discover some significant characteristics of Christian education. The following are examples of these distinctive features.

Because faith relates to the whole person--mind, personality, will and attitudes--it begins to form at birth. In the few years before small children can talk we communicate with them through non-verbal means. We do this by the way we hold, feed, correct, or encourage them. Out of these non-verbal relationships they learn to trust, to have hope and to give love. Thus the foundation of Christian personalities is laid before they can talk. These early years are beyond the reach of words, and the children are too young for school. Yet these early years set much of what the person will need in order to "glorify God and enjoy Him forever." Congregations can do many things to help parents understand the significance of children's first few years of life and encourage them to develop the basis on which their faith, hope and love will develop.

Because faith relates to all of life's experiences, it is a factor in all that happens. As children learn the use of words and can form meaning for the events of life, they need mentors to help them relate faith to life situations. These mentors--parents, Sunday school teachers, pastors and friends--are the people who help growing children understand the role of God in all of life. They help by sharing what faith means to them and by interpreting experiences in the light of faith. Earlier I referred to forgiveness as being central to our faith and pointed out that it had to be experienced to be understood. It is in that sense that mentors can provide the love, concern, forgiveness, or stimulation necessary to help children see the connection between their lives and God's love for them. Sometimes a death, an accident or some other tragedy will defy all explanation. In such cases children need mentors all the more to provide the emotional support necessary to steady their lives.

Because faith relates us to God, we are all on common ground as we listen for a word of guidance from God. This image of our common condition is different from the stereotyped educational image of the teacher telling pupils what they should know. In the faith relationship to God, the important characteristics are openness and expectation of meaningful guidance from God. That is why our Lord told his disciples ". . . unless you turn and become like children, you will never enter the kingdom of heaven" (Matt. 18:3). Thus, age and experience are not as crucial in developing one's faith as is one's receptivity.

Because Christian faith is formed, supported, enriched and corrected in congregations, education must be congregation-centered. We have no New Testament account of an individual Christian standing alone and aloof in solitary splendor before God. What we have throughout the New Testament is an account of the Church as it is lived in congregational units. It is commonly thought by scholars that the four Gospels were written for--or out of--the experiences of congregations. The rest of the New Testament contains letters, mainly written by the Apostle Paul to congregations. What we find in all of this literature is information about the congregations worshiping God, celebrating the sacraments, and helping people to encourage each other to live the Christian life.

The congregation is so obviously the center of our spiritual life that we seldom stop to consider how unique it is and exactly what it does for our faith. The congregation is not like any other human association. It provides fellowship--yet it is not a social club. It provides classes and study opportunities--yet is it not a school. It often gives money and food to the poor and homeless--yet it is not a social agency. It sometimes criticizes the government, or tries to get legislators to pass laws--but it is not a political party. The congregation is unique because it is first of all a group of people with common beliefs. These beliefs make the congregation different from all other groups of people.

What, then, does the congregation provide that gives Christian education a special character? Participating in the life of a Christian congregation provides believers with a world view--an understanding of creation and the nature and destiny of human beings. It provides us with basic attitudes toward sin, forgiveness, justice, mercy, the use of time and money and other values which make up the lifestyle of God's people. Moreover, the congregation is the place where we bring the practical problems we are facing in order to obtain "the mind of Christ" for ethical issues not treated in the Bible. In addition, the congregation provides us with the kind of companionship that encourages and supports our personal quest for God's presence and guidance for the decisions for which we are accountable.

How does all this happen? In general terms it comes about through worship, preaching, celebrating the sacraments, Bible study, service projects in the community in which the congregation is located, and the natural association of people who share their lives because they have shared beliefs. In more specific terms congregation-centered education means we start with the spiritual life of the congregation. Thus, the minister is the principal educator in that the content of the sermons and prayers helps to shape the minds of the people. Christian education by this analysis is never something separate from the work of the minister. Christian education cannot be compartmentalized in the minister's mind as something others do in a different building at another time. It must be equally clear that this view does not mean that the minister leads the congregation as a classroom teacher, nor does it mean that the minister lectures rather than preaches. It only means that the congregation when it gathers to worship is going through an intense learning experience and, if the minister leads that experience well, the minister is developing the faith of believers.

Although the congregation is made up of all ages, it is the adults who make decisions, lead congregational activities, teach, and are the parents of the young. Thus, our first organized, intensive efforts to teach the Bible and the theology of the church should be with adults. Adult Christian education is difficult because adults are slow to change their ways or their mental outlook. But when they do change, even a little bit, that change is immediately communicated to other adults and also to their children. So, the slow but sure way to make a congregation more faithful and to raise children in the Christian faith is through a vigorous and comprehensive program of adult education. If we follow this plan, we will be following Jesus' method; for he selected adults and, after years of living with them and instructing them concerning the kingdom of God, left with the confidence that a community of adult believers was the core from which his church would expand.

Does this theology of education rule out schools or classes for children and youth? No. It only places such classes in a subordinate place to the worship and work of the congregation. Subordination should not imply unimportance. Classes for children and youth are essential because such classes can study the theology and moral standards of Christianity in a more systematic way than can be done in most families. Moreover, classes provide a fellowship for children of a similar age which is very important for their social development. Such fellowship can be for the children a taste of what mature Christian fellowship will be when they become adults. The idea of subordination of classes to congregation also helps orient the work of classes. Classes are to prepare children and youth for full participation in the life of the congregation rather than being an end in themselves. In practical terms this would mean children might prepare prayers or litanies of praise usable for congregational worship and, on occasion, this could be their contribution to the regular worship of the congregation. By this process they both study prayer, learn to write prayers, and relate themselves to the community of which they are a part.

Transformation

Thus far I have been describing Christian education from the standpoint of formation. Formation is the way the congregation forms itself in the Christian faith and--through its life and work--transmits its faith to children and adult converts. Christian education has been the traditional term for all the ways we form and shape the rising generation. Those of us who were born of Christian parents experienced our religion in this fashion as we grew up. The educational process was well-known to Isaiah, for he expressed it in these words: "For it is precept upon precept, precept upon precept, line upon line, line upon line, here a little, there a little" (Isa. 28:10).

However, when we grow up we realize that at the heart of our faith is--according to Jesus--the God of the living (Matt. 22:32). The living God continues to reveal God's self to people in special ways to meet new conditions. The most common experience of the living God is conversion. People who are converted are people who have had such a profound sense of God's acting in their lives that they turn from evil or destructive activity to a life in which they find forgiveness and a consuming desire to live as Christ would have them live. Conversions, or the kinds of commitment individuals make when they confess their sins and join the church, are transforming experiences. This transformation is from a secular orientation to the new being in Christ (2 Cor. 5:16-18). Since such experiences cannot be planned or scheduled, all we can do is to teach people to expect such experiences and help them understand it when it occurs. The end result of the conversion experience is a person who has made Christ the center of life.

A less common form of transformation comes when a Christian experiences the living God in relation to some particular life situation. Christian educators seldom discuss religious experiences of this nature, yet such experiences are fairly common in the Bible. It was such an experience of God by Moses that caused him to give up the comforts of home and take on the arduous, lifelong task of leading the Hebrew slaves out of Egypt (Ex. 3-4:20). From Moses' experience of God, the whole history of the world was changed. Although Peter was the first to confess Jesus as the Christ, he retained his Jewish diet and prejudice against gentiles until he had a special experience with the Holy Spirit which opened him to a clearer understanding of what the living God wanted for the church (Acts 10). From that experience, the newly created Christian church broke out of its Jewish setting and became an independent church destined to preach the good news to all people of every nation. From these and scores of other biblical illustrations, we realize that God is constantly stimulating people to a new and different understanding of God's will for the world. Since the meaning of life is often transformed when Christians experience the leading of God's Spirit, we must understand the role of transformation in education.

Why is it necessary for God to reveal God's will from time to time?

Do we not have enough knowledge of God from the Bible and history to satisfy our needs? Yes we do, but we also know from the Bible and from history that all is not well with human nature. The stories in the first part of Genesis, for example, show how human beings forgot that God was in charge of the world as they sought power to suit their own selfish desires. Becoming discouraged with human disobedience, God sent a flood and then started over again with the descendants of Noah. The same theme of disobedience appears in Isaiah when he tells how God made a fine vineyard of Israel; but, rather than being a vineyard for the glory of God, the Israelites used their favored place for their own selfish gain (Isa. 5). Our Lord, just before going to the cross, used the same story to show how God had sent him to Israel; but rather than accept him, they had rejected him and his teachings. The story indicates that God was going to bypass Israel and take the message of Jesus Christ to all the people of the world (Matt. 21:33-46).

These biblical stories are a mirror reflecting our own image. We, too, tend to forget God as we try to arrange life to suit our own desires. There is always a tendency to place ourselves and our needs ahead of God's concerns for the world. God's way of reminding us of our first responsibility is to send us preachers, prophets, missionaries, and others who have had a special experience with God to remind us of our first loyalty.

But not all of our problems came from our natural desire to serve ourselves. There are many sincere Christians who are eager to do God's will but who are unable to discern that will for their situation. Our modern world is very complex. We are facing problems that were not known in biblical days. Today we are required to consult the Bible, discern the basic intention behind the teachings, and then apply that intention to completely new situations. This is an intellectual and spiritual task that is unusually difficult because so many of our modern ethical problems are caused by science. For example, we now have such powerful insecticides that we can and do poison the earth and the air. Should we do so in order to provide more food for the greatly increased population of the earth? We now have such effective medical methods we can keep people alive even though they will never be able to live a normal life. Should we? We now have large corporations which can command labor and natural resources from all over the world in order to keep prices low. Should there be any restraint on these corporations? We could continue with similar examples of how the problems of our modern world are complex in contrast to those of the agrarian society of biblical times.

Although the problems are new because of new scientific achievements, the matter of translating the Christian faith from one mentality to another or of seeking God's guidance for new situations is not. John's gospel is an illustration; for the writer, although steeped in Jewish thought and customs, wrote a gospel for people who had a mentality shaped by Greek philosophy. John also solved the problem of how to deal with new situations by assuring us that the truth we needed would be supplied by the Holy Spirit (Jn. 14:12-15). One of the major functions of the Holy Spirit is to guide us into all the truth we will need about new things which will come into the world (John 16:12-15). As the Spirit guided John in writing a gospel for a different cultural situation, so we have the promise that the Spirit will lead us to a Christian response to the new scientific mentality which dominates our lives.

Transformation, therefore, is a broad term to cover these two major areas of our life that need the continuing presence of God: the need to remind ourselves that our first allegiance is to seek God's will for our lives and the need to have God's guidance in the perplexing problems we face day by day.

Come, Holy Spirit

In theological language we are talking about the role of the Holy Spirit, for the Spirit is the experience of God in our lives. Since the goal of Christian education is growth "in the grace and knowledge of our Lord Jesus Christ," it is strange that Christian educators seldom mention the Holy Spirit (2 Pet. 3:18). I assume this is because the Spirit is independent, working when and where and how the Spirit pleases rather than being dependent upon our teaching programs or predetermined curricula. But this elusiveness of the Spirit is more a reminder that God's will is not necessarily our will than it is a reason for omitting the Spirit from our conception of Christian education. It may be that Christians avoid a discussion of the Spirit because such a discussion may move to a consideration of the doctrine of the Trinity. That doctrine is extremely complex and has been the source of much controversy. But we can experience the work of the Spirit in our lives apart from a theological doctrine about the Trinity. There is little explicit teaching about the Trinity in the Bible, but a lot of the experience of the Spirit; so we will follow that example in this lecture. In some cases, Christians avoid thinking about the Spirit because they think it means speaking in tongues and they do not understand how such behavior can be useful in the church. We must be careful at this point--as the apostle Paul was--not to violate the feelings of Christians for whom ecstatic speaking has some value. Yet following Paul, we must observe that speaking in tongues is a rare occurrence and when it happens it must be understood to be useful for the edification of the church (1 Cor. 14). Rather than discussing the doctrine of the Trinity or the rare occurrence of speaking in tongues, let us consider what we know about the Spirit that relates to the educational work of the church.

Paul said to the Christians in Rome that "Any one who does not have the Spirit of Christ does not belong to him" (Rom. 8:9). To the Christians at Corinth where there was great concern about the Spirit, Paul instructs: ". . . no one can say 'Jesus is Lord' except by the Holy Spirit" (1 Cor. 12:3). He continued by affirming that one was baptized, served Christ in the church, and received power for a new life in Christ as a result of the Spirit's activity. Because the Spirit provides the experiential side of our faith, let us note three major functions of the Spirit, which have a practical relation to the educational work of the church.

First, the Spirit relates us to Christ. In Paul's theology the Spirit and Christ are almost identical. One cannot understand the Spirit except in relation to Christ; so, at times, Paul uses "Spirit" interchangeably with "Christ." The work of the Spirit is to reproduce Christ in peoples' lives. It is important to root personal experience in the historical Jesus because in him we have the story of salvation, moral teaching, and a pattern of living that is full of particular meaning. In New Testament times Christians told what the Spirit did to relate them to Christ and guide them in their discussions to live for Christ. They did not talk of a spirit which made them feel good, a general desire to be good, or the spirit of nature that renews the earth at springtime. The Holy Spirit led them to Christ and guided them in efforts to continue the ministry of Christ in the world in which they lived (John 14:25-26).

Second, the Spirit relates us to each other and forms the church. One of the most dynamic and dramatic accounts of the Spirit is the formation of the church at Pentecost. There the Spirit is clearly defined as God's representative to certify that Jesus is the Christ and to form the church out of those who believe. The Spirit gathers the community of believers and resides in the community. There is no account of the Spirit being given to any one disciple, except that the Spirit worked through individuals to form and instruct the church. Thus, the community of believers is the natural home for the Spirit. The Spirit can, of course, work outside the church; but the work the Spirit does is to form or reform the church (Acts 1-2).

Luke's account of the work of the Spirit through the preaching of Peter concludes with this summary: "And they devoted themselves to the apostles' teaching and fellowship, to the breaking of bread and the prayers" (Acts 2:42). The word "fellowship" used to characterize their life together in the newly formed church is difficult to translate. It means "sharing," "joint possession," "participation in," or "holding things in common." What they held in common and jointly possessed was a common experience of Christ by means of the Spirit. In order to preserve the original meaning we sometimes use the Greek word "*koinonia*" to remind us that the fellowship was in Christ and was not just companionship of people who enjoyed each other. In writing to the Corinthians Paul used the same term to characterize the church. It was a secular term used in the market place to describe business partners who worked together for a common cause. Paul used the common word *koinonia* to tell us that when we live and work together for Christ the Spirit will be present.

Third, the Spirit shapes the ethical characteristics of the congregation. The Spirit's interest in ethical behavior is a continuation of the work of Christ. Jesus lived the life of a teacher and most of the gospels are taken up with his parables and other teachings. Disciples, friends and enemies all refer to him as teacher, and what he said about the moral aspects of life is widely admired even by those who reject him as Savior. This concern of the Spirit for ethics has two aspects.

One aspect is the relationship of Christians to each other. This aspect of ethics is outlined by Paul to the Christians in Galatia. He said that they should live by the Spirit, rather than by ". . . the desires of the flesh." He then lists what human life is like when people live only to gratify their natural instincts. They engage in sexual activity without concern for anyone else, they give themselves to false gods, they seek power over one another, and they drink to escape reality. In contrast he affirms ". . . the fruit of the Spirit is love, joy, peace, patience, kindness, goodness, faithfulness, gentleness, self control; against such there is no law" (Gal. 5:16, 22-23).

From the formation of a congregation which exhibits the fruit of the Spirit, another aspect of the Spirit's ethical work emerges: a place where ethical decisions can be made. This aspect of the Spirit's work is often overlooked or under used. We have a strong tendency to think of ethical problems as puzzles which individuals should solve in their heads. But most ethical problems we face are deeply enmeshed in life and are not amenable to clear-cut, logical solutions. Rather, they are problems we have to live with as we patiently try different solutions within a community. The community in which the ethical problem is formulated and discussed is just as important as the attempted solution. This is particularly true of new problems brought on--as indicated earlier--by science. We need a congregation where a problem can be understood and where possible solutions can be discussed over a period of time in order slowly but carefully to find the mind of Christ. By this analysis, a congregation is required in order that we have the leading of the Spirit for complex ethical issues.

Lead, Holy Spirit

If this brief overview of the biblical testimony about the Spirit is accurate, then we have an environment for Christian education that is different from what most people expect. Education as an activity which forms people in the Christian pattern is expected. But education that assumes the Holy Spirit as an agency of transformation is not well-known. What difference will it make for a congregational education program if we expect the Spirit to transform our lives?

1. Since the Spirit leads the church and activates faith, Christian educators are not the masters of the process with which they work. This is a humbling statement, but to say more would be arrogant. We use the best educational methods we know and we vary methods according to the human conditions we face; but becoming a Christian is still a mystical experience we do not completely understand. There is an element we cannot control or predict in the Christian education process. Therefore, education in the church can never become a science.

To what extent can the social sciences, especially psychological data regarding education, be used? We can use psychological data to create the optimum condition for learning. We can use research data to help us prepare the best curriculum according to the psychology of human development. However, after using the best educational methods, we cannot rely on those methods to create the spiritual life.

2. The relationship of trust and confidence in Christ which we seek to foster is a sentiment deep within a person's being--deeper than words can adequately describe. If we are successful agents of the Spirit in helping people know God within themselves, then we can never be dogmatic about what God ought to mean to another person; for this is the work of the Spirit. This does not mean that we abandon our pupils. It means that we must be careful not to superimpose our religious experience on others so that they cannot easily have their own experience of God. There is a razor-edge distinction here, but it is extremely important. It is one thing to testify that the Spirit is real and available, but it is quite a different thing to supply what the Spirit will say to another person. In the Christian religion all believers are expected to become personally related to God.

I am emphasizing this point because it is difficult to convey to Presbyterians. We are the managers and organizers of society. We are the ones who get things done in the community. This middle-class mode of life carries over into our church work so that we have an almost irresistible urge to shape other people's response to the gospel--thinking that, if they don't see it our way, something is wrong. We must resist this urge and see ourselves more as catalytic agents trying to fuse a soul to Christ so that the person will become less dependent on us.

Perhaps a better illustration is that of a coach. A coach is one who helps an athlete become better in a sport. A coach works personally with athletes, analyzing their style, showing how to improve, pointing out what should be changed, and in other ways trying to perfect their skill and ability. Athletes know they must absorb and use these suggestions, for they will play the game--not the coach. I think we who teach in congregational schools should consider ourselves as coaches. Our relation to our pupils is personal and is based on our experience and knowledge; but we have no authority except as we can help pupils know that the Spirit will help *them* live a Christian life.

3. To speak as we have of the Spirit changes the nature of educational evaluation. Anyone who has tried to teach anything knows the need for evaluation. Either by questions in class, by examination at the end of a course, by interview, or by other devices, the teacher seeks to discover what the pupils have learned. The instructor also wants to know what can be done to improve the teaching and to motivate interest.

We in Christian education have used all of these evaluative methods, including the testing of church school pupils' knowledge of the Bible. If we say the only real stimulator of--and guide toward--spiritual life is the Holy Spirit, do we not abandon all evaluative devices and say that spirituality is something that can't be measured? I think not. We must use evaluative devices or we will lose our way in the educational work of the church. However, we must change both the way we use them and also develop some different techniques for evaluating.

For example, we can use paper and pencil tests to find out how well our pupils understand the facts of our faith. Here would be the difference: we would not assume that because a person knows *about* God he or she knows God. We would use psychological tests for diagnostic purposes; but we would not assume that, because we know *something* about a person, we would know *all* about him or her.

Now let's consider some different ways of evaluating our work which conform to our understanding of the Spirit. The first has to do with *intention*. To what extent do our pupils seek to understand and follow God's will for their lives? Although that phrase sounds idealistic and impossible to judge, we must ask that question of ourselves or we will miss the purpose of the education we are sponsoring.

The second has to do with *affectional relations*. To what extent does the fruit of the Spirit appear? Note that these are more "feeling" states than they are an inventory of information. They grow out of interpersonal relations and they are expressed in personal relations. We cannot create the Spirit by an attitude of love; but, if the Spirit is present, the result will be love. Of course, all of these emotional states are relative, and they fluctuate in a person from day to day; but our problem is to gauge the trend. Is our Christian education work with our class or group producing a *trend* toward mutual acceptance? Are people in our class finding that they can honestly share their fears as well as their hopes, and in these shared experiences do they grow? If you want to try something unusual but clearly biblical in your church school class, let me suggest that you get together a few students to discuss whether there is a trend in the class toward the fruit of the Spirit. If such a trend is not felt, have your group discuss why these qualities of human experience are not manifest; and perhaps the discussion in itself will lead to a more profound and pertinent type of Christian education.

The third has to do with *decision*. Decision in life's problems and commitment of one's self to a cause come from the deepest level of our personality. Here the Spirit works to lead a person to Christ. We might ask this question: "To what extent do our pupils seek the mind of Christ for their lives?" Children will certainly not understand this phrase and we should not use it with them. Yet the idea that our life is not our own but is rather a trust from God to be used in God's service is a fundamental Christian affirmation. We communicate this belief best when we help our pupils work through their day by day decisions in the light of their developing Christian conscience.

The fourth has to do with *responsibility*. We can judge the effectiveness of our Christian education effort by the extent to which our pupils accept and properly discharge responsibility. For a person to understand God is for a person, within the limits of his or her ability, to want to assume responsibility for the Christian enterprise. We will note this in practical chores done in the classroom. At a more mature level, we will be able to judge by the way people assume more and more responsibility for other people, whether they seek to interest others in the Christian faith, and whether they attempt to apply their faith in their own families or in the neighborhoods where they live.

4. The church as a living social organism is a method in itself because the living relationships within the church are the ones that go deepest in a person's being. The church must, therefore, self consciously engage in the experience of repentance, mercy and obedience in order to fulfill her mission and thereby to refresh her relationship to her Lord. Believers thus engaged grow in grace. Faith cannot be stockpiled and it is nontransferable, but it can be shared in a living community.

Although this statement about the living church as method seems vague, it is probably the most practical comment I can make. Just as we cannot say precisely how a child picks up mannerisms from the family life, we know the family experience is the most influential factor in the development of a child, especially during the earliest years. The church has existed for a long time and in many remote places without articulating a theology of education. Yet it has been capable of reproducing faith generation after generation because Christians living together and sharing their lives coach each other in how to be Christian.

From a Christian education point of view the church was described by Matthew when he said, "Where two or three are gathered together in my name, there am I in the midst of them" (Matt. 18:20). This passage reveals the unique relationship between Christ and believers when they come together. Christ is the schoolmaster, the believers are his pupils, and the church is the organization that seeks to learn from Christ and to live for Christ.

17

Education for Congregational Leadership

There is general agreement that seminary education in the United States has improved greatly during the past fifty years. However, in spite of all the progress that has been made, seminaries are criticized for their inability to prepare ministers to lead congregations. This situation is often referred to as the gap between the ethos of the seminary and the ethos of the congregation, or as crossing the boundary between the academic study of religion and the leadership of lay Christians who have a practical interest in the way their faith relates to their hopes, fears and the tragic events which they see all about them.

This criticism comes from three sources. (1) Graduates of seminaries complain that they are not prepared to lead a congregation. They voice this assessment by saying that, in their first pastorate, they had to learn how to practice ministry by trial and error or that older ministers taught them how to survive in the parish. (2) Professors, especially in the more academic areas, often wonder whether the main purpose of their teaching is to help students understand the subject or to use the subject in the practice of ministry.[1] (3) Congregations with newly ordained ministers often find their expectations for leadership are not met and register their dissatisfaction with denominational officers.

The problem of the gap between seminary training and the realities of leading a congregation has been recognized since seminaries were founded; but its importance has become more widely recognized in the past fifty years. During this time seminary officials and denominational leaders have sponsored various programs to help solve the problem,

---

A paper prepared for the International Seminar on Religious Education and Values (ISREV) meeting in Banff, Alberta, Canada, August 23-28, 1992.

especially during the 1970s. However, in recent years mainline protestant denominations have become preoccupied with their decline in membership and influence. Seminaries of those denominations have shared those concerns as well as the added burden of raising money as denominational support has diminished. As a result, this gap in the system of education for ministers has drifted out of sight. In order to bring this problem back into view and to probe the possibilities of the solution, I obtained a grant from the Lilly Endowment. This grant paid the expenses of a small group of denominational leaders and consultants to discuss the problem and to review what denominations and seminaries were doing in response to the criticisms noted above. From those meetings have come these questions: (1) why has seminary education become more academic? (2) what have seminaries and denominations done to help newly ordained ministers lead congregations? (3) what additional educational experience is needed to help ministers learn how to lead congregations?

The purpose of this paper is to answer each of these questions but the underlying concern is for newly ordained ministers in their first pastorates. This is because during the first two or three years ministers form study habits, a style of ministry, a way of dealing with personal affairs and a basic pattern for dealing with the congregations they serve.

Seminary Development

The answer to the question "Why has seminary education become more academic?" lies in the way seminaries developed in the United States. In the United States prior to 1808, Protestant ministers studied Bible and theology in college, under the supervision of a minister, or in a "log college."[2] This method changed with the founding of Andover Theological Seminary in 1808 as a three year seminary independent of any college, with its own library, faculty and governing body.

According to Glenn T. Miller, who has written the definitive history of the founding of seminaries, Andover set the academic standards by which later theological schools would be judged.[3] Miller also observed that Princeton Theological Seminary, which was founded in 1812 on the Andover model, had more influence on other schools than Andover did because Princeton was a school owned and controlled by the church. During the 19th century as denominations expanded with the growing population and as they struggled to make their interpretation of

Christianity supreme, they copied the Princeton model because it produced ministers loyal to the denomination's faith and practice.[4]

Seminaries rapidly became the institutions for training ministers in mainline protestant denominations, although Bible institutes and college departments of religion supplied training for ministers for churches without formal educational requirements.[5] At the end of World War I a conference of theological seminaries was convened to discuss theological education in the light of the war experience. This conference met biennially and during its 1922 meeting heard a report from Robert Kelly. The Kelly study of seminaries, sponsored by the Institute of Social and Religious Research, showed the state of seminary education, including the lack of admission and academic standards. This survey was followed by a more comprehensive study of schools dedicated to the training of ministers conducted by Mark A. May and William A. Brown. The May-Brown study, published in 1934, recommended that the Conference of Theological Seminaries become an accrediting agency. In 1936 the conference became the American Association of Theological Schools, adopted standards for accreditation and in 1938 published a list of schools which met those standards. In the early 1970s the name was changed to the Association of Theological Schools (ATS).

Accreditation

Seminaries, from their establishment in 1808 until the late 1930s when AATS began the accreditation process, were closely tied to the denominations which founded and supported them. Accreditation made no sudden change in that relationship. In fact, accreditation was a desirable development. It moved the seminaries out of the shadow of higher education institutions into the open, where the quality of their academic work could be judged. Moreover, the standards gave administrators and boards of trustees goals by which they could improve libraries, provide adequate physical facilities and secure adequate administrative staff. The standards also supplied guidelines for enriching the curricula and for establishing criteria for selecting faculty. Although accreditation is neutral, it has affected the character of denominational seminaries in terms of their self image and professors in terms of their teaching goals.

The Kelly and the May-Brown reports had shown seminaries as schools of the church--small, unresponsive to the best educational methods, not respected in the academic world and not careful about maintaining admission standards. Now, over fifty years after the beginning of accreditation, denominational seminaries are respected in the academic world, for almost all are also accredited by the association which accredits colleges and universities in their region. This move, from being primarily responsive to the church, to a concern for accreditation has been a mixed blessing. As indicated above, it stabilized and improved education. However, it diverted the seminaries' attention from training ministers as leaders of congregations to the more academic goal of providing well planned courses on subjects ministers should know.

The effects of fifty years of accreditation on the goals of the seminary professors are somewhat easier to identify. J. Christiaan Beker, professor of New Testament at Princeton Theological Seminary, writing recently in the *Christian Century* states that he is "deeply alarmed" at the trend toward professionalism in biblical studies. "Faculty feel enormous pressure," he writes, "to impress their peers in various segments of the biblical disciplines in order to secure economic well-being and promotion within their departments. Indeed, the way to impress colleagues is to conform to the standards of the learned societies which are guided by the model of the scientific study of religion--a model that shuns or looks down upon any confessional commitment." Beker continues with a plea for seminary professors to teach with the goal of serving "the well-being of the church."[6]

The professionalism about which Beker writes developed during the past fifty years as denominational seminaries modeled themselves after accredited graduate professional schools. This model has influenced the criteria for the selection of seminary professors, their advancement in rank, tenure, policies for sabbatical leave, workload, specialization and institutional loyalties. Tenure, for example, is a status borrowed from secular higher education which protects a professor's freedom to explore a subject and the right to hold unconventional opinions. Tenure functions the same way in seminaries but it creates a special problem because seminaries were founded to communicate certain beliefs. Seminaries may require adherence to creedal statements before granting tenure, but seminaries are limited in what they can do if professors change their beliefs after they achieve tenure. Unless the seminary is able to show that professors have deviated from a doctrinal position to which they have subscribed, the seminary is not free to dismiss them.

In practice this allows a considerable amount of freedom for the interpretation of beliefs and morals.

Many seminary professors of the 1920s and 1930s grew up in congregations which retained some of the evangelical ethos of the 19th century, and they often served as pastors before they became professors. They were selected to teach because of their character, beliefs and their flair for academic work. A doctor's degree was desirable but was not required. Today's professors grew up in congregations more pluralistic in beliefs, and they probably elected teaching as a vocation while in college or seminary. In many cases they enrolled in the department of religion of a large university for their Ph.D. degree. Thus, early on the role of professor and the academic study of religion became the major interest of many seminary teachers. It is from that pool of candidates that seminaries usually select their professors. Moreover, seminary policies for advancement in rank, workload and sabbaticals are formulated to increase academic productivity--usually publication. This development of academic specialization does not mean that seminary professors are uninterested in the church or unconcerned about practical problems in religions life; but the seminary does not reward these interests as it does the academic.

Although most professors in denominational seminaries are deeply concerned about the church and teach for the well-being of the church, they are not always selected for these values. It is not unusual for a seminary faculty to be made up almost entirely of professors who have had little or no experience in pastoral ministry, the vocation for which their students are preparing. As a result, seminary students are well educated in subjects but are not necessarily well oriented to the leadership role they are expected to play in a congregation. In general terms, seminary professors are not role models for their students, for professors are not responsible for or to congregations.

Institutional Independence

Although accreditation was the formal process which pulled seminaries into the mainstream of graduate professional schools, other circumstances at the same time caused them to become more independent. During the past fifty years denominational seminaries have expanded their sources of funding and they have become more ecumenical.

Each denomination has a different story about the way it finances its theological schools. The Presbyterian story may be somewhat unusual but the changes in sources of funding are typical. During the 1940s Presbyterian seminaries received from 40 to 60 percent of their funding from church benevolences. This amount dropped to about 20 percent in 1970 and to five percent in 1990. Christa Klein, who made a study of seminary policy issues for the Association of Governing Boards of Universities and Colleges in 1991, found that denominational funding for seminaries "continues to decline while costs continue to rise."[7]

When the decline in funding from denominational benevolences became obvious in the early 1970s, the schools responded by employing more fund raising personnel. Seminaries found that they had a cause church people would support. Protestant seminaries tripled their income and expenses in the decade from 1970 to 1980.[8] These schools have continued their fund raising efforts--and in the case of the Presbyterians--have become financially semi-autonomous. Although none of the schools want to lose denominational support, none would close if that source of funding were withdrawn.

Fifty years ago our denominational seminaries were rather parochial in that the professors and most of their student body were of one denomination. Today almost all of our seminaries, including the large evangelical ones, are ecumenical, for such is the spirit of our era. During the past half-century we've seen the formation of the National and World Councils of Churches, both of which have affected church life in America. When the Roman Catholic Church opened itself to a new dialogue with other Christian denominations as a result of Vatican II, the spirit of cooperation was greatly expanded. In addition to this ecumenical movement in the churches, many professors in our seminaries were trained in the non-denominational environment of universities. As a result, today denominational seminaries often have professors from several denominations. It is not unusual for Roman Catholics to teach in Protestant seminaries and vice versa. There is at least one case of a Jewish professor teaching New Testament courses in a Protestant seminary. This situation of financial semi-independence and ecumenical outlook in academic affairs creates a feeling among some administrators that they and their boards of trustees are primarily responsible for the institution. The phrase "church-related" rather than "church-sponsored" seminary is being used increasingly to express that feeling. Such a turn of events is not necessarily undesirable. But it allows the seminary to define itself more in terms of quality of professors and academic programs than in terms of the original meaning of a seminary as "the seed-bed" of the church.

Ministerial Role

The focus of seminary programs for ordination has become fuzzy during the past fifty years. In the 1930s the role of ministers was rather well defined. They performed this role through preaching, teaching, advising (pastoral counseling was not yet in vogue) and administering a program that fitted the expectations of most members of a congregation. By the 1950s the uncertainty about the role of ministers prompted H. Richard Niebuhr to term it a "perplexed profession."[9] After reviewing the recent history of ministry, Niebuhr concluded there was an "emerging new conception of the ministry" which he described as the "Pastoral Director."[10] Much of what Niebuhr wanted in a Pastoral Director makes sense today, but the term did not stick. By the 1960s there was a strong move to consider the minister a "professional." After the social unrest of the late 1960s and 1970s there was a movement to consider the minister a "change agent" in society. During the 1980s there was a recognition of the minister as a "manager" of a congregation.

A certain amount of this effort to identify the central thrust of a minister's role is faddish and represents only a minority view. But the Niebuhr judgment that the ministry is a "perplexed profession" is a correct assessment of the lack of clarity about the role of ministers. The seminaries reflect this ambiguity. They simply add courses and lectures, or sponsor conferences on the various models of ministry and expect students and ministers to select the model that suits their inclination.

This brief overview of seminary development in terms of the effects of accreditation on the schools, their success in finding additional financial support and the ambiguous role of the minister contributed in different ways to their becoming graduate professional schools.[11] Seminaries have maintained their interest in the church and its ministry but in ways that flow naturally from the kind of schools they have become.

Entry Into Ministry

Our second question is "What have seminaries and denominations done to help newly ordained ministers lead congregations?"

Seminary Answer

The development of seminaries into graduate professional schools should not be interpreted as a lack of interest in the work of their graduates. Rather, this development should be considered as the seminaries' interpretation of how they can best serve the church. Compared to fifty years ago, our seminaries today have better prepared professors, richer and more diverse curricula, larger libraries--often stocked with audio and visual resources--and have created opportunities for students to participate in archaeological digs or projects in cultural contexts other than their own.

In addition to becoming better schools, seminaries, including non-denominational ones, have become of increasing value to the institutionalized church. The most obvious contribution is in the work of professors who produce books on theology, Bible and special studies designed for use in church schools. Some seminaries have developed instructional programs for officers and lay persons on topics such as evangelism, stewardship, church growth or the training of Bible teachers. Several seminaries have secured large endowments to produce video-cassette courses to be used by adult study groups in congregations. The list of ways seminaries relate to denominational headquarters and help congregations is long. We cannot imagine how poorly informed denominations would be or how bleak congregational life would be without the contributions of the seminaries.

As the ethos of the seminary became more academic, it demonstrated more concern about the practice of ministry. There was an extensive growth in courses in the "practical field" and some form of field experience became a requirement for the B.D. degree. Professors in the practical field formed an association in 1950. Meeting biennially until 1982, these professors carried on a lively discussion about problems and opportunities of education for the practice of ministry.

The seminaries' concern for, yet caution about, their part in training for the practice of ministry is illustrated in the story of the ATS-sponsored *Readiness for Ministry* project. The immediate motive for the study was the desire of ATS during the 1970-72 biennium to revise its standards for accreditation[12] and a growing desire on the part of theological educators to formulate a common understanding of the work of the ministry. The research summarized the need for clarity about the role of the minister in these words:

> Some theological students were hesitant about entering certain parochial ministries, being ignorant of the ministerial expectations held by the laity of their church body, but usually fearing the worst. Lay leaders in turn were occasionally bewildered as some young clergy seemed to ignore community expectations and plunged into activities that did not include the primary objectives of the church. Theological schools often felt uncomfortable in seeking to educate young clergy in ways that changed their perceptions of the goals and objectives of ministry with the result that service within a congregation or parish of the related church became extremely difficult.[13]

The project was carefully conceived and conducted with the guidance of a first-class group of researchers. With the help of 2,000 people, one-half of whom were lay people from forty-seven denominations--the number later growing to 5,131 persons--the researchers were able to identify and describe sixty-four basic characteristics of ministers. The researchers then turned their attention to ways of assessing the readiness of a seminary student for ministry. During the 1976-77 academic year forty schools in the ATS administered the assessment instrument in order to perfect its use.

As a research project, the *Readiness for Ministry* study is a textbook example of excellent social research. Moreover, when part of the research was repeated fifteen years later to see whether the original findings had been too much influenced by the events of the time, very little difference in the criteria by which people judged the work of the minister emerged.[14]

The importance of the *Readiness for Ministry* project for this paper is the way it was received and used by seminaries. Originally the purpose of the research was to identify criteria of readiness so that seminaries could plan their educational programs to help their students acquire the proper skills and abilities of a minister. The planners of the study described the purpose in these words:

> There is a growing conviction that the only valid test of an educational system lies in the results it effects in its graduates. Denominational leaders are also coming to share this conviction. They find that the questions a congregation raises about a potential minister do not concern the number of courses completed but revolve

about such areas as wisdom and knowledge, pastoral skills, psychological maturity, and the strength of faith.[15]

Notice that the conviction of denominational leaders and the needs of congregations are used to justify a shift of attention from courses to competencies. The planners of this study then went on to suggest that:

> The Commission on Accrediting of the ATS is shifting the focus of its investigations from evaluation of institutional resources--whose contribution to educational excellence has not been precisely demonstrated--to evaluation of the graduates of the institution.[16]

The seminaries did not respond favorably to the idea of a "competencies-based" curricula on which accreditation would be judged. That proposal was abandoned, showing how committed the seminaries were to an academic model of education. The seminaries, however, recognized the value of the research on criteria for ministry and the tests that were developed to assay a student's fitness for ministry.

In short, the seminaries' answer to the question of how they help ministers lead congregations is this: they have provided the kind of education in Bible, theology and history that will help ministers understand the Christian faith; they have provided courses and field work opportunities to introduce students to the practice of ministry; and they have maintained a variety of continuing education courses on specific issues and problems which ministers must address.[17]

Denominational Answers

The problem of helping newly ordained ministers during the formative years of their work is not the most pressing concern of church leaders. This comes about because a good number of seminary graduates make the transition to the practice of ministry with their own native ability and the help of friends. Others who do not fare so well go to another pastorate after a few years and attempt to make a fresh start. Those who fail or who suffer through a bad first experience are usually faulted for personality problems, insensitivity to human relations, inability to lead, or other negative characteristics. Since one's first pastorate is considered a test, church leaders tend to fault the individual who fails or flounders and to commend those who move through the experience successfully. Thus, this period in a minister's career is not clearly seen as a responsibility of the seminary or of the denomination.

Each denomination has its own answer to the question of how it helps newly ordained ministers. This project examined the policies of three large mainline denominations: Lutheran, Methodist and Presbyterian.

The newly formed Evangelical Lutheran Church in America (ELCA) has within it some Lutheran denominations which had required an intern year before ordination. There seems to be an understanding within the Lutheran tradition that the minister is a pastor, for the term pastor is constantly used as a name prefix instead of "Reverend" or "Doctor." The descriptive term "Pastor" expresses not only the church's expectation of a minister but implies a responsibility of the denomination to provide pastoral experience before ordination. The Lutheran denominations which required an intern year were demonstrating a partnership with their seminaries. The denomination shared responsibility for the part of the minister's training that the seminaries could not provide alone.

The newly formed ELCA continues the idea that the denomination has a special responsibility for the support of its ministers after ordination. This is provided for all ministers in a well planned program of continuing education. The "Letter of Appointment" requires congregations to provide funds and time for the pastor's continuing education. The denomination supplies a nationwide program in continuing education centers and its seminaries, and ministers are required to file a report each year on their continuing education activities.

The ELCA has developed a "Growth in Excellence in Ministry" (GEM) program for newly ordained pastors. The program assumes that the role of pastor can be properly learned only as one plays that role in a congregation. It also assumes that most newly ordained ministers are unclear about the role they are to play, will probably experience conflict with some parishioners and suffer from an overload of duties. The GEM program, sponsored by the synod (Lutheran regional administration), provides a trained leader for groups of three to five newly ordained ministers. These groups meet monthly for one or two years to discuss all aspects of their ministry including cases that are prepared in advance which may be helpful for the whole group. Very detailed manuals have been prepared for leaders, consultants and the sponsoring synod.

Leaders of the Division of the Ordained Ministry of the United Methodist Church in the late 1960s discussed the importance of the first few years of ministry and decided that the third to fifth years were critical. They planned a "young pastors" pilot project during 1970-71 to test their assumptions. The center of the program was a "cluster group" consisting of five to eight pastors usually meeting biweekly. The purposes of the group were to provide support for each other and to help each other to develop ministerial abilities. Each cluster had a pastoral associate--a more experienced colleague--who functioned as a facilitator of the group process, sharing his ministerial experience and helping to maintain a good support environment. Three times during the two-year period the cluster groups met together in a region for a three-day program to discuss human relations, theological issues or social problems.

One of the important aspects of the pilot project was the decision to have Edgar W. Mills evaluate the results of this project. Mills' evaluation is a thorough assessment of the value of the experiment and contains many important suggestions.[18] For our purpose, we will note that the most important change in the lives of these young pastors was "an enhanced ability to work collaboratively on issues and problems of their ministry and support each other in the process."[19] Mills' evaluation did not show any direct positive effect on "established patterns of continuing learning" and only "a tiny influence on the ordering of their role priorities."[20]

The United Methodist Church has a two-phase ordination policy. When candidates for ministry complete the M.Div. degree and are appointed to a full-time position, they are ordained as deacons with full power of ministry in their appointment. As "probationary" members of the annual conference they are "assigned a counseling elder with whom they will establish a covenant around the development of vocational goals. . . . "[21] Each annual conference is free to set up whatever supervisory structures and groups it desires to provide the guidance required by the denomination. The handbook suggests four models for peer group supervision--two of which are cluster groups. I have examined the handbooks or printed materials from six conferences representing different regions of the United States. These materials are well written policy and program statements reflecting years of experience in dealing with newly ordained ministers during their two years of probation. One of the handbooks is 53 pages in length and includes sample copies of all of the forms the supervisors and probationers are to use. After the probationary period there is a formal review and evaluation of the candidate. If the probationer's record is satisfactory, he or she is ordained an elder and is in full connection with the annual conference.

The United Presbyterian Church in the mid 1950s began a series of Young Pastors Conferences for ministers in their third to fifth year. These were planned on the theory that newly ordained ministers enter their first pastorate with considerable enthusiasm and with confidence that what they had learned in the seminary could be applied to a congregation. After three years many ministers found their enthusiasm waning, their seminary learning not of top priority with the church members and their image of ministry out of harmony with what the congregation desired. The purpose of the conferences was to help young pastors gain a more realistic understanding of ministry and to provide some support and guidance for them as they settled into a more mature notion of their role. These Young Pastors Conferences have continued in various forms.

After the union of the major Presbyterian denominations in 1983, a study of what Presbyterians were doing to help pastors "start up" a new pastorate was sponsored by the Vocation Agency. The report, *After the Call*, is an excellent survey of what presbyteries and synods were doing in this regard.[22] In the summer of 1991 I wrote to the executives of the sixteen synods asking for an update of programs in the presbyteries since the 1985 survey. The replies showed considerable interest in problems related to newly ordained ministers. The literature most widely used consists of booklets by Roy Oswald of the Alban Institute. The method most often used is a conference or seminar during which issues and problems of being a minister are discussed. These conferences often include an orientation to the Presbyterian method of work and to the resources available for use in a congregation.

Learning to Lead a Congregation

This review of what seminaries and denominations are doing to help ministers in their practice leads us to our third question, "What additional experience is needed to help newly ordained ministers learn how to lead congregations?"

Seminaries have found their niche as graduate professional schools. The seminaries will probably continue to improve their training in "practical" courses and units of supervised field work. The seminaries will probably continue to expand their service to the church according to the interests of the professors, for the church is the basis of their support. There is no reason to expect them to change and no movement among church people to cause them to expand into something different. The seminaries, therefore, should be considered as resources for the church rather than agencies that will design and sponsor educational programs based on the needs of individual ministers of particular congregations.

Denominational leaders who work directly with ministers and congregations have tried a wide variety of programs since the 1950s to help newly ordained ministers. Except for the Methodist's "Young Pastors" program of 1970-71, I do not know of any programs that have been thoroughly evaluated. The programs currently sponsored by the ELCA, the United Methodists and the Presbyterian Church (U.S.A.) all must have received favorable response or they would not have been continued. The lack of competent evaluation of these programs is not a serious problem. What is important is that the denominational leaders have identified a gap in the education of ministers and have done what they could to fill that gap.

Because denominational leaders have demonstrated a concern for this gap for a long time, I will propose in the last section of this paper that they plan, sponsor, and evaluate more vigorous programs for the first few years of ministry. The denominational programs we have reviewed tend to follow the seminary model of education. That is, leaders--by survey or through knowledge of the problem of newly ordained ministers--identify an area of concern and abstract it into a topic. Illustrations would be stewardships/budget-making or developing a mission statement for the congregation. Then in a conference setting of a few days the topics are discussed by experts. Except for the practical focus of the topic, this is the seminary classroom method of education. What is needed is a different type of education more suited to the nature of the gap. Let us note the nature of the gap, the elements that must be involved in an educational project and then an educational program that might be suitable.

The Gap

The gap between seminary training and the practice of ministry has been described in various ways. Some point to the academic nature of the seminary and contrast it to the practical needs of the congregation.

Others stress the difference between the protected environment of the seminary and the exposure of the minister to criticism. The seminary honors ideas and information while congregations give a high priority to a pleasing personality. A seminary grades on the basis of a student mastering a subject, but the church honors ministers who can resolve sticky personal relations and attract new members.

All of the above contrasts between seminary and the practice of ministry are true, and much has been done by seminaries in their field education programs and by the denominations in their conferences to help smooth out the transition. But the gap continues to exist because (1) the practice of ministry calls for a style of learning not available in the seminary and (2) the theology of church members is existential rather than systematic.

1. The practice of ministry can be learned only when one is the designated leader of a congregation. Although seminaries can replicate this situation to some degree in courses on preaching or teaching, they cannot replicate the leadership role in a congregation. A congregation is a dynamic social organization that has its own history and characteristics. When a minister assumes responsibility for leading a congregation in worship and work, he or she finds that there are few direct connections between seminary courses and the particular problems that must be addressed. A person under these conditions must learn how to learn within real life situations. Many young ministers do so; but others need help to understand what is happening, how it happened, and what their behavior should be toward the people involved.

2. Most church members are not seriously interested in systematic theology, theories of Christian ethics or any other academic entry into religion. Church members are more concerned about what Christianity has to offer them in dealing with problems and issues in which they are involved. This life centered interest puts a premium on the minister's ability to relate to people in their sorrows, celebrations, choices, temptations, loneliness, or fears. The seminary prepares ministers as well as can be expected to deal with these matters, but it cannot replicate the congregational situation in which ministers must interpret the faith.

The Elements

Because the style of learning and the substance of what is learned are rooted in the practice of ministry, we need to examine the elements that make up the learning situation: (1) the congregational/ministry equation, and the two components, (2) the congregation and (3) the minister.

1. The congregational/ministry equation. It is fruitless to argue that one element in this equation is more important than the other. It is critical, however, to know that there is a symbiotic relationship between these two elements. In addition, the variables that describe the minister (such as gender, age, education, interests, ability and personality) are many. The variables which characterize a congregation (such as size, location, budget, history, sense of mission and program) are likewise numerous. The equation becomes more complex when we realize that some of these variables are constantly changing.

Because the congregation/ministry equation is so dynamic and complex, most entry into ministry programs avoid it. I will assume that this is the reality which should be at the center of an educational experience designed to help newly ordained ministers.

2. The congregation. Not all world religions have congregations. Buddhism, Confucianism and Animism do not require a congregation, and congregations in Islam do not function as congregations do in the Jewish or Christian religions. The congregation in the Christian religion is a community with common beliefs about God, uniting in worship and work in such a way as to define and support a style of life.[23] How congregations function as small face-to-face communities is not well-known. One source of information is ministers who have distilled wisdom about congregations from years of experience. This wisdom can be shared with young ministers; but too often the experience is little more than stories which are not applicable to all congregations. Another source is studies done by researchers who describe the life of a congregation and explain why it functions the way it does. Unfortunately, we have very few of these studies. Most of the literature about congregations is about what they ought to be or how they can be more efficient in some aspect of their work. Although this literature may be inspirational or suggestive, it does not help us understand why particular congregations are as they are or what might be done to change them.

During the past twenty years a variety of scholars have studied different aspects of congregational life. As a result we have more confidence in our ability to describe the characteristics of a congregation and a better understanding of why congregations develop the way they do. Although we are not far enough along in congregational studies to prescribe treatment for problems, we assume that methods are now available whereby a young minister can, often with the help of lay leaders, achieve a realistic description of a congregation's self-image and some indication of what its mission should be.[24]

3. The minister. The role of the minister as preacher/pastor/leader of a congregation was not seriously questioned until the Niebuhr/Williams study of theological education in the 1950s. Since then, as described in the seminary development section of this paper, a variety of descriptive titles have been proposed. This ambivalence about the minister's role reflects the uncertainty of our time about the mission of the church and the lack of clarity inherent in ministerial work. The issue is not what characteristics church members want in their minister. The *Readiness for Ministry* study identified the five top characteristics as ministers as (1) an ability to provide "service without regard to acclaim," (2) a person of integrity (3) who sets a Christian example, (4) is competent in pastoral skills and (5) can develop the congregation into a community.[25] The issue is how shall the minister's role be played?

My review of the most widely used manuals, booklets and studies of conference programs designed to help newly ordained ministers leads me to conclude that they are based on the notion of the minister as a professional person who has skills and knowledge to apply to congregational life. Much of this literature is about survival. The cover picture of a 1992 leaflet describing a major conference for young ministers shows a minister up to his neck in water sweating profusely while two sharks circle around him! Some advice has been summarized as to how to "tiptoe through the tithers." There is some excellent writing about how to analyze the power structure and struggle in a congregation, but the coaching is about how to deal with the politics of conflict rather than with the issues. The more helpful literature and conference programs focus attention on personal and professional growth. Personal growth items include management of time, care for family, formation of a support group, avoiding "burn-out" and similar matters. Professional growth stresses the importance of gaining competence in managing stewardship programs, counseling, teaching, leadership of worship and other activities of the minister.

The interpretation of the minister as a professional gained recognition in the 1960s and has endured because our society has become more complex.[26] We have learned to depend on professionals--people who have expert knowledge and skill in a restricted field. This attitude influenced the development of seminaries as graduate professional schools and it informs lay people in congregations who select ministers. It has also endured because the idea of professionalism has value. One wants a minister who knows how to visit the sick, perform a wedding ceremony, and lead a well-planned worship service with a helpful sermon. Moreover, the target for improvement--the minister--is obvious. So, programs proliferate to help ministers become better professionals.

The goal of professional competence will continue because ministers must master their role in church and society. But this goal for ministers needs to be more precisely defined at two points. The first is that ministers must know how to relate to the congregations they are serving as well as to their individual members. Without a proper relation of care, concern and sharing of the minister's own faith in God, not much of spiritual importance will occur. How to establish and maintain such a relationship is quite different from development of one's skills, which is the goal of professionals. The second is that ministers must understand themselves as leaders of congregations. This means ministers must learn how to understand the congregations they serve, how to help congregations understand themselves in relation to the community in which members live and to lead congregations into a self-selected mission.

Jackson Carroll has provided us with an excellent analysis of ministers as leaders of congregations. Ministers, Carroll insists, have three central tasks: (1) ensuring Christian identity, (2) formation of community, and (3) empowering a public ministry.[27] This task oriented conception of ministry means ministers must evaluate their competency on the basis of what congregations become under their leadership, not on the basis of their reputation as good professionals.

Education For and In the Gap

If the first few years of ministry are critical for the lifetime service of a minister and if this period presents an opportunity for learning not available prior to ordination, what should an educational program for this period be? At this point in the development of educational programs for the gap we cannot give a final answer. What we need is a variety of well-planned and evaluated programs in order to build up a body of experience from which an effective model might emerge. The following outline of an educational program based on the previous discussion of the nature of the gap and the elements that should be involved is offered as a suggestion that may be tried and evaluated.

1. Sponsorship. It is important that the church's administrative agency responsible for congregations and that the seminaries both be involved in planning and supporting an experimental program. The church agency--be it a conference, presbytery, synod or diocese--has knowledge of and experience with congregations under its supervision. Seminaries have institutional stability, means of raising money, and experience in long range planning of educational programs. Which of these two agencies should take the initiative or how the responsibility should be divided will depend on the interests of leaders and local conditions. In some situations the church agency will have the leadership, money and desire to sponsor an experimental program, with seminaries being junior partners. In other situations a seminary may be jointly involved in every phase of such a program.

2. Interpretation. The project should be interpreted to the newly ordained as education based on experience. Although theological beliefs, historical references, psychological principles, ideas, theories and data from research will be used, the minister's experience as the installed leader of a congregation will be the data for discussion. Since ministerial experience is the substance and focus of this project, it is different from seminary education.

The project should be explained to the churches served by the ministers as an experimental program designed to fill the gap between seminary education and the practical needs of a congregation. The congregation, through its official board, must agree to allow its minister to participate and must approve his or her attendance at the scheduled meetings. The congregation should be assured that its normal activities will continue although the minister may ask members' help in understanding the church's history and mission.

3. Educational environment. The selection of participants in an experimental program should be decided by the planning committee. Much will depend on the number of newly ordained ministers in the area and their interest in such a project, funds for transportation and time available. It is better to select individuals for an experimental project on the basis of their interest and promise for ministry than to require all eligible people to participate.

The program should be designed for a minimum of two years' duration. Learning from experience is difficult because it involves one's whole person, especially one's attitudes. It takes time for a person to realize that he or she is too aggressive or shy in personal relations or is overly anxious about adhering to an agenda. Psychologists who have worked with groups of this type report that it takes about a year before individuals begin to loosen up and become amenable to attitudinal change.

A small peer group is the center of the educational process. If a small group of peers forms the right kind of association, it will support and help members of the group. One of the negatives of the ministry, especially in the first few years, is loneliness and a lack of peers in whom one can confide. The small peer group is, therefore, much more than a class; it may be the beginning of the finest kind of collegial relationships. Conventional wisdom places the number in such a group between five and ten: if the group is fewer than five, there is not enough interaction; and if the number is above ten or twelve, there is not enough time for all in the group to share their ideas and experiences.

The style and frequency of meetings deserves careful attention. If funds are available for an overnight meeting, then a meeting from noon one day until about noon the next would allow for a three hour seminar in the first afternoon, a second seminar and recreation in the evening and a three hour seminar the next morning. A church camp might be a good location. If the group met in a large metropolitan area, it could meet from 9:00 a.m. to 3:00 p.m., giving about five hours of discussion time. If the location is a church, the group should agree to stay away from the telephone and not allow other interruptions.

The group should meet no less than seven times per year. If the group started in September and met monthly except in December and the month of Easter (usually April), the seventh meeting would be in May.

4. Program. The basic program would consist of three seminars, each with a well-defined purpose and with leaders trained to work in that area.

(1) The Leadership Seminar. The leadership seminar would be designed to help ministers learn (a) how to understand the congregations they serve and (b) their role in the congregational/ministry equation.

Since the ministers are new to each other and to the congregations they serve, it may be well to use the first year on a somewhat objective analysis of both goals. Each minister might use some of the recently developed guides for describing the congregation. Members of the congregation could help and could thus provide a way for the minister to learn to relate to his or her parishioners. The description of a church's self-understanding of its history and mission leads directly to its idea of what characteristics the minister should have and the role he or she should play in the congregation and community. So during the first year, the ministers could use seminar time defining their role in relation to the expectations of the congregation.

Exactly how the leadership seminar would function would have to be worked out by the leaders. One way would be for all the ministers to work on one phase of their congregational description and use their discussion time to compare and contrast their different situations. Another would be for each minister to present the congregation he or she serves as a case study so the group could discuss what ministry should be like under the conditions described. Regardless of method used, the purpose is to help the minister learn how to understand the congregation and the expectations which that congregation has of its minister.

A natural outgrowth of the first year should be a heightened awareness in the congregation of some fairly specific goals which fit its history and interest. These could be formalized either by the official board or by some adult class and could become the center of attention the second year. Reports on how well this process worked and the minister's leadership role would be the substance for the seminar discussions. Ministers in their second year may be ready to report to the seminar their efforts to work on the central tasks of leadership as defined by Jackson Carroll or their efforts to be "reflective leaders" using the cases in Carroll's book, *As One With Authority*, as a model.[28]

(2) The Self-seminar. The purpose of the self-seminar is to help the ministers understand themselves, their motives for ministry, their expectations in ministry, and some assessment of their strengths and weaknesses in the practice of ministry. The method would be that of group counseling. The material discussed would be the "feeling" part of one's ministry. The ministers could express their responses to the problems and people in their congregations. This might be done by general discussion of each person's experiences with interpersonal matters common to all congregations--such as conflicts between groups in the church. Perhaps a better way would be for each minister to present a written account of an occurrence or a counseling problem on which help was needed. The discussion would help members of the group learn how to deal with such pastoral problems and it might open the reporter to deeper levels of self-understanding.

Some meetings of the self-seminar should be planned with spouses in order to deal with family matters and the relationships of the family to the congregation.

The feeling side of ministry (such as anxiety, stress, loneliness, or vocational expectations of a person entering ministry) are all within the normal range of one's emotions and can be discussed in the self-seminar. We know, however, that if a person has deep personality problems and has been able to hide or suppress them in the protected environment of the seminary, they may emerge when he or she becomes a minister and is accountable for his or her total lifestyle. When this happens, the leader of the self-seminar should arrange for whatever psychotherapy or counseling is needed.

(3) The Professional Seminar. Some time should be allocated for professional development. The peer group should be in charge of this period and request what they need. Some of the time, especially at the beginning, may be an orientation to the ways the administrative unit above the congregation operates and what resources it offers congregations. Time could be devoted to a display of "how-to-do-it" manuals for various church activities, reviews of recent books, or new curriculum materials, including videocassettes. The group could ask for a person to critique a sample sermon from each member or for some other leader to help them work through an issue of common concern.

5. Evaluation. An experimental project of this nature, which from its planning through completion will last three to four years, needs formative evaluation. This is a style of evaluation in which an evaluator works with the project from its inception. At set intervals, the evaluator by interviews or questions ascertains how well the purposes are being realized and reports back to the people in charge. Changes are made while the project is in progress in order to improve it.[29]

6. Leaders. The project requires an evaluator, a psychologist and two or three ministers with special training.

(1) The evaluator should be a person with training in social research and knowledge of and sympathy for the work of a minister. A person with proper qualifications can be located in psychology or sociology departments of colleges or universities.

(2) The leader of the self-seminar should be a certified psychologist or psychiatrist who has had experience in group counseling, has a concern for the work of ministers and has personal knowledge of how congregations function. This person should also be acquainted with

the counseling resources in the community in order to make referrals. A person with these qualifications can be found in colleges, universities, counseling centers or in private practice.

(3) The staff for the leadership seminar will be the most difficult to locate. These leaders must be ministers with broad experience with congregations and experience in helping others learn from experience. There is no model for this position.[30] The idea of a "supervisor" conjures up the image of one who knows how to show a less experienced person how to act. Such is not appropriate because the staff person does not know all the factors the inexperienced ministers are facing in their congregations. The term "mentor" has the same liabilities. The term "coach" is helpful in that these persons make suggestions and support the athletes, but coaches have authority over the players which is not true in this ministerial relationship. Perhaps the term "colleague" suits the relationship, for the purpose is to help the newly ordained ministers learn from the experiences they are having in their congregations, not to duplicate experiences the staff person had.

I suggest that the leadership seminar have two or three colleagues, depending on the number in the seminar group. Two or three colleagues will provide some variety of viewpoint so that a dialogue may be maintained about the way the seminar is progressing. The colleagues responsible for the leadership seminar should organize a training/planning period of about six months. It would be highly desirable for the evaluator and the psychologist to meet with them for most of these sessions. These leaders will work out the details of the program. The colleagues responsible for the leadership seminar should set up and perhaps test whatever protocols they plan to use in helping the ministers learn about their congregations. They will also need to review recent studies about congregations and theories of organization applicable to congregations.

Experience, the Great Teacher

The above suggestions for an experimental program assume that the practice of ministry in a congregation is sufficiently different from both the newly ordained minister's previous experiences and the training received in seminary as to merit a special educational program.

Since the proposed program is experience based, the exact nature of the program should be open to experimentation. For example, the colleagues who are in charge of the leadership seminar might test the value of visiting the congregations served by ministers in the peer group. A visit to the congregation at worship, during a church night supper and perhaps at an officers' meeting would provide a perspective the young ministers may not have. But that procedure may change the relationship of the colleague to the minister to that of a supervisor--thus continuing the dependence on "experts" which characterized seminary education. Also, the congregation may develop false expectations from such a visit. However, it is only by testing this and other procedures that we will build up a body of experience which will shape an educational program this gap in minister training deserves.

Notes

1 J. Christiaan Beker, "Integration and Integrity in New Testament Studies," *The Christian Century* May 13, 1992: 515-517.

2 James W. Fraser, *The Development of Protestant Theological Education in the United States 1740-1875* (Lanham MD: University Press of America, 1988) 3-23.

3 Glenn T. Miller, *Piety and Intellect* (Atlanta: Scholars Press, 1990) 79.

4 Miller 113.

5 Miller 187-202.

6 Beker 515-516.

7 Christa R. Klein, *Perspectives on the Current Status of and Emerging Policy Issues for Theological Schools and Seminaries* (Washington: Association of Governing Boards of Universities and Colleges, 1991) 29.

8 John C. Fletcher, *The Futures of Protestant Seminaries* (Washington: Alban Institute, 1983) 53.

9 H. Richard Niebuhr, *The Purpose of the Church and its Ministry* (New York: Harper, 1956) 48.

10 Niebuhr 79.

11 A review of issues that have emerged as seminaries developed from the mid 1950s to the late 1980s was done by James M. Gustafson in "Reflections on the Literature on Theological Education Published Between 1955-1985," *Theological Education* 24 Supplement 11 (1988): 9-86.

12 David Schuller, Milo L. Brekke and Merton P. Strommen, *Readiness for Ministry*, Vol. 1. (Vandalia, Ohio: The Association of Theological Schools, 1975) vi.

13 *Readiness for Ministry*, Vol 2 (1976) 8.

14 Daniel O. Aleshire, "ATS Profiles of Ministry Project," *Clergy Assessment and Career Development*, eds. Richard A. Hunt, John E. Hinkel, Jr. and H. Newton Malony (Nashville: Abingdon Press, 1990) 99-100.

15 *Readiness for Ministry*, Vol. 1, vi.

16 *Readiness for Ministry*, Vol. 1, vi.

17 Within the seminaries professors have carried on a lively discussion about theological education. The major issues are discussed in Joseph C.

Hough, Jr. and John B. Cobb, Jr., *Christian Identity and Theological Education* (Atlanta: Scholars Press, 1985). Responses to the Hough/Cobb thesis that seminaries should produce practical theologians will be found in Don S. Browning, David Polk and Ian S. Evison, *The Education of the Practical Theologian* (Atlanta: Scholars Press, 1989).

18 Edgar W. Mills, *Peer Groups and Professional Development* (Nashville: Division of the Ordained Ministry, United Methodist Board of Higher Education and Ministry, 1973).

19 Mark A. Rouch, *Young Pastors* (Nashville: Division of the Ordained Ministry, The United Methodist Board of Higher Education and Ministry, 1973) 25.

20 Rouch 31-32.

21 *Board of Ordained Ministry Handbook* (Nashville: Division of Ordained Ministry, United Methodist Board of Higher Education and Ministry, 1988) chapter 13, page 10.

22 David W. Danner, *After the Call* (New York: The Vocation Agency, Presbyterian Church [U.S.A.], 1985).

23 Bruce C. Birch, "Memory in Congregational Life," *Congregations: Their Power to Form and Transform*, ed. C. Ellis Nelson (Atlanta: John Knox Press, 1988) 20-43.

24 The following books will be useful in helping a congregation identify itself and its mission. Jackson Carroll, et. al., *Handbook for Congregational Studies* (Nashville: Abingdon Press, 1986). Carl S. Dudley, *Basic Steps Toward Community Ministry* (Washington: The Alban Institute, 1991). Denham Grierson, *Transforming a People of God* (Melbourne: The Joint Board of Christian Education of Australia and New Zealand, 1984). David A. Roozen, et. al., *Varieties of Religious Presence* (New York: The Pilgrim Press, 1984). James P. Wind, *Places of Worship* (Nashville: American Association for State and Local History, 1990).

25 *Readiness for Ministry*, Vol. 1 6-7.

26 Charles R. Feilding, *Education for Ministry* (Dayton, Ohio: The Association of Theological Schools, 1966). This study of seminary education found that "The gap between the working ministry as seen in the seminary and practiced in the parish is alarmingly wide." (See page 29.) The study urges seminaries to design and support a more vigorous program of supervised field work. It had been assumed that if seminaries educated professionals, the gap would be closed.

27 Jackson W. Carroll, *As One With Authority* (Louisville: Westminster/John Knox, 1991) 97-118.

28 Carroll 119-147.

29 C. Ellis Nelson, *Using Evaluation in Theological Education* (Nashville: Discipleship Resources, 1975) 25-41.

30 James B. Conant, *The Education of American Teachers* (New York: McGraw-Hill, 1963) 137-145. This book is the report of a study conducted for the Carnegie Foundation for the Advancement of Teaching. Conant considered the gap between the academic preparation of teachers and the practice of teaching to be of critical importance. The gap, he concluded, could not be bridged by more or different courses offered in university departments of education. He recommended that a new position be created called a "clinical professor." This person must be an excellent teacher who would supervise new

teachers and must keep up with theories and research findings related to teaching.

There is a rough analogy between the preparation of teachers and ministers. The *practice* of teaching and ministry must deal with people in an institutional setting. Although congregations are more complex than classrooms, Conant's suggestion that we need a new type of educator to bridge the gap is true. For our purpose the word colleague seems appropriate.

18

Be of Good Cheer

I want to thank the Governing Cabinet of the Association of Presbyterian Christian Educators (APCE) and through them the whole Association for my being selected "Educator of the Year." To be honored by one's colleagues is of special significance. You are the people I admire and respect because you work day in and day out to help adults, teenagers, and children develop faith in God. I am delighted to see so many of you gathered here to support and to instruct each other in the educational work of the church.

Fifteen years ago when APCE met in Louisville, the church situation was discouraging. Both streams of the Presbyterian church had reorganized in the early 1970s and had reduced the visibility and effectiveness of Christian education. Both denominations were forced by economic circumstances to piece together a denominational curriculum out of what was available rather than designing what the church needed. The committee planning the 1977 meeting of APCE asked me to make the opening address on the topic "Where Have We Been? What Does it Mean?" The leaders of APCE wanted a historical perspective and any hope I could offer for the future. After reviewing the reasons for the uncertainty in the church, I urged APCE members to stick to our mission: educating church people in a congregational setting, supporting activities that strengthen family life and training teachers and group leaders.

During the past fifteen years since I spoke to you, conditions have changed. The Christian education situation today is most encouraging. Three events support this optimistic appraisal.

First, when the two streams of Presbyterians flowed together in 1983, the General Assembly took time to identify what was truly important for

---

Comments to the Association of Presbyterian Christian Educators meeting in Cincinnati, Ohio, February 13, 1992.

the future of our church. Christian education was assigned a top priority and the General Assembly authorized the funding necessary to produce a new curriculum for our church schools. The structural design for the mission of the denomination restored visibility to our work in the Education and Congregational Nurture Ministry unit. Moreover, this ministry unit has a fine staff in Louisville which is increasingly taking hold of the educational work of our church.

Second, the new Brief Statement of Reformed Faith recognizes teaching as central to the ministry of Jesus and thereby certifies teaching as the church's responsibility. When the committee commissioned to compose a Brief Statement sent its first draft out to the church for comment, I was dismayed to read that Jesus was described as preacher, healer, and savior but nothing was said of his vocation as a teacher or of his teachings. I wrote the chairperson that such an omission was serious and I proposed that a line be added to the description of the life and work of Jesus. I supported that proposal with several pages of reasons why Jesus's role as teacher and the substance of his teachings were absolutely essential for understanding the Christian faith. I sent copies of that correspondence to some of you asking for your response and your help in getting this concern into the Brief Statement. The committee accepted my suggestion and added a line so that the official version of our Brief Statement of Faith affirms that our Lord "taught by word and deed." Thus, every time we stand and repeat what we believe, we honor teaching as a vocation in the church.

Third, the church-at-large understands the importance of Christian education. Last April the Research Services office of the General Assembly released the results of a study of what Presbyterians consider our primary concerns. Over three-fourths of church members, officers, and pastors said membership growth was primary and almost the same percent also selected Christian education. The two go together, for proper church growth depends on enrolling children and youth in our church schools and teaching Christian beliefs to adults.

I do not mean to suggest that our denomination has stopped its decline in membership or that we have regained our theological focus. I do, however, want to affirm that the Presbyterian Church (U.S.A.) is slowly coming to realize that Christian education is essential if the church is to revitalize itself. This is encouraging news. It prompts me to conclude these comments with the words of John ". . . be of good cheer. . . ." (John 16:33.)

Writings of C. Ellis Nelson

The notation "NcMHi" on the following references means the manuscript or a copy of the publication is on file in the Presbyterian Historical Foundation, Montreat, NC.

1941

"A Minister's Responsibility to Youth." Address. Austin Presbyterian Seminary Alumni Association. Austin, Texas, May 1941. NcMHi.

1944

"Guidance Principles Applied to Theological Education." M.A. thesis. University of Texas, Austin, 1944.

1947

"Guiding Youth in Evangelism." *The Earnest Worker* July 1947. NcMHi.

1949

"The Importance of Christian Education for Adults." Installation address as Professor of Christian Education, Austin Presbyterian Theological Seminary, Austin, Texas 15 Sept. 1949.

1950

State of Texas. Legislative Council of the 51st Legislature. *Public Higher Education in Texas*. Ed. and research coordinator. Austin: Legislative Council, 1950.

1951

"What Christians Owe to the World." *The Presbyterian Outlook* 12 Feb. 1951.

"The Purpose of the Teaching Program of the Church." *The Presbyterian Survey* Sept. 1951: 7-9. NcMHi.

Jesus and His Teachings. Richmond, Virginia: Board of Christian Education, Presbyterian Church, U.S., 1951. NcMHi.

A Study of Texas Presbyterian Ministers, Officers and Churches. Austin, Texas: Committee on Program, Publicity and Research, Synod's Council, Presbyterian Church, U.S., 1951. NcMHi.

1952

"The God of the Bible," "The Role of Theology and Education in the Christian Nurture of Children," and "The Glory, Jest and Riddle of the World--Man." Children's Work Section, Division of Christian Education. National Council of Churches Convention, Columbus, Ohio, 10-12 Feb. 1952.

1954

"The Relation Between Theology and Education in Christian Education." Address. Board of Christian Education, Presbyterian Church, U.S. Richmond, Virginia, May 1954. NcMHi.

1955

"Religious Negativism As a Contributing Agent in Functional Disease, v. The Clergyman's Viewpoint." *Texas State Journal of Medicine* April 1955.

"Some Procedures Examined." *The Presbyterian Outlook* 11 July 1955.

A Diagnostic Survey of Certain Attitudes and Values Related to the Development of Day Schools in the Presbyterian Church, U.S. Diss. Columbia U, 1955. Ann Arbor: UMI, 1955. 00-12456.

1956

"4,720 Man-Years for the Lord." *The Presbyterian Survey* April 1956.

Rev. of *Anxiety in Christian Experience*, by Wayne E. Oates. *The Presbyterian Survey*. Jan. 1956. NcMHi.

Rev. of *The Gift of Power*, by Lewis J. Sherrill. *The Austin Seminary Bulletin* June 1956: 29-30. NcMHi.

Rev. of *Holiness is Wholeness* and *Individuation* by Josef Goldbrunner. *The Austin Seminary Bulletin* Oct. 1956: 25-27. NcMHi.

1957

"The Relation Between Theology and Education in Christian Education." *The Austin Seminary Bulletin* July, 1957: 5-20. NcMHi.

Rev. of *The Nature of Prejudice*, by Gordon W. Allport. *The Austin Seminary Bulletin* July, 1957: 22-25.

"Report of Ad Interim Committee on Education of Lay Leaders." *Minutes of the Ninety-Seventh General Assembly of the Presbyterian Church, U.S.* Atlanta: Office of the General Assembly, 1957. 134-147.

"The Divine Constraint of Christian Education for Adults." *Union Seminary Quarterly Review* 13.1 (1957): 41-49.

1958

"Existential Christian Education." *Union Seminary Quarterly Review* 13.4 (1958): 19-29.

"Adult Classes Get Out of Their Ruts." *The International Journal of Religious Education* 35.2 (1958): 8-10.

1959

"Toward Better Methods of Communicating the Christian Faith." *The Future Course of Christian Adult Education*. Ed. L. C. Little. Pittsburgh: U of Pittsburgh P, 1959. 202-219.

"The Basis and Purpose of Christian Education." The Robert F. Jones Lectures, Feb. 1959. Austin: Austin Presbyterian Seminary Library. Reel-to-reel audiotape.

1960

Rev. of *The Rise and Fall of the Individual*, by W. P. Witcutt. *Religious Education* 55(1960):318.

"Choosing a God." *The Pulpit* 31.9 (1960).

Introduction. *Evaluation and Christian Education*. Ed. Helen F. Spaulding. New York: Bureau of Research and Survey, National Council of Churches, 1960. NcMHi.

"Group Dynamics and Religious Education." *Religious Education*. Ed. Marvin Taylor. New York: Abingdon Press, 1960. 173-184.

1961

Rev. of *Church Education for Tomorrow*, by Wesner Fallaw. *Pulpit Digest* April 1961: 64-66.

"The Christian Education of Conscience." *The Princeton Seminary Bulletin* 55.1 (1961): 37-48.

"The Vocation of the Professor of Christian Education." *Religious Education* 56:6 (1961): 413-414.

Growth in Grace and Knowledge. Five lectures published for use of students at Union Theological Seminary and Teachers College, Columbia University, 1961.

1962

"Church in Community." *The Presbyterian Outlook* 9 April 1962: 7.

Rev. of *Christian Nurture and the Church*, by Randolph C. Miller. *Union Seminary Quarterly Review* 17.4 (1962): 404.

"The Changing Curriculum in America." *The Presbyterian Survey* 52.9 (1962): 14-16.

"Criteria for Judging the Quality of Christian Education for Adults." *Wider Horizons in Christian Adult Education.* Ed. L. C. Little. Pittsburgh: U of Pittsburgh P, 1962. 257-278.

1963

"Machine-Taught Religion." *The Christian Century* 2 Jan. 1963: 12-15.

The Quiet Revolution. WRVR, New York. 21 March, 1963. NcMHi.

Love and the Law. Richmond, Virginia: John Knox Press, 1963.

"Adult Education." *The Westminster Dictionary of Christian Education.* Ed. Kendig Brubaker Cully. Philadelphia: The Westminster Press, 1963.

1964

"The Divine Constraint of Christian Education for Adults." *The Christian Educator* 7.2 (1964): 5-7.

"Not Apart From Life." *International Journal of Religious Education* 41.1 (1964): 8-10.

1966

Rev. of *The Church's Educational Ministry: A Curriculum Plan.* Cooperative Curriculum Project. *Church School Worker* 16.11 (1966): 40-41.

"The Curriculum of Christian Education." *An Introduction to Christian Education.* Ed. Marvin Taylor. Nashville: Abingdon Press, 1966. 157-169.

What's Right. Richmond, Virginia: John Knox Press, 1966.

1967

"Dare You Think About 1980-1990?" *The Church School* 20.9 (1967): 6-8.

Rev. of *Catechesis of Revelation*, by Gabriel Moran. *Union Seminary Quarterly Review* 22.4 (1967): 369-370.

"Religious Education in an Era of Radical Pluralism." *Religion in Life* 36.1 (1967): 128-139.

"Church Education and the Teaching of Religion in the Public Domain." *Theological Education* 3.3 (1967): 384-396.

"Christian Moral Education." *Dictionary of Christian Ethics.* Ed. John Macquarrie. Philadelphia: The Westminster Press, 1967.

"The A.B.C.'s of a New Venture in Church Education." *Christian Faith and Action.* Philadelphia: Board of Christian Education, The United Presbyterian Church, 1967: 26-32. NcMHi.

Where Faith Begins. Richmond, Virginia: John Knox Press, 1967.

1968

"Innovations for the Education Mission of the Church." *Dimensions in Christian Education* 17:6 (1968): 10-17.

"The Relation of Seminary Training to Congregational Education." *Religious Education* 63:4 (1968): 301-308.

"What is Happening to Christian Education?" *Colloquy* 1.8 (1968): 22-24.

Rev. of *Christian Education in Mission*, by Letty M. Russell. *The Union Seminary Quarterly Review* 23.2 (1968): 213-214.

Issues Facing Christian Educators. Geneva: World Council of Christian Education, 1968.

1969

"The Premature Arrival of the Future." *Dimensions in Christian Education* 19.1 (1969): 15-18.

"Can Protestants Make It With the "Now" Generation?" *Religious Education* 64.5 (1969): 376-383.

Rev. of *A History of Religious Education*, by Robert Ulrich. *Union Seminary Quarterly Review* 24.3 (1969): 281-284.

1970

"Once Gentle Nudged From His Heaven." *The Tower.* New York: Union Theological Seminary, Spring, 1970.

"Religious Instruction in the Protestant Churches." *Toward a Future for Religious Education.* Ed. James M. Lee and Patrick C. Rooney. Dayton: Pflaum Press, 1970. 154-182.

1971

"Reflections, U.S.A." *Colloquy* 4.1(1971):13.

"Athens and Jerusalem Revisited." *Spectrum-International Journal of Religious Education* 47.1 (1971): 21-31.

"Are There Ten Righteous People?" *Colloquy* 4.3 (1971): 28-33.

"Wanted: New Shell for Old Kernel." *Face to Face* Nov., 1971.

1972

"Is Church Education Something Particular?" *Religious Education* 67.1 (1972): 5-16.

"Sanctification Sociology." *Religion in Life* 41.3 (1972): 302-311.

"A Protestant Response to the Directorium Catechisticum." *The Living Light* 9.3 (1972): 85-94.

1973

"What Kind of Moral Life Does Your Congregation Have?" *Colloquy* 6.5 (1973): 26-29.

"Soul Education." Address. The Michigan Association of Non-Public Schools. Lansing, Michigan. 23 Aug. 1973. NcMHi.

"What Has Religion To Do With Morality?" *The Living Light* 10.3 (1973): 327-340.

Rev. of *The Present Revelation*, by Gabriel Moran. *The Review of Books and Religion* 3.3 (1973).

Rev. of *Moral Nexus*, by James B. Nelson. *Religious Education* 68.6 (1973): 765-766.

"An Appeal to Professors and Researchers in Religious Education." Presidential address. The Association of Professors and Researchers in Religious Education. 1973.

Conscience: Theological and Psychological Perspectives. Ed. New York: Paulist Press, 1973.

1974

Rev. of *The Flow of Religious Instruction*, by James Michael Lee. *The Living Light* 11.1 (1974): 146-148.

Introduction. *Generation to Generation.* By John Westerhoff and Gwen Kennedy Neville. Philadelphia: United Church Press, 1974. 21-24.

Using Evaluation in Theological Education. Nashville: Disciples Press, 1975.

1976

"Curriculum as Theological Fallout." *Alert*. 5.4 (1976).

Rev. of *A Theology of Christian Education*, by Lawrence O. Richards. *Religious Education* 71.6 (1976): 652-653.

"Conscience, Values, and Religious Education." *Foundations for Christian Education in an Era of Change*. Ed. Marvin J. Taylor. Nashville: Abingdon Press, 1976. 68-80.

1977

Rev. of *Will Our Children Have Faith?* by John Westerhoff. *Religious Education* 72.1 (1977): 91-92.

"Where Have We Been? What Does It Mean?" *Life At Louisville*. 8.4 (1977).

"The Habitat of the Spirit." *The Princeton Seminary Bulletin* 1.3 (1977): 112-116.

"Trends in Society and Culture Related to the Catachesis of Youth." *Catechesis: Realities and Visions*. Eds. Berard L. Marthaler and Marianne Sawicki. Washington, D.C.: United States Catholic Conference, 1977.

1978

Rev. of *The Wing-Footed Wanderer*, by Donald Miller. *Religious Education* 73.3 (1978): 369-370.

Rev. of *McGuffey and His Readers*, by John Westerhoff. *Religious Education* 73.4 (1978): 490.

Rev. of *Lying*, by Sissela Bok. *Right and Wrong*, by Charles Fried. *The New Review of Books and Religion* 3.2 (1978): 6.

Rev. of *Foundations of Religious Education*, ed. Padraic O'Hare. *The Living Light* 15.4 (1978): 561-562.

Don't Let Your Conscience Be Your Guide. New York: Paulist Press, 1978.

1979

"Issues for Christian Educators Related to the Development of Conscience." Address. Association of Professors and Researchers in Religious Education. Toronto, Canada, 23-25 Nov. 1979.

"Our Oldest Problem." *Tradition and Transformation in Religious Education*. Ed. Padraic O'Hare. Birmingham: Religious Education Press, 1979, 58-73.

1980

"What is Worthwhile in our Sunday School History?" Address. Scarrett College, on the occasion of the 200th anniversary of the founding of the Sunday School. 20 June 1980. NcMHi.

"Why is Christian Education at the Center of the Church's Life?" Address. Presbyterian School of Christian Education. 10 Sept. 1980. NcMHi.

". . . Make Disciples. . . ." *ACPE Advocate* Aug., 1980. NcMHi.

1981

"Last Words: Be an Advocate of Unity in Christ." Address. 1981 graduating class of Louisville Presbyterian Seminary. 31 May 1981. NcMHi.

"Christian Education is More Than Church School." Response when given the Margaret Walker Bowen Award for distinguished service to Christian Education. 2 June 1981. *The Presbyterian Outlook* 22 June 1981: 4.

Rev. of *Christian Religious Education*, by Thomas H. Groome. *Pacific Theological Review* Fall, 1981.

1982

Rev. of *The Theory of Christian Education Practice*, by Randolph C. Miller. *Theology Today* 38.4 (1982): 520-522.

"Does Faith Develop? An Evaluation of Fowler's Position." *The Living Light* 19.2 (1982): 162-174.

1983

"Forgiveness: Homily on Matthew 18:21-35." *Pacific Theological Review* Fall, 1983: 14-16.

"Toward Accountable Selfhood." *Modern Masters of Religious Education*. Ed. Marlene Mayr. Birmingham: Religious Education Press, 1983. 160-174.

"Tuning in the Divine." A response to "Religious Education as Growth in Practical Theological Reflection and Action," by Don S. Browning. Indianapolis: National Faculty Seminar, 1983. NcMHi.

1984

"Formation and Transformation." Address. The Centennial Celebration of the Presbyterian Church of Korea. Seoul, Korea, Aug. 1984.

"Has the Sunday School Movement Played Out?" *Austin Seminary Bulletin* May 1984: 37-45.

"From the Third to the Fourth Generation." *Pacific Theological Review* Winter, 1984: 13-15.

"Toward the Year 2003." *Religious Education* 79.1 (1984): 101-109.

"Educating Ministers for the New Presbyterian Church." *The Princeton Seminary Bulletin* 5.2 (1984): 122-130.

"Theological Foundations for Religious Nurture." *Changing Patterns of Religious Education*. Ed. Marvin J. Taylor. Nashville: Abingdon Press, 1984. 10-23.

"The Role of Teaching Within the Church." Indianapolis: The National Faculty Seminar, 1984. NcMHi.

1986

"Research in Faith Development." *Faith Development and Fowler*. Ed. Craig Dykstra and Sharon Parks. Birmingham: Religious Education Press, 1986. 180-205.

1988

"Some Educational Aspects of Conflict." *Tensions Between Citizenship and Discipleship*. Ed. Nelle G. Slater. New York: Pilgrim Press, 1988. 195-219.

Congregations: Their Power to Form and Transform. Ed. Atlanta: John Knox Press, 1988.

"Religious Education? Yes, Indeed!" *Does the Church Really Want Religious Education?* Ed. Marlene Mayr. Birmingham, Ala.: Religious Education Press, 1988. 102-124.

How Faith Matures. Louisville: Westminster/John Knox Press, 1989.

1990

"Congregational Life," "Conscience," and "Lewis Sherrill." *Encyclopedia of Religious Education*. Ed. Iris V. Cully and Kendig Brubaker Cully. San Francisco: Harper & Row, 1990.

"Educational Mission." A Report to the General Assembly Special Committee to Study Theological Institutions, Presbyterian Church (U.S.A.). Eds. Lawrence N. Jones, Sara Little, Robert W. Lynn and C. Ellis Nelson. Oct. 1990. NcMHi.

1991

"Congregation's Educational Strategy." *The Congregation as Carrier of Religious Tradition*. Ed. Carl Dudley, Jackson Carroll and James Wind. Louisville: Westminster/John Knox Press, 1991. 156-171.

1992

"Leadership of Theological Seminaries: The Case of David Stitt at Austin Presbyterian Seminary." *Proceedings of the Presbyterian Historical Society of the Southwest*. Ed. Thomas W. Currie, Jr. Austin, Texas, 29 Feb. 1992. 103-111.

Helping Teenagers Grow Morally. Louisville: Westminster/John Knox Press, 1992.

"Essential Ingredients." *The Presbyterian Outlook* 13 April 1992: 5-6.

"Be of Good Cheer." *APCE Advocate* 17.1 (1992).

"Education for Congregational Leadership." Lecture. International Seminar on Religious Education and Values (ISREV). Banff, Alberta, Canada, 23-28 Aug. 1992.

Curriculum vitae

C. Ellis Nelson

Personal data:

Birth:	7 March 1916 at Galveston, Texas.
Education:	Austin College, Sherman, Texas, A.B., 1937.
	Austin Presbyterian Theological Seminary, Austin, Texas, M.Div. 1940.
	University of Texas, Austin, M.A., 1944.
	Columbia University, New York, Ph.D., 1955.
	Research Fellow, Mansfield College, Oxford University, England, 1964.
	Research Fellow, Christ Church College, Oxford University, England, 1972.
Marriage:	Nancy Gribble, Austin, Texas 8 July 1941.
Children:	Ellis Stark, 1944; Joy Elizabeth, 1949; Martha Karin, 1950.

Professional Service:

Research professor, Austin Presbyterian Seminary, 1990 to date.

Visiting professor, Ormond College, University of Melbourne, spring 1990.

Distinguished visiting professor, University of Dubuque, fall, 1989.

Visiting professor, Austin Presbyterian Seminary, January 1984-1988.

Interim President, Austin Presbyterian Seminary, January 1984-July 1985.

Visiting professor, San Francisco Theological Seminary and Graduate Theological Union, Berkeley, CA 1981-1983.

Louisville Presbyterian Theological Seminary, President and professor of Christian education, 1974-1981.

Union Theological Seminary, New York, Skinner and McAlpin Professor of Practical Theology, 1957-1974; Dean, 1969-1970.

Austin Presbyterian Theological Seminary, Instructor in religious education, 1940-1943; Assistant professor, 1943-1945; Professor, 1948-1957.

Director of Research, Texas Legislative Council's Study of Higher Education, 1950.

Director of Youth Work, Board of Christian Education, Presbyterian Church, U.S., Richmond, VA 1945-1948.

Instructor in Bible, University of Texas at Austin, 1943-1945.

State School for the Blind, Austin, Chaplain, 1940-1942.

University Presbyterian Church, Austin, Texas, Associate Minister and Minister to students, University of Texas 1940-1943.

Ordained by Central Texas Presbytery, Presbyterian Church, U.S., 7 May 1940.